THE THIRD OPTION

THE THIRD OPTION

The Emancipation of European Defense, 1989–2000

Charles G. Cogan

Foreword by Lawrence S. Kaplan

Humanistic Perspectives on International Relations
Cathal J. Nolan, Series Editor

Westport, Connecticut
London

Library of Congress Cataloging-in-Publication Data

Cogan, Charles.
  The third option : the emancipation of European defense, 1989–2000 / by Charles G. Cogan ; foreword by Lawrence S. Kaplan
    p. cm.—(Humanistic perspectives on international relations, ISSN 1535–0363)
  Includes bibliographical references and index.
  ISBN 0-275-96948-7 (alk. paper)
    1. Europe—Defenses. 2. World politics—1989– 3. North Atlantic Treaty Organization. 4. European Union. I. Title: 3rd option. II. Title. III. Series.
  UA646 .C643 2001
  355'.03304—dc21   2001032910

British Library Cataloguing in Publication Data is available.

Copyright © 2001 by Charles G. Cogan

All rights reserved. No portion of this book may be
reproduced, by any process or technique, without
the express written consent of the publisher.

Library of Congress Catalog Card Number: 2001032910
ISBN: 0–275–96948–7
ISSN: 1535–0363

First published in 2001

Praeger Publishers, 88 Post Road West, Westport, CT 06881
An imprint of Greenwood Publishing Group, Inc.
www.praeger.com

Printed in the United States of America

The paper used in this book complies with the
Permanent Paper Standard issued by the National
Information Standards Organization (Z39.48–1984).

10 9 8 7 6 5 4 3 2 1

Contents

Series Foreword	vii
Foreword	xi
Preface	xiii
Abbreviations	xv
Introduction	1
1 From the Fall of the Berlin Wall to the Change in the Nature of NATO (November 1989–July 1990)	17
2 From the Gulf War to the New Strategic Concept (July 1990–December 1991)	39
3 From the Bosnian War to France's Move Toward NATO (1992–December 1995)	61
4 From the AFSOUTH Imbroglio to the Madrid Summit (1996–July 1997)	83
5 The Turn Toward Autonomy: St. Malo to Kosovo to Cologne (July 1997–June 1999)	97
6 The European Union Becomes a Defense Organization (July 1999–December 2000)	117

7 Epilogue	133
Appendix	153
Selected Bibliography	161
Index	167

Series Foreword

International relations is a thoroughly humanistic subject. All its actors are human beings, or they are institutions and organizations built and controlled by human intention and maintained by daily decision-making. Individual states, which emerged as the most powerful and decisive actors on the world stage over the past 350 years, are not reified constructs with an independent will or social reality beyond human ken or volition. Properly regarded, they are wholly human constructs. All states are designed for, and are bent to, the realization of goals and aspirations of human communities. That is true whether those ambitions are good or evil, spiritual or material, personal or dynastic, or represent ethnic, national, or emerging cosmopolitan identities. So, too, is the international society of states a human construct, replete with its tangled labyrinth of international organizations, an expansive system of international law that creates binding obligations across frontiers, ancient norms of diplomacy and ritualized protocol, webs of economic, social, and cultural interaction, and a venerable penchant for disorder, discord, and war.

Immanuel Kant observed with acute accuracy: "Out of the crooked timber of Humanity, no straight thing was ever made." The endless drama of human affairs thus gives rise to motley events, decisions, and complex causal chains. At the international level, too, we encounter the foibles of human beings as individuals and in the aggregate, and come upon a mix of the rational and irrational in human motivation. All that makes formal "modeling" of international politics a virtual impossibility—a fact that is itself a source of deep frustration to idealistic reformers and social scientists alike. On the other hand, precisely because international relations is so deeply humanistic a subject, it is a rich realm for the exercise of broad political and moral judgment. It is a natural arena for serious ethical reflection by and about those who frame foreign policies and practice statecraft. It is proper for scholars and informed citizens to praise or censure leadership decisions and actions. In short, as in all realms of human endeavor, moral judgment is not only implicit in every decision or action (or inaction) taken in international relations, it is a core duty of leadership, an apt function of scholarship, and a basic requirement for any educated citizenry.

These facts are clear, and even self-evident. At its classical best, political science understood them, and therefore drew its questions from the conversation across time of the great political thinkers as well as from current policy debates, to examine both in a rich discourse that was historically and philosophically aware, even as it was rigorous and well-grounded empirically. In contrast, much contemporary political science purports to describe and explain international relations through elaboration of objective "laws" of politics or economics, which entirely overlook its humanistic character. At its modern and "postmodern" worst, the discipline is prone to mere methodological preoccupations, striking elaborate poses about arcane topics, and impenetrable prose. For instance, positivism's search for a "rational choice" model of human conduct assumes that individuals are "rational actors" who purposively seek to maximize their interests. In seeking a universal, deductive theory (broadly modeled on academic economics, where similar methodologies are employed with little explanatory success), too many political scientists eschew historical or philosophically informed case study in favor of a crude reduction of all politics to formal models. These usually engage extreme simplifications, couched in an obscurantist terminology, which model what was already known, or is obvious, or are so generalized that they account for nothing specific. Over that thin substance is then spread a thick veneer of false rigor, packaged in mathematical formulae that are, and are intended to be, intimidating to the uninitiated. Left out is the fact that most things of lasting importance in human affairs may be explained not by "rational choices," but by ideology and ignorance, blundering and stupidity, courage and self-sacrifice, enlightened vision, fanaticism, or blind chance (what Machiavelli called *fortuna*).

Alternately, the "critical theory" school in political science rejects any epistemology holding that reality exists separately from the academic observer, and is therefore objectively knowable to any real degree. All knowledge about international relations instead merely reflects the biases and power interests of the observer (the usual suspects are racial, class, or economic elites). Scholars are warned against the attempt to achieve objective knowledge of the reality of international relations, which traditionally was the moral and intellectual raison d'être of their profession. Rather than seek to impartially map out, explore, and explain the international society of states and its complex subsystems and mores, a feat said to be impossible, scholars are to directly engage and change the world (even though that, too, ought to be impossible, if they are unable to understand it in the first place). Too often, this leads to polemical studies that purport to unmask elites whose pervasive and corrupt power is said to sustain and operate a fatally unjust international system. There is much intolerance and angry posturing here as well, in calls for "exposure" of "fellow-traveling" academic approaches identified as legitimizing and reinforcing irredeemably illicit power structures. In sum, in its epistemological assertion that all knowledge is radically subjective or merely political, critical theory denies the possibility of objective knowledge or the value of other scholarly traditions.

This series does not support the contention that all significant political action is reducible to rational choice or that it is impossible to acquire objective knowledge about world affairs. Instead, it promotes a classical, humanistic approach to international relations scholarship. It is dedicated to reviving and furthering the contribution to understanding made by classical studies—by knowledge of history, diplomacy, international law, and philosophy—but it is agnostic regarding the narrow ideology or specific policy conclusions of any given work. It supports scholarly inquiry that is grounded in the historical antecedents of contemporary controversies, and well versed in the great traditions of philosophical inquiry and discourse. The series recognizes that, at its most incisive, international relations is a field of inquiry that cannot be understood fully outside its historical context. The keenest insights into the meaning of economic, legal, cultural, and political facts and issues in contemporary world affairs are always rooted in appreciation that international society is a historical phenomenon, not a theoretical abstraction or a radical departure from prior experience. Hence, the series welcomes interdisciplinary scholarship dealing with the evolution of the governing ideas, norms, and practices of international society. It encourages a dialectic rooted in abiding intellectual, ethical, and practical interests that have concerned and engaged intelligent men and women for centuries, as they tried to reconcile the historical emergence of modern states with wider or older notions of political community.

This series is especially interested in scholarly research on the varied effects of differences in power—whether economic, political, or military—on relations between nations and states. The causes of war and the supports of peace, both in general and concerning specific conflicts, remain a core interest of all serious inquiry into international relations. Similarly, there is an enduring need for studies of the core requirements of international order and security, and of international political economy, whether regionally or globally. Scholarship is also welcome that is concerned with the development of international society, both in the formal relations maintained by states and in broader demands for political, economic, social, and cultural justice on the subnational and even individual level. Finally, the series promotes scholarly investigation of the history and changing character and status of international law, into international organization, and any and all other means of decentralized governance that the states have invented to moderate their conflicts and introduce a measure of restraint and equity to the affairs of international society.

Cathal J. Nolan

Foreword

It is only in recent years, essentially since the end of the Cold War, that American historians have identified NATO as a subject worthy of study as a significant chapter in the history of United States foreign relations. Inasmuch as the signing of the North Atlantic Treaty in 1949 marked the first entangling alliance with any European nation since the termination of the Franco-American treaty in 1800, the minimal contribution of historians to our understanding of NATO's role in American history is at first glance surprising. Reasons for their neglect may have been the scarcity of primary materials and the need for more temporal distance from the subject. But a more persuasive explanation has been their subsuming the treaty under the Truman Doctrine and then marginalizing it as a lesser factor in the nation's containment policy.

European historians, by contrast, have taken the alliance and organization more seriously. Important centers of NATO scholarship have developed in most of the Allied countries where NATO studies have been integrated into the history of Western Europe since the end of World War II. Comparable developments may be in store for American centers. Historians have revised their estimate of the alliance's role in American diplomatic history over the past decade, and it is likely that they will consider NATO a key element in the history of the Cold War. Charles G. Cogan's work is a product of this new direction in American scholarship. In his case it has been strengthened by his familiarity with European, particularly French, sensibilities.

Cogan brings a perspective to his studies that has been refined by experience in Europe as chief intelligence officer with the Central Intelligence Agency in Paris. After retiring from the agency a decade ago he began a new career as a scholar, first with his doctoral degree from Harvard University in 1992 and then with a burst of significant publications, concentrated for the most part on Franco-American relations within the Atlantic Alliance. As a senior research associate at the John F. Kennedy School of Government and as visiting scholar at the John M. Olin Center for Strategic Studies, both at Harvard, he has produced two major publications: *Oldest Allies, Guarded Friends: The United States and France since 1940* (1994) and *Forced to Choose: France, the Atlantic Alliance, and NATO—Then and Now* (1997). Both books reflect an understanding of France's position in NATO and attitude toward the United States not often encountered among American scholars. In his preface to *The Third Option* he identifies his current book as a sequel to his earlier work, carrying the Franco-American relationship from the end of the Cold War to the end of the century.

But Cogan also observes that this book is broader in scope. France and the United States are major actors, but the central questions raised are where Europe is headed in the twenty-first century and, consequently, what places the United States and NATO will occupy in realignments of relationships. Given the obvious difficulties in finding documentary sources the author has made skillful use of interviews with major leaders and of articles and essays from European as well as American journals. He has followed the tortuous course of NATO's history in the 1990s from summit to summit, from crisis to crisis, and has provided a perceptive account of its evolution in a style that should attract a wide readership in the academic community.

It was inevitable that the passing of the Communist threat would alter NATO's functions. It was not simply that the organization would seek new missions, at it did at the Rome summit in 1992. The internal relationships themselves would be changed as Europe moved toward unification and toward achieving a defense identity that could liberate European allies from American domination. In light of the near reality of a United States of Europe, Cogan offers alternative options that the alliance might adopt in future crises. The first would be full use of the NATO machinery in an American-led operation. The second would see that the European Union (EU) would operate with NATO assets under a NATO chain of command but without American participation. This would fit a scenario of "separable but not separate." Cogan foresees a third option as another likely path given the direction a French-stimulated Europe may follow. This would have the European allies function independently of NATO, using their own growing capabilities.

Whether the EU is capable of operating outside NATO is, in the author's judgment, an open question. Britain's concern about maintaining the Atlantic connection and France's concern over an increasingly powerful German role in the EU may serve as a centripetal force limiting the divisions between NATO and the EU. While the outcome of this uneasy relationship is not clear, Charles Cogan provides a compelling and persuasive analysis of Europe's movement toward a credible defense identity.

Lawrence S. Kaplan
Georgetown University
Director Emeritus,
Lyman L. Lemnitzer Center for NATO and European Union Studies,
Kent State University

Preface

This book is a sequel to an earlier work of mine, *Forced to Choose: France, the Atlantic Alliance, and NATO—Then and Now*,[1] which focused on the period of the late 1940s and the origins of Europe's defense relationships. My objective then was to demonstrate how the initial arrangements that were made for the Alliance profoundly affected the ambivalent and reserved way in which the French eventually came to regard NATO.

This present book, by contrast, examines the period since the end of the Cold War, during which France's defense policy has been profoundly, though quietly, altered, with nuclear dissuasion giving way to "projectable" intervention forces as the keystone of that policy. In the same period France's attitude toward NATO underwent a series of swerves, alternating between rapprochement and distancing, as the French sought different ways of coping with the end of the Cold War and the resulting overwhelming strategic position of the United States, or what French Foreign Minister Hubert Védrine has dubbed "hyperpuissance."

I would like to thank, in particular, Cathal J. Nolan of Boston University's International History institute for having included this work in the International Relations collection of the institute's new book series, published by Praeger and, as in my previous writing endeavors, Stanley Hoffmann, ready with his unparalleled experience and insight, as well as his unfailing goodwill, to offer advice and encouragement. In addition, there have been many others who have helped me in this project by pointing me in the right direction for research and by imparting what was often direct knowledge. They are too numerous to be included here, but I will cite a few names: Jolyon Howorth of Bath University; Bertrand Lavezarri and Jonathan Daly, fellows at the Weatherhead Center for International Affairs during 1999–2000 and NATO experts in France and the U.K. respectively; and in Washington, Ronald Asmus, Ian Brzezinski, Fred Beauchamp, Keith Dunn, Philip Gordon, Gen. George Joulwan, Ambassador

Robert Hunter, Lawrence S. Kaplan, Peter Rodman, Robert Simmons, Lt. Gen. (Ret.) Bernard E. Trainor, and Hoyt Yee.

In contrast to my book cited earlier, as well as my initial book on the French-American relationship, *Oldest Allies, Guarded Friends: The United States and France since 1940*,[2] this work is a contemporary one and is based largely on interviews, secondary sources, and published documents and statements. I wanted to assess where we are in terms of European defense after the tumultuous decade of the 1990s. Also, I wanted to envision what might be the future relationship between Europe and the United States now that the Cold War is over.

This is a book, unlike the two previous ones, which is not just about France but also about the larger Euro-American relationship. Although France is perhaps more emblematic of the European side of this relationship than is any other European country, in this work it is not just a question of examining France and NATO. The book looks as well at the larger Euro-American framework and, extending beyond that, at the Western relationship with Russia.

Due to the near-current nature of the events I am describing and because I have talked to a number of officials of the United States and other Western governments, some of the statements of my interview sources must remain anonymous. In this regard, I would like to salute my sources—American, French, and others—who prize objectivity and accuracy and therefore are willing to give of themselves in order to set the record straight as they see it.

NOTES

1. Charles G. Cogan, *Forced to Choose: France, the Atlantic Alliance, and NATO—Then and Now* (Westport, Conn.: Praeger, 1997).

2. Charles G. Cogan, *Oldest Allies, Guarded Friends: The United States and France since 1940* (Westport Conn.: Praeger, 1994). See also *Alliés Eternels, Amis Ombrageux: les Etats-Unis et al France depuis 1940* (Brussels: Bruylant, 1999), (original French version of *Oldest Allies*, with adaptations).

Abbreviations

ACE	Allied Command Europe
AFSOUTH	NATO'S Southern Command at Naples
AMF(L)	Allied Command Europe Mobile Force (Land)
ARRC	Allied Rapid Reaction Corps
AWACS	Airborne Warning and Control System
CAP	Common Agricultural Policy
CEA	Commissariat for Atomic Energy
CFSP	Common Foreign and Security Policy
CINCLANT	Commander-in-Chief Atlantic
CJTF	Combined Joint Task Force
CSCE	Conference on Security and Cooperation in Europe
CVF	Aircraft Carrier of the Future (British terminology)
DPC	Defense Planning Committee
DSACEUR	Deputy Supreme Allied Commander Europe
EC	European Community
ECSC	European Coal and Steel Community
ECSDP	European Common Security and Defense Policy
EDC	European Defense Community
EEC	European Economic Community
EMU	Economic and Monetary Union
ESDI	European Security and Defense Identity
EU	European Union

FAR	Rapid Action Force (Force Action Rapide)
FRY	Federal Republic of Yugoslavia
GDP	Gross Domestic Product
GDR	German Democratic Republic
GPS	Global Positioning System
IFOR	Implementation Force
IGC	Intergovernmental Conference
IHEDN	Institute of Higher Studies of National Defense
IPSC	Interim Political and Security Committee
JRRF	Joint Rapid Reaction Forces
JSF	Joint Strike Fighter
KFOR	Allied occupation force in Kosovo
KLA	Kosovo Liberation Army
KVM	Extraction force based in Madedonia
MLF	Multilateral force
NA	National Archives
NAC	North Atlantic Council
NACC	North Atlantic Cooperation Council
NATO	North Atlantic Treaty Organization
OSCE	Organization for Security and Cooperation in Europe
PfP	Partnership for Peace
PSC	Political and Security Committee
QMV	Qualified majority voting
SACEUR	Supreme Allied Commander Europe
SACLANT	Supreme Allied Commander Atlantic
SDR	Strategic Defense Review
SFOR	Stabilization Force
SHAPE	Supreme Headquarters Allied Powers Europe
SRG	Strategy Review Group
STOLV	Short Takeoff and Vertical Landing
UN	United Nations
UNPROFOR	United Nations Protection Force
WEU	Western European Union

Introduction

> The affirmation of a European strategic identity has in effect represented for 40 years the constant ambition of the diplomatic and strategic action of France, which legitimately believes that the European upheavals of 1989 have increased both its necessity and its possibility.
>
> Frédéric Bozo, writing in 1991.[1]

THE EUROPEAN DEFENSE COMMUNITY (EDC) AND ITS AVATARS

At the dawn of the new century, with the Cold War having ended more than a decade ago, and with a new world power relationship described as "unipolarity," the French are closer paradoxically to the realization of the goal cited above by Bozo than ever before. By a curious turn of the wheel of history, the emerging European defense identity is coming to resemble in some ways the European Defense Community that was rejected in the mid-1950s by the French National Assembly in an outburst of nationalist fervor. The difference between the two is that the EDC would have been a *communitarian* or *supranational* (some would use the term *federal*) European institution, whereas the European defense identity, as it is being developed, consists of a capability run conjointly by the member states of the European Union (EU) and is therefore *intergovernmental*.

Had it been allowed to come into existence, the EDC today would have been in Pillar One—the supranational element of the EU—where decisions are taken by a qualified, that is, weighted, majority vote in which the more populous countries count for more than the less populous ones, though not in an overwhelming way. The European defense identity, now known under its new name—the European Common Security and Defense Policy (ECSDP)—is in an intergovernmental category of the EU (Pillar Two), where decisions, with very few exceptions, have to be arrived at by the unanimous vote of the member governments. European defense officials are emphatic on this distinction, as in this statement by French Defense Minister Alain Richard on June 16, 2000:

> We never use the term communitarian... the definition by the European Council of capabilities objectives does not mean that Brussels would take over the determination of what intervention capabilities would be used in crisis management [operations]. Military planning will remain a national competence. Neither does the definition of joint capabilities objectives imply the constitution of a European Army. We have very much in mind the unfortunate experience of the European Defense Community. The rule will remain for the European Union as it is for NATO: [it will be] a national decision to participate or not in an operation. Each nation will fix the nature and level of its involvement.[2]

The killing of the EDC by the French National Assembly on August 30, 1954, and its rapid replacement by the admission of West Germany into a strengthened NATO, had the effect of suppressing the impulse toward a European defense identity for nearly forty years. Of the two objectives behind the Assembly's vote, only one was preserved: preventing the French Army from being largely subsumed in a supranational entity. The other objective, preventing German rearmament, was quickly overridden in a joint diplomatic effort led by French Prime Minister Pierre Mendès France and British Foreign Minister Anthony Eden: West Germany was admitted into the Brussels Pact (along with Italy), and this defensive alliance of 1948 grouping Britain, France, and the Benelux countries was now designated the Western European Union (WEU). At the same time, West Germany was brought into NATO. After some hesitation the French National Assembly approved these new arrangements on December 30, 1954.

The irony of the 1954 rejection of the EDC was not lost totally on French parliamentarians at the time. As Marie-Pierre Subtil noted, "A number of parliamentarians affirmed [after the December 30, 1954, vote] that if they had known, they would have chosen the EDC, and thus Europe. Too late."[3]

However, it was too much to expect France to give up part of its sovereignty over French military forces to a supranational or "communitarian" institution.[4] Although it would have created a European Army separate from the United States (and Britain), the EDC was too far ahead of its time. The wounds of the 75-year-old enmity between France and Germany, and their three wars in that period, hardly had time to heal in the early 1950s. People were not ready at that time for the creation of a "supranational" European Army made up of a majority of German and French troops.

THE FAILURE OF THE WEU EXPERIMENT

During the Cold War, the WEU withered in the face of the all-encompassing presence of NATO as the primary security organization for Europe. In one sense the Brussels Pact had served its essential purpose: as modified in 1954, it had enabled West Germany and Italy to become members of the WEU, which in turn provided more congruence and rationale for West Germany also becoming a member of NATO. Put another way, and in retrospect, the Brussels Pact served as little more than a cover for the admission of West Germany into NATO.

Though marginalized, the Brussels Pact had nevertheless remained throughout the Cold War as the one European security organization that had escaped integration into an American-led security system. However, although it remained intact, it was in an emasculated state, with no military forces. The bulk of Europe's forces, excepting those of France after its departure from the NATO integrated military command in 1966, were at the disposal of the Supreme Allied Commander Europe (the SACEUR)—as always, an American general. In sum, as long as NATO was around, the WEU was superfluous.

Moreover, the WEU was cast in the form of dependent relationship to NATO. According to the modified Brussels Treaty, which created the WEU in 1954, the latter is supposed to "rely" on NATO, to wit: "In the execution of the Treaty the High Contracting Parties and any organs established by them under the Treaty shall work in close cooperation with the North Atlantic Treaty Organization. Recognizing the undesirability of duplicating the Military Staffs of NATO, the Council [of the WEU] and its agency will rely on the appropriate Military Authorities of NATO for information and advice on military matters."[5]

In the 1980s, as a way out of the dilemma of Europe's strategic powerlessness, the members of the WEU, led by the French, attempted to set up through the WEU a European defense identity as an alternate instrument to NATO. The year 1987 saw the emergence of this attempt in the so-called platform declaration of the Council of the Brussels Pact at a meeting in The Hague. The declaration stated in part, "[We] recall our commitment to construct a European Union.... A major instrument in reaching this objective is the Modified Brussels Treaty [of 1954] ... which instituted obligations of a considerable import with respect to collective defense [and] constituted one of the first stages in European unity. ... Thus we aim at developing a European identity in the defense area."[6]

The renewed impulse to create a European defense identity around the Brussels Pact and its clause of "automatic" response by its members to an enemy attack did not, however, spring from nowhere. As indicated by the observation of Frédéric Bozo quoted at the beginning of this introduction, it has been a consistent tenet of French policy for the past half-century. The term "European Security and Defense Identity" (with "policy" now replacing the word "identity") has for the French come to signify a euphemism for achieving some form of independence from the NATO integrated military command.

Beginning in the mid-1980s, under the aegis of the WEU, European ships took part alongside those of NATO in surveillance activities in the Gulf during the Iran-Iraq war. Similar operations took place during the Gulf War and its aftermath and later in the Adriatic in the 1990s during the enforcement of the embargo against belligerents in the former Yugoslavia (e.g., Operation Sharp

Guard, run jointly by the WEU and NATO). But these were marginal military activities. The only independent activities carried out by the WEU were the administration of the city of Mostar, a purely civilian operation, and the effecting of an embargo on the Danube against Serbia-Montenegro.[7] Gradually the idea of resuscitating the WEU was given up. As Hubert Védrine, a former Élysée (presidency) official who was later to become foreign minister, ruefully stated in his book on President Mitterrand published in 1996:

In fact, the other Europeans [have] never shared our way of looking at [the WEU] and our hopes [for it]. They think it is perfectly fine that the United States assure the security of Europe, and for reasons that are at once political, psychological and budgetary, they have no desire to assume heavier responsibilities. Apart from their Chancellor, the Germans see it as a French whim, and [they] only support it to maintain a good élan in our bilateral relations.[8]

In the late 1980s, France and West Germany, with France in the lead, sought to create combined forces that would symbolize their new postwar relationship, forces that would not be connected directly with the dormant WEU. In July 1987, Helmut Kohl proposed the creation of a 4,200-man French-German brigade, and it officially came into being in January 1988.[9] It was placed under the aegis of a new organization, the French-German Defense and Security Council, inaugurated on January 22, 1988, on the twenty-fifth anniversary of the Franco-German Treaty of Friendship and Cooperation (known as the Élysée Treaty).[10]

On October 14, 1991, President François Mitterrand and Chancellor Helmut Kohl took a further step and announced plans for a purely European force, with the French-German brigade as its nucleus: "French-German military cooperation will be strengthened beyond the existing brigade. The augmented Franco-German units could thus become the nucleus of a European Corps, which could include forces from other member states of the WEU. This new structure could also become the model for closer military cooperation between member states of the WEU."[11]

Although the aim was to create a European force from among WEU members, the new military formation was not tied organically to the WEU but rather to the French-German Defense and Security Council. Once more, in the absence of a European consensus, the French-German "locomotive" had taken over to drive forward the construction of Europe.

At the French-German summit at La Rochelle on May 21–22, 1992, the new formation was created officially. It was no longer the French-German Corps but was rebaptized the Euro-Corps.[12] Three other European nations, Belgium, Spain, and Luxembourg, subsequently joined the Euro-Corps, whose headquarters was placed at Strasbourg and whose strength was projected at 50,000. In January 1993, France made a major concession, at the instance of West Germany, in agreeing that, should a military crisis arise in Europe, the Euro-Corps would be placed under the command of NATO. Though concession it was, the agreement was in line with previous accords that had been drawn up with NATO since France's break with the integrated command in 1966 and that governed the use of French troops in the event of war in Europe (i.e., the Ailleret-Lemnitzer and Valentin-Farber agreements).[13]

THE PERDURING OF NATO

Although by the logic of things, the end of the Cold War should have seen a return to peaceful institutions, and in particular the extension of the European Union to encompass the "common European house," to use the phrase of Mikhail Gorbachev,[14] the opposite effect was produced: a military alliance (NATO), which was the West's defensive instrument during the Cold War, persisted in its existence and developed new roles outside the zone that was originally defined in the Washington Treaty of 1949 and that has never been amended per se. These roles include peacekeeping, peace enforcement, crisis management, and outright military intervention for reasons related not to the common defense of Western Europe but to humanitarian ends (as in Bosnia, Kosovo). What is more, NATO came to be regarded, or regarded itself, as *the* instrument for the spread of democracy, moving its territorial domain to the east (Czech Republic, Poland, Hungary).

On the one hand, the extended postponement of the European Union's avowed initial vocation of extending itself to all of Europe, and, on the other hand, the transformation of NATO's role into that of an expanding security community (an about-face palpably reflected in the deliberations of the Clinton administration itself), are events that should not be considered in isolation but rather in a dialectical relationship to each other. The complicated interaction between these two regional organizations that have only recently begun speaking to one another as institutions needs to be the subject of greater illumination in order to assist in an understanding of the unforeseen events of the first decade of the post–Cold War era.

In general, one can distinguish three broad phases in the dialectic of enlargement between NATO and the EU. The first was from the fall of the Berlin Wall in November 1989 to the Brussels NATO Summit of January 1994; the second was from the Brussels NATO Summit to the Washington NATO Summit five years later in April 1999; and the third was from that latter moment through four EU summits (Cologne, Helsinki, Feira, and Nice) to the end of 2000. All these phases took place against a background of regional conflicts involving the Western powers such as had not occurred since the American retreat from Vietnam in the early 1970s.

The 1990s saw an extended delay in the European Union's outreach to Eastern Europe. Instead of significantly "enlarging," the EU chose "deepening"—which essentially meant putting in place the mechanism for an Economic and Monetary Union (EMU). In the same period, NATO chose enlargement. As the decade of the 1990s drew to a close, these two tendencies—a deepening economic and monetary union in Western Europe and an expanded "Atlantic" security community spreading into Eastern Europe—came to fulfillment with the entry in force of the Euro on January 1, 1999, for a three-year transitional period and the admission of Poland, the Czech Republic, and Hungary into NATO three months later, in March 1999.

The assertion that there is a dialectical relationship between NATO and EU enlargement is a subject of debate among scholars and government officials, and such an assertion is contested more in Europe than in the United States. On one level, the two processes *are* unrelated. EU expansion, as one French official has said, is a bottom-up exercise. There are criteria to be filled, starting at the microlevel on up, questions such as whether the goods of a candidate country can be competitive with the borderless flow of goods from existing EU countries and whether the banking and investment structures can be reconciled with those of the EU member countries. On this side of the argument, there is the theme that these two institutions, NATO and the EU, do not compare: enlargement of NATO only required a resolution at the NATO Summit in Washington in April 1999 that the three Eastern European nations be admitted, whereas the twelve countries currently negotiating for membership in the EU (which include the aforementioned three) must satisfy the *acquis communautaires* contained in some 80,000 pages of EU documents.

But in the larger political (and security) sense, the two institutions have a dialectical relationship in the effects they produce. Few can doubt that, had the European Union been more forthcoming toward prospective new members in the immediate aftermath of the end of the Cold War, the move toward NATO enlargement would not have taken place in the same way, or at least with the same precipitation. The reluctance of certain powers, including and especially France, to extend the European Union to the Visegrad countries (Poland, Hungary, the Czech Republic, and Slovakia) led ineluctably to an intensive look at NATO enlargement, which would have seemed quite improbable at the start of the 1990s.

The turn toward NATO also was given impetus by the successive wars in Yugoslavia that broke out at the beginning of the decade and that demonstrated over time not only the impotence of the UN in contrast with the effectiveness of NATO as an instrument of regional coercion but also a growing divergence in strategic perceptions between the United States and its West European allies. The incoherence and indecisiveness of the Europeans, as perceived by the Clinton administration, was to have an effect on the United States gradual decision to go forward with NATO enlargement.

Richard Holbrooke, who was to become one of the prime movers behind NATO enlargement, had by his own account not given much thought to this possibility before his tenure as U.S. ambassador to Bonn (1993–1994): "When I arrived in Germany in September 1993, I believed that EU membership was more important and would arrive first. What turned me around was the realization that the EU, mired in its own Euro-mess (the common currency, the endless arguments about process, its inner-directedness, and its failure on Bosnia), was not going to invite any of these countries in, at the earliest, before 2003."[15]

To put it in another way, if the countries of Central Europe had been given some encouragement early on about joining the European Union, the existential threat that they perceived as still coming from Russia might have been lessened in their eyes. Instead, President Mitterrand, in his unfortunate "European confederation" initiative, first mooted on December 31, 1989, and then officially presented at Prague in June 1991, told their representatives at the Prague gathering that it might take "decades and decades" before they became members. He proposed the "confederation" as a way station on the route to a far-distant EU membership. Had these countries been able to anticipate early on the "existential" protection that EU membership could provide, they might not have turned their attention and their efforts so intensively in the direction of NATO.

THE DEVELOPING DEFENSE ROLE OF THE EUROPEAN UNION

The European Union has been a work in progress for some fifty years, a progress that has been slow and sometimes unsteady, but looking back on it, rather remarkable. Through its various incarnations, starting with the European Coal and Steel Community (ECSC), the Union was built on the premise that economic arrangements between the Western European states would be easier to set up than political and military ones. Nevertheless, the aims of its originator, Jean Monnet, were political and strategic: to tie Germany and France so closely together that there never again could be a great European war and to make Western Europe economically and politically sound and self-sufficient.

The political arrangements that were to follow the economic ones were never far from Monnet's mind, and he even conceived of a European Political Community in the early 1950s.[16] But his hastily conceived European Defense Community, intended to bring German troops into the defense of Europe but not to create a German Army per se, went down to defeat in the French National Assembly in August 1954, as noted previously, and the Political Community project had to be abandoned as well.

As it was, it took a very long time for communitarian or "supranational" relationships between the Western European states to spread over the bulk of the economic and monetary area. The Common Agricultural Policy (CAP) of subsidies and other compensations to European farmers and the policy of "Structural Funds" for the less-developed states on the periphery (Greece, Portugal, Ireland) were milestones in the sacrifice of sovereignty to the supranational European Community,[17] as was the decision embodied in the Single European Act of December 4, 1985, to institute a free circulation of goods, persons, services, and capital throughout the European Community by 1993.[18]

The Single Market started to go into effect in July 1987,[19] and in a report by European Commission Chairman Jacques Delors on accompanying financial measures to be taken, published on April 17, 1989, it was specified that a first phase of the free movement of capital should be effected by July 1, 1990. The Delors Report named two other stages for the creation of the Economic and Monetary Union without placing dates on them: the creation of a European Central Bank and the introduction of the single currency.[20]

There followed the critical decision at the Strasbourg European Council in December 1989 to set a timetable for starting the process of transforming the European Monetary System into the European Monetary Union (EMU) by means of the single currency. To this effect, it was agreed at Strasbourg that an Intergovernmental Conference (IGC) would be convened before the end of 1990.[21] A year after that, in December 1991, it was agreed at the European Council in Maastricht, that the Euro would be introduced on January 1, 1999, and that it would become the sole medium of exchange by the year 2002.

The Maastricht Treaty of December 1991, signed in February 1992 and ratified a year later, emerged from twin IGCs, one on the EMU and one on the political union, the latter having been proposed jointly by François Mitterrand and Helmut Kohl on April 19,1990, and approved at the European Council in Dublin that June. Both conferences began on December 15, 1990, following the next European Council meeting, at Rome. Out of the political conference, and as incorporated into the Maastricht Treaty, the concept of an eventual European defense identity was sketched out for the first time, linked with the simultaneously announced Common Foreign and Security Policy (CFSP). The CFSP, placed in the intergovernmental Pillar Two of the EU's treaty corpus, was heir to the abortive European Political Community of the 1950s which in turn had been resurrected as a loose, consensus-based mechanism in 1970, known as European Political Cooperation.[22] The key passage in the Maastricht Treaty that instituted these changes is the following: "The common foreign and security policy shall include all questions related to the security of the European Union, including the framing of a common defense policy, which might in time lead to a common defense."[23]

It was the fall of the Soviet imperium that had reopened in earnest the question of a European defense identity. In the 1990s, the frozen peace of a superpower standoff gave way to a succession of minor wars on Europe's doorstep. From the end of the Cold War and the consequently easy coalition victory against Saddam Hussein in the period 1989–1991 through the war in Bosnia in the middle of the decade to the air campaign in Kosovo at the end of it, Europe's military forces, mainly those of Britain and France, but later those of Germany, Italy, and others, became engaged, though seldom as principal actors and often in dispute with their main Western ally, the United States.

The decade of the 1990s, which is the central focus of this book, saw many twists and turns in France's defense policy, as the French sought to cope with the principal international experiences of the decade: the end of the Cold War, the reunification of Germany, the collapse of the Soviet Union, and the enduring and overwhelming military power of the United States. Yet French *strategy* remained remarkably the same throughout the period: a quest for autonomy in defense matters as expressed through Europe. Witness these two statements, nearly ten years apart, by leading French policymakers:

- The [European] Community ... at the same time that it undertook its economic and monetary union, became engaged on the route towards political union.... Political union will lead ineluctably, in terms of foreign policy, to the creation of a proper European defense capability.—President François Mitterrand, April 1991.[24]
- With the Euro [in being], it appears more and more of an anomaly that the European Union remains inexistent in the area of defense [and] that it cannot even speak about it!—Foreign Minister Hubert Védrine, December 9, 1999.[25]

What both Mitterrand and Védrine were saying was that it was entirely logical that the European Economic and Monetary Union, set in train by the Maastricht EU Summit of December 1991, would be followed by other steps toward integration, including some in the defense area. This, moreover, was a conscious policy of François Mitterrand: making the emergence of a political union within the EU contingent on the dynamic that would be created by the EMU.[26]

This causal chain hardly should have come as a surprise to Washington. However, the U.S. government, perhaps because it has the optic of a *hyperpuissance*, to use Mr. Védrine's phrase, seems habitually surprised and disconcerted by Europe's desire for an autonomous defense capability. And, despite Védrine's rhetorical plaint, the "fifty-year-old French dream," as Jolyon Howorth has put it,[27] of an independent European defense identity was not only alive but closer to realization then ever before as the twenty-first century opened.

It was not just *logical* to expect that the EMU would lead ineluctably to an autonomous European defense: the very size of the European Union, which finally committed itself in principle to a major expansion with the decision of its Helsinki Summit in December 1999, seems to demand it. The EU eventually will reach the point where its economic and demographic weight will far exceed that of the United States. Can it not be expected that the EU will seek to make this weight felt internationally? As a French Foreign Ministry statement put it in December 1999, "By the end of the next enlargements, the Union will have the necessary dimension to weigh in on the equilibrium of the European continent and on world affairs. It is necessary from this moment to exploit this historic chance to give the Union a more coherent and more operational diplomacy, so that it can assure its proper security, and to give it the means to act, if necessary, beyond its frontiers."[28]

The admission of thirteen more countries into the EU has now been accepted in principle. At the Helsinki Summit, at least in part in response to European public opinion, the EU somewhat precipitously decided to put six postulant countries into the same basket with the six already accepted candidate countries and not to exclude a thirteenth—Turkey—from eventually being considered for membership: "The European Council confirms the importance of the enlargement process started at Luxembourg in December 1997 ... [and] reaffirms the inclusive character of the adhesion process, which now groups together 13 candidate countries into a single category. The candidate countries participate in this process on an equal footing."[29]

However, the enlargement of the European Union had not been set quite in concrete. At Helsinki, no firm timetable was set for any new admissions. There was only the forecast that "the [EU] should be in a position to welcome new state members starting at the end of 2002."[30] Another signpost was that by the end of 2004 at the latest, the European Council would make an overall review of the enlargement question. Although no firm promises were made, the Helsinki Summit raised expectations, and this came at a time when the EU was only beginning to address anew the unwieldiness of its institutions, stemming from the fact that its structures were designed for its original six members and not the present sixteen nor the future twenty-eight or more. This restructuring was supposed to be done by a new Intergovernmental Conference, which completed its work by December 2000, in time for the Nice Summit under the French EU presidency. At Nice, the EU took the significant step of assigning voting weights to incoming members while still holding off on a date certain for membership. In sum, *when* the new candidates will be admitted, assuming they all will be, is still far from certain. In other respects, notably the extension of qualified majority voting and the streamlining of the European Commission membership, the Nice Summit did not make significant advances.

What all this means, as far as expansion of the EU into Central and Eastern Europe is concerned, is that the decade since the fall of the Berlin Wall can be said to have been lost. As a group of European intellectuals stated in a declaration in early August 1999, "The war in Kosovo should compel the European Union to rethink its future. [It should] redirect an institution that is introverted and wrapped up in its economic program towards a pan-European political plan. ... Ten years after the fall of the Berlin Wall, the vision of a reunified Europe seems to have disappeared."[31]

THE FRANCE-NATO PROBLEM

Why is it, in this search for a European defense identity, that France distinguishes itself from all the European allies in the intensity of its desire to be free of American command and control? The reasons are complex and many. In one respect, it stems from the fact that France, Great Britain, and the United States are the three major countries representing both Western values in general and a democratic political culture in particular. In this respect, France considers itself to have an equal validity alongside its "Anglo-Saxon" partners and, therefore, resists any sign that it is not being taken seriously.

But apart from the fact that historically French political culture differs significantly from and rivals that of the Anglo-Americans, there are more contemporary reasons for setting the French apart. In modern times, it is only France among the three that has been overrun, conquered, and subjugated. As Stanley Hoffmann has put it, France became obsessed with independence because she lost it in 1940.[32] The French experience differed sharply from that of Britain, which had successfully defended itself during World War II. This difference, among many other reasons, has made it easier for Britain, not suffering from the stigma of World War II as France had, to accept an American lead in strategic and defense matters.

The "fifty-year-old French dream" of a European defense identity, to which Jolyon Howorth has referred,[33] was consistently opposed by a Britain traditionally suspicious of any coalescing of powers on the Continent and careful not to run afoul of its traditional *special relationship* with the United States. In part also, this British rebuff of French ambitions had to do with the millennial rivalry between Britain and France. But the Britain of Prime Minister Tony Blair ended his country's opposition to France's "fifty-year-old dream" with the St. Malo Declaration of December 1998, which stated that the European Union "must have the capacity for autonomous action, backed up by credible military forces [and] the means to decide to use them . . . in order to respond to international crises."[34]

Another reason for France's unique and consistent search for a European defense identity stems from the bad hand France was dealt at the time of the creation of NATO and its transformation from an alliance on paper to a military organization in being.[35] According to the Gaullist argument, the North Atlantic Alliance and NATO are two distinct movements and, therefore, two distinct entities. The transition from the Washington Treaty of 1949 to the creation of the NATO organization of 1950–1951 took place against a background of ever-increasing threats by the Soviet Union, culminating in the North Korean invasion of June 1950. In the face of the Soviet menace, France willingly abandoned hopes of building a defense of Europe by Europeans alone (the Brussels Pact of 1948) and threw itself into the arms of the United States—partly to escape the onerous tutelage of Great Britain in defense matters. But in 1951, when the NATO integrated command was put in place and General Dwight D. Eisenhower returned to Europe as Supreme Commander (SACEUR), the French wound up with not even a major subordinate command, even though France was supposed to furnish the bulk of the troops for the defense of Western Europe. Although General Alphonse Juin eventually, in 1953, became the chief of the Regional Central Command, at the outset Eisenhower kept this key post for himself.

Although at the beginning the French welcomed the American-led integrated command as a way of escaping British hegemony, they soon became uncomfortable with the arrangements. Already, in July 1951, General Juin described the Central Command he was about to join as "too subjugated to SHAPE."[36] In essence, the French came to regard the integrated military command as a sort of zero-sum game in which their sovereignty was whittled away and a sizeable portion of their defense forces was placed under the orders of an American officer (the SACEUR). This was a situation that Charles de Gaulle, after his return to power in 1958, was gradually to undo. By 1966, de Gaulle was able to achieve independence from the NATO command without leaving the Atlantic Alliance.

In March 1959, de Gaulle fired his first warning shot: in case of hostilities, the French Mediterranean Fleet would not come under the integrated NATO command. In June 1963, de Gaulle withdrew from the integrated command French naval forces in the Atlantic and the English Channel. In September 1965, de Gaulle indicated that he would pull out entirely of the integrated command by 1969 at the latest. On March 7, 1966, de Gaulle did just that in a letter stating that all Allied forces should leave France. But though leaving the integrated command in unceremonious fashion, de Gaulle remained within the Alliance. France continued to attend North Atlantic Council meetings and reaffirmed its intention to abide by the Washington Treaty's clause on mutual defense (Article V).[37]

De Gaulle's successors saw the disadvantage to France of its isolation from NATO's military structures, and they undertook a discreet rapprochement with these structures while at the same time trying to revive the Brussels Pact structure (the Western European Union) in order to create a purely European defense system.[38] The latter effort failed because of the unwillingness of France's European partners to dilute the NATO system. The French then turned in the 1990s to NATO itself, hoping to work from within to increase Europe's autonomy in defense and to lessen U.S. dominance by modifying the SACEUR (integrated command) system.

The SACEUR system had been fashioned to defend against the threat of a massive attack from the East during the Cold War. The imperative of efficiency required that there be a highly centralized command for the use of both conventional and nuclear weapons. Whether this system should continue has been the subject of intermittent debate since the end of the Cold War. The unreconstructed school of thought in France, particularly since the end of the Cold War, is that the integrated command should go.

Although the integrated command theoretically was an anomaly with the end of the Cold War, it nevertheless turned out to be the case in Bosnia (and later in Kosovo) that nothing was possible until the Americans intervened and exercised the facilities of the integrated command. The virtue of the integrated command—American participation and know-how—was once again seen as crucially important, despite its vice—the increasingly anachronistic deficit of sovereignty for Western Europe in defense matters, in an era when the Cold War was over.

France's *outsider* situation, difficult operationally after the break with the integrated command in 1966, became more and more onerous as the Cold War wore off. As the other major power in Europe, along with Britain, willing to join in foreign interventions in the free atmosphere of the post–Cold War, France was impelled to take steps to overcome the disadvantages of its isolation from the NATO military bodies.

Several agreements had been concluded between France and NATO following de Gaulle's rupture in 1966. These were aimed at arranging the disposition of French forces in the event of hostilities in Europe. The first was the Ailleret-Lemnitzer accord of August 1967 on operations in the central zone of Europe, and probably the most politically important was the Lanxade-Naumann-Shalikashvili agreement of January 1993 on placing the Euro-Corps under NATO in a time of emergency.

While the tendency of the French military was to harmonize its relationship with NATO, President Mitterrand was wary of encouraging a rapprochement. In a restricted Defense Committee meeting on January 16, 1990, Mitterrand stated that previously in his presidency, during the first "cohabitation" government (1986–1988), headed by his political rival, Jacques Chirac, France was "within the snap of a finger of returning to integration with NATO. It was my refusal that prevented this."[39]

Later in the decade, when Jacques Chirac returned to the scene, this time replacing Mitterrand as president in June 1995, he began a sharp turn toward NATO, announcing in December of that year that France was rejoining the Military Committee (while still holding itself apart from the integrated command). As Hubert Védrine was to observe in 1996, "[In] announcing the withdrawal of France from the NATO military command . . . de Gaulle [in 1966] created a fait accompli which was to impose itself on his successors until 1995."[40]

However, the French rapprochement with NATO stalled in 1996–1997, in general over the U.S. refusal to grant what the French saw as a necessary degree of autonomy to a European Security and Defense Identity (ESDI) within the Alliance, and in particular over U.S. rejection of a French bid for a redistribution of NATO command appointments in Europe's favor. Nevertheless, the question of France's position vis-à-vis NATO remained open, and some see the return of France to NATO as more or less inevitable. One particularly knowledgeable NATO official expects it to happen around 2002.[41]

France both represents Europe, as the most vociferous defender of its autonomy in defense, and is rejected by much of conservative opinion in the Old Continent. The France-NATO relationship forms a significant part of the defense relationship between the United States and Europe. But France, too weak ever to take on the United States alone, must use its formidable diplomacy in a constant search for allies, particularly Britain and Germany, as it tries to assert Europe's strategic identity, as evoked by Frédéric Bozo.[42] For France, this strategic identity has come to be symbolized in the so-called "third option"—military operations not conducted together with NATO, nor with the use of NATO assets by the Europeans, but by the Europeans alone with the use of their own resources.

The issue of the comparison, or the relationship, between the two institutions of NATO and the EU now, at the beginning of the twenty-first century, has been transformed. The EU has taken on for itself a role in defense, supplanting the Western European Union. In this manner, the relationship between NATO and the EU—these two organizations that inhabit the same city, Brussels, but scarcely spoke to each other over the past decades—has moved to the top of the agenda. It is no longer a question of whether NATO and the EU *compare*; they now recognize that they must *relate*, and they have taken steps to bring this about. They have to coordinate their respective enlargements, and, because they are both now defense organizations in the European space, they have to coordinate their planning and force postures so as to avoid duplication of resources and efforts. Such coordination is complicated by the facts that eight members of NATO are not members of the EU[43] and that five members of the EU are not members of NATO.[44]

And finally, the European Security and Defense Identity—now called the European Common Security and Defense Policy[45]—as it gains in substance and in autonomy, is only one issue among many in the relationship between the United States and the European Union, a relationship which, by all odds, holds the key to world peace and stability. But having taken on the crucially important role of defense, the EU's prestige as an institution is now engaged to crown this new initiative with success. It is not difficult to divine what should be the long-range projection of the EU's new role. As Stanley Hoffmann has put it, "Europe must not remain an economic giant and a diplomatic and military dwarf; in the long run, its weakness in the latter domains will sap its force in others."[46]

NOTES

1. Frédéric Bozo, *La France et l'OTAN: de la guerre froide au nouvel ordre européen* (Paris: Masson, 1991), p. 195.

2. Speech in Paris to the Association Eurodefense. ⟨http://www.defense.gouv.fr/actualites/communiques/d170600/170600b.htm⟩.

3. Marie-Pierre Subtil, "L'échec du projet de défense européenne," *Le Monde*, August 20–21, 1989, p. 2.

4. Italy had also failed to ratify the EDC Treaty by the time the French National Assembly killed it in a procedural vote on August 30, 1954.

5. This is the text of Article IV of the revised Brussels Treaty (*United Nations Treaty Series*, Vol. 211, 1955, p. 346).

6. Bernardette d'Armaillé, *L'Architenture européenne de sécurité* (Paris: CREST, 1991), p. 47.

7. Nicole Gnesotto, *La Puissance et l'Europe* (Paris: Presses de Sciences Po, 1998), p. 33.

8. Hubert Védrine, *Les mondes de François Mitterrand. À l'Élysée 1981–1995* (Paris: Fayard, 1996), pp. 728–29.

9. Pascal Boniface, "Révolution stratégique mondiale, continuité et inflexions de la politique française de sécurité," in Samy Cohen, ed., *Mitterrand et la sortie de la guerre froide* (Paris: Presses Universitaires de France, 1998), p. 180.

10. Louis Gautier, *Mitterrand et son armée 1990–1995* (Paris: Grasset, 1999), p. 19.
11. *Le Monde*, October 17, 1991, p. 4.
12. Boniface, "Révolution stratégique," p. 182.
13. Ibid., p. 178.
14. Daniel Vernet, "Mitterrand, l'URSS et la Russie," in Cohen, *Mitterrand et la sortie de la guerre froide*, p. 36. According to Vernet, the phrase had originated with former Foreign Minister Andrei Gromyko.
15. Letter to the editor, "Correspondence," *World Policy Journal*, vol. 14 (winter 1997/98): 100. (Cited in James M. Goldgeier, *Not Whether But When: The U.S. Decision to Enlarge NATO* [Washington, D.C.: Brookings Institution, 1999], p. 69.)
16. Charles G. Cogan, *Oldest Allies, Guarded Friends: The United States and France since 1940* (Westport, Conn.: Praeger, 1994), p. 93.
17. With the ratification of the Maastricht Treaty in February 1992, the European Community became the European Union (EU).
18. Pierre Favier and Michel Martin-Roland, *La Décennie Mitterrand, Vol. 3, Les Défis (1988–1991)* (Paris: Seuil, 1996), p. 78 (hereafter cited as *DM*).
19. Christian Lequesne, "Une lecture décisionnelle de la politique européenne de François Mitterrand," in Cohen, *Mitterrand et la sortie de la guerre froide*, p. 129.
20. *DM*, Vol. 3, p. 187.
21. Lequesne, "Une lecture décisionnelle," p. 137.
22. Gnesotto, *La Puissance et l'Europe*, p. 72.
23. Maastricht Treaty text, Article J.4, paragraph 1. ⟨http://www.defense.gouv.fr/europe/traites_fondateurs/maastricht.htm⟩.
24. Speech closing the Ecole de Guerre Forum, "The State of European Security at the Dawn of the 21st Century," April 11, 1991. (Cited in *Politique Etrangère de la France, Textes et Documents*, April 1991, p. 118.)
25. Interview of December 9, 1999, in *Libération*.
26. François de la Serre, "La politique européenne de François Mitterrand," in Cohen, *Mitterrand et la sortie de la guerre froide*, p. 119.
27. Remarks made on December 4, 1999, at a conference on "France in Europe—Europe in France," at Harvard University.
28. "La politique étrangère et de sécurité commune: un outil et une ambition." (Cited from ⟨www.diplomatie.fr/europe/politique/fiches8.html⟩, December 17, 1999.)
29. ⟨http://www.diplomatie.fr/actual/evenements/helsinki/cl.html⟩, p. 1.
30. Ibid.
31. *Le Monde*, August 5, 1999, p. 10.
32. Conversation with Stanley Hoffmann, May 21, 1992. Also see Cogan, *Oldest Allies*, p. 207.
33. See p. 9.
34. ⟨http://britain-info.org/bistext/fordom/defence/4 dc98–2.stm⟩, p. 1.
35. For a development of this argument see the Charles G. Cogan, *Force to Choose: France, the Atlantic Alliance, and NATO—Then and Now* (Westport, Conn.: Praeger, 1997).
36. Vincent Auriol, *Mon septennat 1947–1954* (Paris: Gallimard, 1970), p. 354. (Letter from Juin to President Auriol, July 10, 1951). N.D.L.R. SHAPE stood for the Supreme Headquarters Allied Powers Europe, where Eisenhower as SACEUR was located, at Rocquencourt, outside Paris.
37. Gautier, *Mitterrand et son armée*, p. 17.

38. See pp. 3–5.
39. Jacques Attali, *Verbatim III, 1988–1991* (Paris: Fayard, 1995), p. 399.
40. Védrine, *Les mondes de François Mitterrand*, p. 143.
41. Gunnar Riberholdt, Danish Defense Minister. (Talk at Harvard University, September 23, 1999.)
42. See p. 1.
43. Poland, the Czech Republic, Hungary, Turkey, Iceland, Norway, Canada, and the United States.
44. Ireland, Luxembourg, Austria, Finland, and Sweden.
45. See pp. 1–2.
46. *Le Monde*, June 6–7, 1999, p. 14.

CHAPTER 1

From the Fall of the Berlin Wall to the Change in the Nature of NATO (November 1989–July 1990)

EXPECTATIONS OF THE POST–COLD WAR

The end of the Cold War, as with other such periods in history, had brought with it both uncertainty and conflicting theories of what had happened and what was to come. In the debate in the United States, the "declinists," led by the British historian Paul Kennedy,[1] likened America's situation to that of previous colonial empires that had "overstretched" their resources and had gone into decline. This thesis was contested by Joseph Nye,[2] who argued that the U.S. share of the world's Gross Domestic Product (GDP) differed little from what it was early in the twentieth century. Furthermore, the United States had a unique asset, that of "soft power"—its value system, its technology, its intellectual freedom—which, as a complement to its military or "hard power," destined it to retain its position as world leader.

From another angle, Francis Fukuyama[3] viewed the decline of Communism and the West's irresistible ascendancy as proof that ideological conflicts had subsided and that history had "ended" with the permanent triumph of the democratic-capitalist system. Samuel P. Huntington, by contrast, saw the ideological struggles of the past replaced by new conflicts over cultural values—a "clash of civilizations" among the major civilizations that he identified: Western Christian, Orthodox Christian, Islamic, Hindu, Sinic, Japanese, Latin American, and (possibly) African.[4] Even though Huntington's thesis was criticized widely, including by one reviewer as that of a "garden-variety essentialism,"[5] his worldview appeared to be vindicated chillingly with the outbreak of wars in the Balkan peninsula in the 1990s along the fault-lines of Western Christian, Orthodox, and Muslim societies.

Whether the world was returning to the multipolar chaos of pre–1914 Europe and whether the United States was up to the role of global gendarme were subjects of continual debate in the United States, but few influential voices called for a return to American isolationism. Such a call would hardly have found resonance in an administration that was in the hands of the moderate, internationalist wing of the Republican Party and its leader, George H. W. Bush. That the United States was not going to retreat from Europe or from the world was made clear repeatedly by the president himself, by Secretary of State James Baker, and also by others prominent in the administration—Secretary of Defense Dick Cheney, and the Chairman of the Joint Chiefs of Staff, General Colin Powell.

GERMAN REUNIFICATION: IMPLICATIONS FOR BRITAIN AND FRANCE

The events of 1989 in Central and Eastern Europe left the principal Western European allies, Britain and France, not only unprepared for, but also wary of, a change in the status quo. On November 28, 1989, scarcely more than a fortnight after the fall of the Berlin Wall, Chancellor Helmut Kohl announced—unilaterally—his own plan for a rapid reunification of Germany. The West, and France in particular, was not expecting such a swift dénouement. As Stanley Hoffmann wrote, "Those who, like de Gaulle, had deemed German unification likely in a world that would have overcome the Cold War, expected it to result from an orderly process firmly controlled by Germany's neighbors and by the major powers."[6]

France, the chief complainant against Yalta and its division of Europe into two blocs, seemingly came to regret the stability and ascendancy that this division had afforded her. In almost nostalgic terms, François Mitterrand had this to say to Prime Minister Hans Modrow during a visit to East Germany in December 1989: "A too-rapid pace of events carries with it the risk that the order existing in Europe for the past 40 years could collapse and lead to an unstable situation.... It is up to the [German Democratic Republic] to make the case that its 40 years of existence as a State represents a durable political reality."[7]

With memories of the two world wars still ingrained in the collective conscience, neither Britain nor France was ready to accept with equanimity a reunified and resurgent Germany. But Britain, unlike France, had never accomplished a necessary epiphany of a reconciliation with Germany. On the geopolitical plane, and quite apart from the average Briton's sense of rancor against the Germans remaining from World War II, London retained its centuries-old concern about an all-powerful nation arising on the European continent. As if to demonstrate the point, British Prime Minister Margaret Thatcher brought to a meeting with French Prime Minister François Mitterrand in Strasbourg on December 8, 1989, maps of Greater Germany as it existed on the eve of World War II. She feared that Germany wanted to reconstitute the "Grand Reich" and suggested that there be regular French-British meetings as a counterweight to Germany.[8] It is perhaps not too much to say that this moment foreshadowed the pivotal declaration of St. Malo nine years later, when Britain and France came to a meeting of the minds concerning European defense.

At their meeting in Strasbourg, in the margins of the European Community's semiannual council meeting, Mrs. Thatcher was more categorically against West German Chancellor Helmut Kohl's efforts to force the absorption of East Germany than was her French counterpart, President François Mitterrand. According to what Mitterrand related to authors Pierre Favier and Michel Martin-Roland, the British prime minister was "in a rage. [She] wanted to prevent the reunification. I understood her concerns, but it seemed to me unrealistic to oppose reunification. [It] would be better to concentrate on negotiating the issues."[9]

Mitterrand's confidence was accorded in a retrospective interview on January 21, 1994. In the heat of the moment, his reaction may well have been different. According to Jacques Attali, one of his advisers in the Élysée (presidency), Mitterrand observed to him on October 2, 1989: "Those who talk of German reunification understand nothing. The Soviet Union will never accept it. It would be the death of the Warsaw Pact. Can you imagine that? And East Germany is Prussia. It would not want to be placed under the thumb of the Bavarians."[10]

France had accomplished its post–World War II reconciliation with Germany in a process marked by a series of variously spectacular and symbolic events: the secret negotiations in 1950 between French Foreign Minister Robert Schuman and German Chancellor Konrad Adenauer that resulted in the creation of a European Coal and Steel Community (ECSC), intended by its author, Jean Monnet, to eliminate the possibility of future conflict between the two countries by the pooling of a key resource; the invitation by Charles de Gaulle, shortly after his return to power in 1958, to Konrad Adenauer to visit him at his home in Colombey-les-deux-Églises; the signing of the French-German Treaty of Friendship and Cooperation by de Gaulle and Adenauer at the Élysée (presidency) in January 1963, eight days after de Gaulle had rejected brutally and publicly Britain's membership in the European Economic Community (EEC); and the impromptu holding of hands between François Mitterrand and Helmut Kohl at Verdun in 1984, on the sixtieth anniversary of that extended and sanguinary battle.

Notwithstanding the reconciliation between these two blood enemies, it was France that held an ascendant position over Germany throughout the entire postwar period, a position that, as the decade of the 1990s opened, she was about to lose. Not since the pre-Bismarckian period had France had the luxury of facing a splintered German nation, as she did in the period 1945–1990. Though France did not hold the western area of Germany in vassalage as she did during the apogee of the Napoleonic era, she did exercise a sort of virtual suzerainty over the Federal Republic by means of her manifold attributes: as one of the four postwar occupying powers in Germany; as a permanent member of the UN Security Council; as chief spoiler, if not chief leader, of the European Community; and as a nuclear weapons power vis-à-vis a Germany prohibited from manufacturing such arms.

ANCHORING GERMANY TO THE WEST: THE EUROPEAN MONETARY UNION

As the Cold War was ending and the Soviet Union was breaking up, anchoring Germany to the West retained even more of the primordial importance that it had enjoyed since the end of World War II. In this manner, deepening the European Union rather than enlarging it became the priority, culminating in the Treaty of Maastricht at the end of 1991 and the march toward the Economic and Monetary Union (EMU). François Mitterrand's expressed intention was to tie Germany permanently to the West by economic and monetary integration and, at the same time, to avoid diluting the European Union by a hasty enlargement.[11] Though the Euro, as it came to be known, predated in its conception the fall of the Berlin Wall, it was only at the end of 1989, at the European Council at Strasbourg, that the EMU process became engaged.

The idea of a European central bank and single currency had been proposed by German Foreign Minister Hans-Dietrich Genscher in a memorandum of February 26, 1988,[12] to his eleven counterparts in the European Community (*EC*). The following April, the report by EC Commission President Jacques Delors,[13] set July 1, 1990, as the date of the first phase of an Economic and Monetary Union), which was to be the free flow of capital. The second and third phases were the creation of a European central bank and the institution of single currency.

By the time of the Strasbourg European Council meeting in December 1989, François Mitterrand, who held the rotating presidency of the EC at the time,[14] had taken the lead in promoting the single currency. Mitterrand's position was in contrast to that of an initially reluctant Helmut Kohl who, though for it in principle, was not eager for electoral reasons to give his countrymen the idea that he was in favor of scrapping the Deutchmark for the Euro. Kohl had his eye on the first free elections in East Germany, which were to be held in the spring of 1990. A victory in these elections for his own Christian Democrats would enhance the party's chances in the elections in West Germany scheduled for December 1990.

At Strasbourg, a deal was struck between Mitterrand and Kohl, whereby an Intergovernmental Conference (IGC) would begin before the end of 1990 for the purpose of implementing Phase 2 and Phase 3 of the Delors recommendations, in return for which the European Council made a statement recognizing the right of the German people to recover "its unity through free self-determination."[15] Despite her objections, Mrs. Thatcher went along with this decision, as she had with the passage of the Single European Act in 1985.[16]

A month before the pivotal Strasbourg meeting that put the single currency on the rails, the Berlin Wall had come down suddenly and without warning on

November 9, 1989. The reunification of the two Germanies and, with it, the liberation of the former satellites of the USSR had been taken over by the people of these countries themselves. Although Mitterrand had declared publicly in Bonn on November 3, 1989, that he was "not afraid" of German unity,[17] he was wary of it. With the fall of the Berlin Wall, and Chancellor Kohl's swift and surprise announcement of his plan to reunify Germany, there was a moment of *flottement*, or hesitation, in Paris. Anxious to get control over events in Germany, François Mitterrand may have overreacted by flying to Kiev to meet with Mikhail Gorbachev on December 9, 1989. The meeting with Gorbachev left the impression that Mitterrand was not in favor of German reunification and that he was trying to slow it down or at least control it by evoking the symbols of the historic Franco-Russian alliance.

During their meeting, Gorbachev told Mitterrand that if German unity took place, he feared he would be overthrown in a military coup.[18] Mitterrand, anxious to preserve stability in Europe, which he felt Gorbachev represented, sought to "contain" the new Germany in two ways: first, as we have seen, by speeding up the timetable for the introduction of the single currency and, thus, locking West Germany into Western Europe; and second, by taking the lead in pressing Helmut Kohl to declare the Oder-Niesse line inherited from 1945 as the definitive eastern border for Germany and, in this manner, to calm the concerns of the Poles and the Russians.

It has become commonplace to criticize Mitterrand, at the fading point of his life, for shortsightedness in being unable to comprehend the irresistible dynamic of German reunification in 1989–1990. But it is easy to ignore in hindsight the problem of the Russian reaction. The Soviet Union, though its empire in Eastern Europe was being challenged seriously, was still a functioning state and a functioning superpower, although so moderated by Mikhail Gorbachev as to make the Brezhnev years look unrecognizable. "Let us not forget," observed Pierre Haski, "that [at the time] there were still nearly 400,000 Soviet soldiers on [East German] soil . . . and there was no certainty as to the manner in which the Communist Bloc leaders would conduct themselves in the face of popular unrest in the East, particularly in East Germany."[19]

Just as John F. Kennedy, aided by a lengthy reaction time and his own prudence, stopped the Cuban Missile Crisis short of war in 1962, so the presence of Mikhail Gorbachev in the Kremlin helped prevent the Cold War from ending in bloodshed. As Robert M. Gates, the former director of U.S. Central Intelligence put it, "Whatever one may think of Gorbachev—and I have criticized him strongly in the past—without his sense of humanity, the end of the Cold War would not have come about in this way."[20]

Mitterrand, too, recognized the importance of Gorbachev's stabilizing role externally as well as the fragility of his position internally, although the latter situation did not become manifest until 1991.

As for George H. W. Bush, Mitterrand, who met with the president on December 16, 1989, on the island of St. Martin, described his outlook in the following terms: "[He] couldn't care less about German unity as long as Germany remained within NATO."[21] Mitterrand did not share Bush's preoccupation with NATO, because he considered the military alliances coming out of the Cold War to be *dépassé*.[22]

Four days after meeting Bush, Mitterrand made one trip too many, holding to a previously scheduled trip to East Germany to visit what was the "fatally ill" Pankow regime.[23] Mitterrand, concerned that Kohl had presented to the Bundestag on November 28, 1989, a ten-point plan for reunification without consulting the Big Four former occupying powers or even his own foreign minister,[24] showed during his visit an undue favoritism toward East Germany. Mitterrand declared on December 20, 1989, that France and the German Democratic Republic (GDR) "still had much to do together."[25]

Mitterrand's trip to Kiev in early December 1989, at which he gave the impression of conspiring with Mikhail Gorbachev to slow down German reunification, and his clearly ill-advised decision to go through with a planned official visit later in the month to the now moribund German Democratic Republic and the consequent appearance that he used it as a counterweight to West Germany were, on the one hand, a reflection of what Jolyon Howorth has described as the phenomenon of France "overestimating her own throw-weight."[26] The real discussions on how to handle the future of Germany were being made by the superpowers, and in particular in the meeting between Gorbachev and President Bush at Malta on December 2, 1989.

But on the other hand, Mitterrand's actions reflected a French desire, based on more than a century of experience, to contain the future of Germany. France's three major wars with Germany over a seventy-five-year time span, and its subsequent alliance relationship with West Germany that had already lasted thirty years, put France in a unique position to make demands on Germany as a condition of its reunification. In addition, France's role as an occupying power, though originally granted almost on sufferance—"out of the goodness of his heart," as Franklin Roosevelt confided to Joseph Stalin[27]—gave France the juridical basis for a voice in the future of a reunited German state.

But there was little Mitterrand could do to stop the rush toward German reunification. As Stanley Hoffmann noted, "It was not until April 1990 that Mitterrand realized—after the elections that swept the Communists out of power in the GDR—that German unity was a fait accompli for all practical purposes; the problem for France was accommodation, not prevention."[28]

Though the rapport between George H. W. Bush and François Mitterrand remained good throughout the period—the exception, not the rule, in French-American summit contacts—they were poles apart on the question of the fate of military alliances at the end of the Cold War. The U.S. leadership had no intention of scrapping NATO. In a speech in East Berlin on December 12, 1989, Secretary of State James Baker spoke of a new European political architecture and a new Atlantism, with a NATO that was to be more "political." He even suggested a treaty between the United States and the European Community.[29]

Baker was intent on reaffirming U.S. leadership and later openly admitted in his memoirs that he had gone to Berlin to make a statement on the importance of the U.S. role: "I knew that President Mitterrand was going there the following week, and I wanted to demonstrate American leadership in going there first."[30] (American leadership was asserted quickly in fact in 1990, in large part due to the imperative necessity to react to Saddam Hussein's aggression against Kuwait, starting on August 2, 1990.)

TRANSFORMING EUROPE

In France there was the expectation, one might say the hope, that with the end of the Cold War there would be a disengagement of the United States, at least partially, from Europe, or at any rate a loosening of American hegemony represented in the NATO integrated command. As Louis Gautier put it, "The end of the Cold War, because it signified the disappearance of the continental adversary, and also in the long run the disengagement of the American ally, offered France new perspectives for its security."[31]

François Mitterrand's view of a new world order was expressed on various occasions in the course of the year 1990. He saw a post–Cold War world developing along the following lines: the Europeans would take charge of their own security; NATO would be continued but remain confined to its traditional geographic zone of Western Europe and North America; the United Nations, free of East-West tensions, would be reactivated as the principal instrument for regulating world order; and France would intensify its role as a champion of peace, democracy, and human rights.[32]

Initially, Mitterrand appeared to look toward the Conference on Security and Cooperation in Europe (CSCE) as an umbrella organization for a new post–Cold War order in Europe. As Louis Gautier has pointed out, the CSCE was one of three basic choices for a security structure in the post–Cold War.[33] The other two were NATO, about which France was reticent, and the European Community, which however did not have a defense role.

At Kiev on December 6, 1989, Mitterrand proposed to Gorbachev that the CSCE be convened in 1990 in order to guarantee Germany's frontiers as tentatively laid down at Yalta. Gorbachev agreed, advancing the view that if a solution could be found in a pan-European framework, it would guarantee Europe against a cataclysm.[34]

But the Organization for Security and Cooperation in Europe (OSCE), as it is now known, was too diffuse to be effective.[35] Decisions had to be taken by unanimity; the organization had no military teeth in it, unlike NATO; and also unlike NATO, it did not have forty years of experience as an organization behind it. NATO, on the other hand, was more homogeneous, had an enforcement capability, and had an acknowledged, but not always respected, leader—the United States. Most fundamentally, the OSCE did not represent a true community of interests, as NATO and the European Union arguably do.

At the end of the year 1989, Mitterrand came up with a proposal that betrayed his intention, as Jolyon Howorth characterized it, "of keeping the USA at arms length from the process of *European* transformation."[36] In his New Year's Eve address, Mitterrand proposed the creation of a European Confederation. Mitterrand started out with the observation that, "Europe, obviously, will no longer be the Europe we have known during the last half-century. Formerly dependent on the two superpowers, she is, like going back to one's own house, returning to her history and her geography."[37]

But, Mitterrand added, to avoid a return to 1919 that would lead to war, the only remedy was the construction of Europe. However, instead of proposing a union of Central and Eastern Europe with the twelve nations of the European Community, he proposed an intermediate stage in which all the nations of Europe would come together in a "European Confederation" that "would associate all the States of our continent in a common and permanent organization of exchanges, of peace and of security." Such a confederation, he said, would welcome any state with pluralistic and democratic institutions.[38]

Explaining his point of view to Helmut Kohl several weeks later, Mitterrand stated:

I spoke of a possible European confederation, because the countries that have liberated themselves from the Communist yoke should not remain isolated, as this will lead to an unhealthy competition among us. It is necessary therefore to have an institution to which all democratic countries will have access. People say that the CSCE already exists for that [purpose]. But it will be very important, for the dignity of these countries, to have a political institution among Europeans alone.[39]

Mitterrand's idea was to fail at an intended founding meeting held in Prague in June 1991. It failed most particularly because the European Confederation would have comprised both Western and Eastern Europe, including the USSR, but would have excluded the United States and Canada. This was not a welcome proposal for those Central and Eastern European countries struggling to achieve complete freedom from the Soviet Union after forty years of occupation. In addition, the proposal was vague. Hubert Védrine, the secretary-general of the Élysée (presidency) at the time, confided, "We were dumbfounded. We found the idea magnificent, but we wondered what it implied, concretely."[40]

The confederation idea would have sidestepped, or postponed, at any rate, the issue of these countries joining the European Union at a time when, in the aftermath of the fall of the Berlin Wall and the collapse of the Iron Curtain, the focus was on the European Union. The issue of their joining NATO had not yet arisen as a serious consideration. Here, as was the case in a number of later instances, the EU was to disappoint the westward-looking countries of Central and Eastern Europe. It was the reluctance of certain powers, chiefly Great Britain and France, to extend the European Union to the Visegrad countries[41] that was to lead ineluctably to an intensive look at NATO enlargement, which would have seemed quite improbable at the start of the 1990s.

RETHINKING A POLITICAL UNION FOR WESTERN EUROPE

Anchoring Germany to the West also had a political dimension to it. Indeed, in the larger sense and as Mitterrand saw it, a political union would flow naturally from an economic and monetary union. The latter was a precondition for the former, Mitterrand declared to the *Nouvel Observateur* on July 27, 1989.[42] With the fall of the Berlin Wall, the impulse toward new political arrangements quickened. In response to a letter from Helmut Kohl on November 27, 1989, proposing a succession of intergovernmental conferences over the ensuing years to deal with economic and monetary union, with institutional reforms, and with an eventual political union, Mitterrand replied, "Like you, I would like, beyond economic and monetary union, a European union."[43]

The post–Cold War goal of a European "political union" was the linear successor to the abortive plan to develop a European Political Community alongside the European Defense Community in the 1950s, which was followed by the attempt to develop greater political cohesion in Western Europe through the failed Fouchet Plan of the 1960s and which finally saw the light again in the loose, consensus-based mechanism of European Political Cooperation developed in the 1970s.[44]

Like most of the EC's initiatives, the "political union" idea was originated by the Franco-German "locomotive" within the EC and, in this case, the leadership of François Mitterrand and Helmut Kohl. By the spring of 1990, the misunderstandings of the period immediately following the collapse of the Berlin Wall largely had gone away. Following the compromise at Strasbourg in December 1989 on German reunification and the Economic and Monetary Union, Mitterrand and Kohl were ready to work closely together again. As Stanley Hoffmann has observed, "After the hesitations of François Mitterrand at the end of 1989, the main lines of [French] policy pursued before that date were maintained."[45]

In April 1990, Kohl and Mitterrand agreed that twin intergovernmental conferences should be held at the end of the year: an economic one to create the mechanism for the Economic and Monetary Union and another one to set in motion an eventual political union.[46] The proposal was made in a joint letter to their EC colleagues on April 19, 1990, in which Mitterrand and Kohl officially put the idea of a political union of Europe on the public agenda.[47] They stated that it was time to "transform the nature of relations between the member states into a European Union and to give it the necessary means of action." In their letter, the two leaders suggested the holding of a conference on political union—including a common foreign and security policy—in parallel with the EC's Economic and Monetary Union conference.

The Mitterrand-Kohl proposal was officially endorsed by the European Council meeting at Dublin on June 26, 1990,[48] at which time the twelve nations of the European Community agreed to work toward a "Political Union," including the progressive unification of their foreign and security policies. (The twin conferences were to begin on December 14, 1990, in the wake of the European Council meeting in Rome.)

RETHINKING NATO

As 1989 drew to a close and the end of the Cold War was evident, a redefinition of the strategy of the Western alliance was inevitable. With the frozen (and stable) atmosphere of the Cold War a thing of the past, the question of who was to be in charge of security in the new Europe now arose.

For the "Europeanists" (1990s style), the reform of NATO was to proceed preferably in the direction of less integration and not more: the eventual strategic goal would be an essentially "bilateral" relationship between a European defense identity on the one hand and the United States on the other.[49] For the "Atlanticists," on the other hand, the conjurer's trick for demonstrating the continuing validity of the Alliance was to find more missions for NATO rather than less. These two conceptions were to come into sharp dispute.

As the Cold War faded away, French strategists were adamant that the U.S. "veto power" over the West's military activities, stemming from its long-dominant position in NATO through the integrated command structure, must not carry over to an emerging European defense identity. Wrote Frédéric Bozo: "the Americans must understand that all right of veto on their part regarding European political or military decisions is excluded because it is contrary to the very nature of the plan [for a European strategic identity]."[50]

When wars end, the expectation is that the alliances created to cope with them go away also. This was not to be with the end of the Cold War, which, of course, was not a typical war in that there never was a direct military exchange between the principal protagonists. There was a widespread feeling, in France in particular, that the momentous events taking place in 1989–1991 meant that Europe was now free to carry on on its own. As François Mitterrand put it in the fall of 1991, after the failed coup in Moscow, "We have just witnessed the deposition of the last empire on our continent. There is no longer an imposed order. Europe is now master of its choices, or it can be."[51] This was to be the mantra of French policy in the 1990s, carried on by Mitterrand and his successor, Jacques Chirac. Indeed, French policy in this regard, remarkable in its consistency despite perceived tactical zigzags, goes much farther back. In the 1990s, with the end of the Cold War, this ambition simply became more pronounced and intense.

While motivations of revenge for past humiliations certainly were never absent from French thinking toward the United States as the Cold War drew to a close, there had been all along a certain logic to French policy that the more pragmatic Americans found difficult to discern, much less accept. That policy, as Frédéric Bozo pointed out,[52] is the search for a "European strategic identity," which France has pursued for nearly half a century.

Yet the affirmation of a "European strategic identity" did not mean that NATO was going to go away. In a speech in Berlin on December 12, 1989, Secretary of State James Baker closed off any notion that NATO should go away with the fall of the Iron Curtain. In a speech that some observers found "hegemonistic" in overtones, Baker in effect preempted the debate. He laid out a vision of an Alliance not limited to the collective defense of its member states under Article 5 of the Atlantic Treaty, but as something more.[53] He proposed, in general terms, a new security architecture for Europe as a whole in which the United States would continue to play a major role.[54]

President Mitterrand, preoccupied by the necessity of a French role in the determination of the future of the two Germanies, at that moment did not enter fully into a debate over NATO. As Frédéric Bozo has observed, "The debate over the maintenance of the [Atlantic] Alliance after the Cold War virtually never took place."[55] Certainly, there was little the French could do to prevent the continuation of NATO as an organization, if indeed this was a serious intention on their part.

Though Mitterrand at that time (end of 1989) did not suggest that NATO not continue as an organization, he felt firmly that it should be contained. The new vision of NATO, as outlined by Baker in his speech at Berlin on December 12, 1989, of reaching out for relationships with the decommunizing states of Eastern Europe, was to be met with resistance by the French president. Although there was no public thinking at the time of incorporating new members from Eastern Europe into NATO, there was a juridical basis for doing so: Article 10 of the Washington Treaty of April 4, 1949 stated in part: "The parties may, by unanimous agreement, invite any other European state . . . to accede to this treaty."

Mitterrand, like nearly everyone else, was not contemplating in late 1989 an expansion of NATO to the east. Rather, he was focused on making sure that NATO would restrict itself to operating in the zone specified in the Washington Treaty of 1949, which mandated a collective defense of the territory of the Alliance's member states. As Jolyon Howorth has pointed out, "the main strategic issue at the heart of all these events [in the weeks following the fall of the Berlin Wall] was the double question of who (or rather which institutions) should assume the management of the transformation of central Europe and what should be the role of NATO in the transformation process."[56]

Mitterrand was opposed to an extension of NATO's role beyond its core function of the collective defense of the territory of its member states, because for France, extending the zone of NATO's competence for intervention meant extending the zone of American domination, via NATO's integrated command, to other areas besides Western Europe. Mitterrand preferred a period of pause, a period of waiting. His appraisal was that the withdrawal of the United States from Europe was ineluctable in the long run, and when the U.S. troop level in

Europe became significantly reduced, the expression of a European identity would take on its full meaning and inspiration.[57]

On April 19, 1990, the French president and President George H. W. Bush met at a bilateral summit at Key Largo, Florida. At such French-American summits, particularly between these two men and particularly in the early years of the Bush presidency, the atmosphere was generally favorable, certainly more favorable than most of the meetings at lower levels between the two governments.

Mitterrand returned from the Key Largo meeting apparently believing he had extracted a commitment from U.S. officials not to press the matter of a new strategic doctrine for NATO until they had a chance for further discussions. In vague but accommodating terms, Mitterrand noted in the joint press conference at the end of the Key Largo meeting that France was "ready to take part in a study aimed at adapting the Alliance to the demands of the forthcoming period." Thus the principle, if not the timing, of a reexamination of NATO's doctrine had been accepted by the French president.[58]

As to how the Alliance should evolve and the role for France in it, Mitterrand made his point of view known through his foreign minister, Roland Dumas, at a meeting of the North Atlantic Council at Turnberry (UK) on June 7, 1990:

France for its part is ready to participate wholeheartedly in a study (on the evolution of the Atlantic Alliance), based on the respect of the following three principles: there should not be a question of pushing out the lines of competence of the Alliance; France intends to retain its autonomy of decision regarding its own defense; it does not intend to call into question its doctrine of deterrence which is of a defensive character. It is open to discussion on everything else.[59]

THE FRENCH NUCLEAR DETERRENT IN THE POST–COLD WAR

France, by its unilateral and harsh withdrawal from the integrated NATO military command in 1966, had signaled its unwillingness—at least politically if not operationally—to recognize American predominance in Europe. Though France had thrown down a marker, it was in no position to make its desires a reality, with the Cold War still in full swing. The 1966 withdrawal from NATO's military structure simply put off a debate that was bound to return in the future. In the meantime, the formula of France being inside the Alliance and outside the military structure remained frozen in place. In the words of Professor Maurice Vaïsse, "All throughout these years, France's defense policy was characterized by a remarkable continuity and the perpetuation of her difference, made easier and encouraged by a national consensus, which allowed her to modernize her [nuclear] deterrent force. With the revolutions of 1990–1991, the 'aggiornamento' was ineluctable: the moment of choice had come."[60]

Though the nuclear imbalance between France and Germany would not change (Germany's nonpossession of nuclear weapons "is the price she pays for the wars she lost in the twentieth century," as Mitterrand observed[61]), the political import of France's *force de frappe* was to diminish markedly, though not altogether vanish, with the end of the Cold War. The overall effect was to emphasize further the nonoperational character of the French nuclear weapon. As Alfred Grosser, writing in 1989, succinctly summed up France's defense dilemma, the French conventional arm was not powerful enough to make itself felt throughout the world, whereas the French nuclear arm was too powerful to be used against weak countries.[62]

France's nuclear weapon had characteristically been presented during the Cold War in the following terms: it could obliterate the population of an adversary at a level equivalent to that of its own: 60 million. Faced with such a prospect, no adversary would choose war against France. This was the famous theory of the "deterrence of the weak against the strong." As Louis Gautier has put it, "The French deterrent has rested almost from the beginning on the idea of the ineluctability of an escalation to nuclear engagement in the case of an unacceptable threat to our interests. The French nuclear arsenal is consequently configured to inflict intolerable damage on an enemy."[63]

Not everyone has agreed with this rather pat (and perhaps too comfortable) theory. Perhaps most notably, as Louis Gautier also pointed out, it was Raymond Aron, France's most prominent critic of Gaullist orthodoxy, who asserted: "I deny that the small [power] can deter any aggression by the threat of massive reprisals. I deny that one can calculate exactly what is at stake and the risks that an aggressor would logically feel authorized to take."[64]

The French nuclear deterrent was implicitly measured against the yardstick of the Soviet Union, although it was intended primarily as a demonstration to the West. As W. Mendl observed, "French nuclear weapons were thought of not so much as a *force de dissuasion* as a *force de persuasion*. French nuclear armament had little to do with a military posture against a principal enemy.... However it had a great deal to do with the French position vis-à-vis the principal allies."[65]

The implicit focus on the Soviet Union contained in the threat of killing France's population equivalent of 60 million people was sublimated, whether intentionally or not, by the doctrine of an "all-azimuth defense," which meant that officially the French *force de frappe* could be used against *any* opponent. Enunciated by General Charles Ailleret in 1967, the "all-azimuth" strategy was officially adopted by General de Gaulle.

The notion of "the deterrence of the weak against the strong" helps explain the remarkably nonwarfighting character of the French nuclear doctrine ("a war is not intended to be fought but to be prevented"), as though it was understood that the French nuclear weapon never would be used against its one yardstick, the Soviet Union. A nuclear "side war" between France and the USSR was, quite simply, unreal.

With the end of the Cold War and the breakup of the Soviet Union, this yardstick was gone. As Louis Gautier put it, "The theory of [the deterrence] by the weak of the strong would seem to be maladapted after the disappearance of the Soviet Union as the main threat."[66] Of what use then was the French nuclear weapon, except to pose an existential threat to its neighbors, principally Germany? In this sense it rests as a reminder, albeit without any real-world meaning, that France can obliterate its ancient enemy, while the reverse is not true.

But above all, as General de Gaulle recognized from the outset (as did some American strategists, notably National Security Adviser McGeorge Bundy), the French nuclear weapon was political. François Mitterrand would tip his hat to his great and hated rival during a Council of Ministers' meeting on October 25, 1988: "Apart from its interest for our security, our nuclear weapon gives us a supplementary diplomatic capability. General de Gaulle had the great merit of conceiving independence as extending from nuclear deterrence. Other men also played an important role, including Pierre Mendès France. . . . This is a French phenomenon. Other choices could have been made; today, none others are possible."[67]

It is worth noting that of the several France-NATO agreements concluded following de Gaulle's rupture in 1966,[68] none touched on the use of France's nuclear deterrent. France's *force de frappe* has remained exclusively French for the thirty years since it became operational. In a conversation with Helmut Kohl on April 26, 1990, François Mitterrand explained his point of view on this exclusivity, focusing on the relationship between France's nuclear deterrent and the NATO integrated command:

France intends to remain faithful to its status as a full-fledged ally, but without taking part in the integrated command. The possession of the atomic weapon is for the purpose of preventing war. Supposing there is an act of folly or, as one might fear from the Soviet side, a land invasion. . . . The only means of balancing is with the atomic weapon. This could mean the physical disappearance of France within a half-hour. The problem is simple: I cannot leave it up to a foreign country to decide in place of us the life or death of France. This explains our basic reserve about coming back to the integrated command. But if our allies are threatened, we will be at their side with all our means.[69]

France's nuclear weapon always has had, of course, a security component, as Mitterrand indicated to Kohl in their 1990 conversation. But first and foremost, this weapon has been the supreme manifestation of France's independence and freedom of action. Conquered and subjugated in 1940, in the postwar period it broke free from foreign (read American) domination, culminating in de Gaulle's rupture with the integrated command in 1966, when all foreign forces were ordered to leave France. De Gaulle took this step after assuring himself that France's nuclear deterrent would soon become operational. (It did, in 1969.)

This process of independence through nuclear power was begun by de Gaulle himself in the brief period after the liberation of France, when he became chief of the Provisional Government. In 1945, de Gaulle created the Commissariat for Atomic Energy (CEA). His Fourth Republic successors decided to weaponize France's atomic capability. The decisive moment came in the Suez crisis in 1956, the only war in the twentieth century in which the United States opposed its principal Western allies, even in the face of implied Soviet threats to drop nuclear weapons on London and Paris. Though criticism of U.S. policy was only marginal within the Eisenhower administration, there were some dissenting opinions on the outside. Writing in the 1990s, Henry Kissinger observed,

> America ought to have shared the British and French perception that [Gamal Adbal] Nasser's brand of militant nationalism represented an insuperable obstacle to a constructive Middle East policy.... From that point of view, it would have been desirable to face down Nasser. But having accomplished his defeat, the United States could not participate in a restoration of British and French colonial dominance. Where America should have separated from its allies—if it were absolutely necessary—was not at the beginning of the Suez crisis but upon its successful conclusion. A demonstration that reliance on Soviet support was disastrous for Egypt should have been followed by support for the reasonable nationalist aims of a moderate successor to Nasser.[70]

In the aftermath of the crisis, and unlike Britain, which drew itself into a position of privileged subordination to the United States, an embittered and humiliated France concluded that the United States could not be depended upon, and it set about creating its own nuclear force. Initially embarked upon in co-operation with West Germany and Italy, the program was changed to an independent and purely French one in 1958, when de Gaulle returned to power.

France, then, has been practicing "independence through nuclear power" for decades, particularly since de Gaulle formalized this situation by breaking with the NATO integrated command in 1966. And in this sense French leaders have traditionally appeared to consider that theirs is the only truly independent country in Western Europe—Britain being too tied to the United States by its *special relationship* and, thus, in no position to declare an "all-azimuth" nuclear policy. Whether France's leaders will consider that the St. Malo declaration of December 1998 represents a definitive turning away by Britain from U.S. tutelage remains to be seen. The puzzle of the relationship of the three major European powers to Washington and NATO has been summed up succinctly by Nicole Gnesotto:

> The *special relationship* between London and Washington represents more than a simple alliance of circumstance: it is the very foundation of British power. America is thus to Great Britain what Europe is to France: the optimal multiplier of a national power that both countries know is relative. In effect, since Suez, and for identical reasons, France made the opposite choice from that of Britain: it is independence in relation to America that structures the identity and influence of France in the world. As for those whose heritage is situated at the other extreme, such as Germany, where the devaluing of power is at the very heart of the culture of the postwar, the Alliance inversely offers the best guarantee against any renationalization of power in Europe. To begin with, in Germany.[71]

The American-centeredness of France, in the role of a foil, is also echoed by Foreign Minister Hubert Védrine in his book of conversations with Dominique Moïsi: "there exists a French conception of relations with the United States.... We cannot say that the approach of most of our partners in Europe is identical to ours. But this is something fundamental for France, because the question of relations with the United States is at the center of international relations today."[72]

THE LONDON NATO SUMMIT, JULY 1990

Although NATO expansion was not on the agenda at this point, during the period immediately following the fall of the Berlin Wall, NATO began looking for ways to expand its horizons beyond that of a primarily military alliance dedicated to the collective defense of its member countries. The Alliance began reaching out to the newly liberated countries of Central and Eastern Europe. There was some basis for this, because, as noted previously,[73] the Atlantic Alliance, like the European Union, had proclaimed a pan-European vocation for itself from the very onset of its existence. However, what set the course for Washington's initial reluctance to consider an outright enlargement of the Alliance was, in part, the fact that the United States and its principal allies had made a gentlemen's agreement with Mikhail Gorbachev and Eduard Shevardnadze, when it was agreed that Germany could be reunited and remain within NATO, that NATO, would not be extended to the east.[74]

The first NATO Summit meeting following the fall of the Berlin Wall was held eight months afterwards at London on July 5–6, 1990. In preparation for this meeting, various NATO organs had been activating themselves in the direction of a new nuclear strategy, a more politically oriented Alliance, and initiatives aimed at extending friendship toward Eastern Europe.[75] In particular, U.S. planners pursued the idea of developing a "new strategic concept" for NATO, given the revolutions that had been taking place in the former Soviet satellite countries. It was over the issue of this new concept that a sharp disagreement between Paris and Washington developed during the summit itself.

At the London Summit, it was evident that NATO was searching for a role that would enable it to break out from the confines of a Cold War military alliance now that the Cold War was ending. The Alliance declared itself, in effect, as much a political institution as an instrument for the collective defense of Western Europe: "We reaffirm that security and stability do not lie solely in the military dimension, and we intend to enhance the political component of our Alliance as provided for by Article 2 of our Treaty."[76]

Furthermore, during the summit the United States pushed for and obtained a statement on the major principles that would be the basis for developing a new NATO strategy. Included were the following key points:

- There will be a significantly reduced role for sub-strategic nuclear systems of the shortest range. They [the Allies] have decided specifically that, once negotiations begin

on short-range nuclear forces, the Alliance will propose, in return for reciprocal action by the Soviet Union, the elimination of all its nuclear artillery shells from Europe.
- In the transformed Europe, they [the Allies] will be able to adopt a new NATO strategy making nuclear forces truly weapons of last resort.
- NATO will prepare a new Allied military strategy moving away from "forward defense," where appropriate, towards a reduced forward presence and modifying "flexible response" to reflect a reduced reliance on nuclear weapons.[77]

France disassociated itself from the section of the London communiqué dealing with the revision of NATO's strategy.[78] In Mitterrand's view, the use of nuclear weapons only as a last resort, as a replacement for the strategy of "flexible response,"[79] further denigrated the value of the French nuclear deterrent and the doctrine behind it. Though the new NATO doctrine seemingly was intended as something that would be less threatening to the Soviet Union,[80] Mitterrand refused to abide by it. He went ahead and signed the summit declaration, with reservations, but made clear that since France had not changed its position of being outside the NATO integrated command, it did not consider itself bound by the strategy of the use of nuclear weapons only as a "last resort."[81]

In a press conference of his own at London on July 6, Mitterrand, concerned at the summit's downgrading of nuclear forces—the cornerstone of French defense policy since de Gaulle—dissociated himself in public from the section of the declaration dealing with the revision of NATO's strategy:

France does not share the strategic conceptions of the Alliance, neither those of yesterday nor those of today: those of yesterday concerning flexible defense and the forward battle, those of today on [the use of] nuclear weapons [only] as a last resort. Deterrence was created to prevent a war, indeed to prohibit it, and not to win it. Therefore any idea which gives the impression that there are degrees in the use of nuclear artillery, that there could be a long process of conventional war which could in a last resort turn into a nuclear war, all this appears to us completely in contradiction with the reality of things.

As we desire that there not be a war, if each one knows that everything is in play from the moment of departure, there will not be one.

They announce that nuclear weapons will not be used except after the fact, after a conventional war.... This seems to me completely antinomic with French strategy, which is not to take the initiative to resort to force, but which keeps the option to use all of its forces at the desired moment, the latter having to as much as possible precede the opening of the conflict.[82]

Or, in an equally dogmatic formulation, Mitterrand is reported to have stated privately to President Bush, in a letter sent in June 1990: "deterrence, in order to be effective, must be early. It is both the most effective and the least perilous solution."[83] (But there is no guarantee, as per the observation by Raymond Aron cited earlier in this chapter, that a rival nuclear power, especially a much stronger one, necessarily would be deterred.)[84]

As with the process of German reunification, Mitterrand found himself clinging to archaic nostrums aimed at retaining France's preeminent position on the Continent of Western Europe. Indeed, there is a kind of "logic displaced from reality" in the orthodox school of French nuclear strategy. Based partly and quite legitimately on the reality of Europe's geographic position vis-à-vis the United States, these constructions nonetheless exhibit a kind of Alice-in-Wonderland quality. Professor Maurice Vaïsse comes close to evoking a sort of frozen assurance that recalls the France of the 1930s, transmuted to the late twentieth century, in the updated (1992) chapter of his and Jean Doise's *Diplomatie et Outil Militaire*:

Nobody dares to touch the military policy inherited from General de Gaulle. But to remain really faithful to his ideas, France—faced with the changes in international strategy—should not put its "diplomacy at the service of its defense," but quite to the contrary retain as a principle that armies are there to maintain the security of states. The political leaders should think over this observation, taken from [de Gaulle's] *The Edge of the Sword*: "Our country has too often in the past lulled itself to sleep in the false security of beautiful constructs of the mind which appear irrefutable until the moment when the shock of reality blows them to bits."[85]

It was clear from the London summit communiqué, with its new position on nuclear doctrine, with its call for "enhancing the political component of our Alliance," and with its statement of readiness to "intensify military contacts, including those of NATO Military Commanders, with Moscow and other Central and Eastern European capitals," that NATO was not moving in the direction that France would have liked. As Jacques Andréani, the French ambassador in Washington, put it, "We don't much like all this. One is losing completely the idea of an alliance, which implies a community of values and common political and economic structures."[86]

For the "Europeanists" in the French leadership there was only a meager compensation in the London Summit communiqué: "The move within the European Community toward political union, including the development of a European identity in the domain of security, will also contribute to Atlantic solidarity and to the establishment of a just and lasting order of peace throughout the whole of Europe."[87]

The use of the term "security" rather than that of "defense" was not by accident. As Hubert Védrine wrote, "We always say 'security' and not defense, so as not to alarm the NATO integrationists. But they're already on their guard. The whole problematic of the 1990's is there [in these two terms]."[88]

NOTES

1. Paul M. Kennedy, *The Rise and Fall of the Great Powers: Economic Change and Military Conflict from 1500–2000* (New York: Random House, 1987).

2. Joseph Nye, *Bound to Lead: the Changing Nature of American Power* (New York: Basic Books, 1990).

3. Francis Fukuyama, *The End of History and the Last Man* (New York: Free Press, 1992).

4. Samuel P. Huntington, *The Clash of Civilizations and the Remaking of World Order* (New York: Simon and Schuster, 1996).

5. Stephen Holmes, "In Search of New Enemies," *London Review of Books*, April 24, 1997, p. 6.

6. Stanley Hoffmann, "French Dilemmas and Strategies in the New Europe," in Robert O. Keohane, Joseph S. Nye, and Stanley Hoffmann, eds., *After the Cold War: International Institutions and State Strategies in Europe, 1989–1991* (Cambridge: Harvard University Press, 1993), p. 128.

7. Pierre Favier and Michel Martin-Roland, *La Décennie Mitterrand, Vol. 3, Les défis (1988–1991)* (Paris: Seuil, 1996), p. 249 (hereafter cited as *DM*). N.B. The citation is from notes of the conversations taken by a colleague of Modrow and published by *Le Monde* and *Der Spiegel* on May 2 and 3, 1996.

8. Ibid., p. 235.

9. Ibid.

10. Jacques Attali, *Verbatim III, 1988–1991* (Paris: Fayard, 1995), p. 313.

11. François de la Serre, "La politique européenne de François Mitterrand," in Samy Cohen, ed., *Mitterrand et la sortie de la guerre froide* (Paris: Presses Universitaires de France, 1998), p. 111.

12. *DM*, Vol. 3, p. 182.

13. See p. 8.

14. The European Community became the European Union with the Treaty of Maastricht, concluded on December 9–10, 1991, and signed on February 7, 1992.

15. Christian Lequesne, "Une lecture décisionnelle de la politique européenne de François Mitterrand," in Cohen, ed., *Mitterrand et la sortie de la guerre froide*, pp. 135–37.

16. See p. 7.

17. *DM*, Vol. 3, photo section.

18. Ibid.

19. Pierre Haski, "Mitterrand et la réunification de l'Allemagne," in Cohen, ed., *Mitterrand et la sortie de la guerre froide*, pp. 9–10.

20. From a seminar conducted by Dr. Gates at Harvard University, May 1, 1992.

21. *DM*, Vol. 3, photo section.

22. Ibid., p. 218.

23. Hoffmann, "French Dilemmas and Strategies," p.130.

24. *DM*, Vol. 3, p. 213.

25. Ibid., photo section.

26. Jolyon Howorth, "Renegotiating the Marriage Contract: Franco-American Relations since 1981," in Sabrina Ramet and Christine Ingebritsen, eds., *U.S.-European Interactions Since the End of the Cold War* (Boulder: Rowman and Littlefield, 2000), p. 8.

27. Jean Laloy, *Yalta: Yesterday, Today, Tomorrow*, trans. William R. Tyler (New York: Harper and Row, 1988), pp. 72–73.

28. Hoffmann, "French Dilemmas and Strategies," p. 130. N.D.L.R. The elections had taken place in March 1990.

29. *DM*, Vol. 3, pp. 241, 254, 283.

30. Ibid., p. 242.

31. Louis Gautier, *Mitterrand et son armée, 1990–1995* (Paris: Grasset, 1999), p. 11.

32. Ibid., p. 42.
33. Ibid., p. 69.
34. *DM*, Vol. 3, pp. 222–23.
35. Known prior to 1994 as the CSCE, the "fifty-two nation OSCE was the only regional 'security' organization that included both the NATO nations and all the countries of the former Soviet bloc." (Richard Holbrooke, *To End a War* [New York: Random House, 1998], p. 290.) It originally had been created to monitor the 1975 Helsinki Accords between the Soviet Union and the West.
36. Howorth, "Renegotiating the Marriage Contract," p. 6.
37. *DM*, Vol. 3, p. 253.
38. Ibid.
39. Attali, *Verbatim III*, p. 427.
40. *DM*, Vol. 3, p. 255.
41. Poland, the Czech Republic, Hungary, and Slovakia are the so-called "Visegrad Four."
42. De la Serre, "La politique européenne de François Mitterrand," p. 112.
43. Lequesne, "Une lecture décisionnelle," p. 139.
44. Catherine Guicherd, *A European Defense Identity: Challenge and Opportunity for NATO* (Congressional Research Service Report for Congress, June 12, 1991) summary page and pp. 76–77. Also see p. 18.
45. Stanley Hoffmann, "La France dans le Monde, 1979–2000," *Politique Étrangère*, no. 2 (2000), p. 4.
46. Cohen, ed., *Mitterrand et la sortie de la guerre froide*, pp. 51–52.
47. Lequesne, "Une lecture décisionnelle," p. 154.
48. Ibid., p. 141.
49. Interview of Jacques Andréani, French ambassador to the United States, on June 26, 1992.
50. Frédéric Bozo, *La France et l'OTAN: de la guerre froide au nouvel ordre européen* (Paris: Masson, 1991), p. 196.
51. Alain Rollat, "Jeu de patience à l'Elysée," *Le Monde*, October 19, 1991, p. 9.
52. See p. 1.
53. Frédéric Bozo, "De la 'bataille' des euromissiles à la 'guerre' du Kosovo: l'Alliance atlantique face à ses défis (1979–1999)," *Politique Étrangère*, no. 3 (1999), p. 593.
54. Howorth, "Renegotiating the Marriage Contract," p. 6.
55. Bozo, "De la 'bataille' des euromissiles," p. 592.
56. Howorth, "Renegotiating the Marriage Contract," p. 6.
57. *DM*, Vol. 4, p. 162.
58. Bozo, *La France et l'OTAN*, p. 187.
59. Gautier, *Mitterrand et son armée*, p. 65.
60. Jean Doise and Maurice Vaïsse, *Diplomatie et outil militaire 1871–1991* (Paris: Seuil, 1992), p. 623.
61. Hubert Védrine, *Les mondes de François Mitterrand. À l'Élysée, 1981–1995* (Paris: Fayard, 1996), p. 406.
62. Alfred Grosser, *Affaires extérieures: la politique de la France 1944–1989* (Paris: Flammarion, 1989), p. 196.

63. Gautier, *Mitterrand et son armée*, p. 91.
64. Ibid., p. 92. Reference is to Raymond Aron, *Le Grand Débat, Initiation à la stratégie atomique* (Paris: Calmann-Lévy, 1965).
65. W. Mendl, *Deterrence and Persuasion: French Nuclear Armament in the Context of National Policy, 1945–1969* (London: Faber and Faber, 1970), p. 18. (Cited in R. E. Utley, *The French Defence Debate: Consensus and Continuity in the Mitterrand Era* [London: Macmillan, 2000], p. 16.)
66. Gautier, *Mitterrand et son armée*, p. 89.
67. Attali, *Verbatim III*, p. 115.
68. See p. 13.
69. Attali, *Verbatim III*, p. 480.
70. Henry A. Kissinger, *Diplomacy* (New York: Simon and Schuster, 1994), p. 533.
71. Nicole Gnesotto, *La Puissance et l'Europe* (Paris: Presses de Sciences Po, 1998), p. 93.
72. Hubert Védrine, dialogue avec Dominique Moïsi, *Les cartes de la France à l'heure de la mondialisation* (Paris: Fayard, 2000), p. 114.
73. See p. 27.
74. Statement of Jack Matlock, former ambassador to Moscow, on "The Connection," WBUR, Boston, February 27, 1997.
75. Guicherd, *A European Defense Identity*, p. 7.
76. ⟨http://www.nato.int/docu/comm/49–95/c900706a.htm⟩, p. 1. N.B. Article 2 of the Washington Treaty of 1949 states in part, "The parties will continue towards the further development of peaceful and friendly international relations by strengthening their free institutions."
77. American Embassy telegram No. 4066 to State, July 6, 1990, pp. 2–3.
78. *Le Monde*, July 8–9, 1990, p. 5.
79. N.D.L.R. With the change of American administrations from that of President Eisenhower to President Kennedy, "flexible response" emerged as a new strategic doctrine replacing that of "massive retaliation." It was aimed at coping with a new situation: the mounting nuclear threat represented by the Soviet Union, coupled with a clear conventional superiority on its part. Under the new doctrine, the Kennedy administration increased the emphasis on conventional forces and sought to find a discriminating use for nuclear weapons. The new doctrine, however, was especially disturbing to the Europeans, because it meant that Europe was now more likely to become the battlefield in a series of conventional escalations, possibly including tactical nuclear weapons, which might or might not lead to a strategic nuclear exchange. This series of escalations could only lead to death and destruction in Europe. It was not until 1967 (by which time France had left the integrated command) that NATO finally endorsed, with some reluctance, the doctrine of "flexible response."
80. "To prove to the Soviets that NATO was no longer the aggressive military organization of the Cold War, Washington decided to renounce the doctrine that incarnated this threat." (*DM*, Vol. 3, p. 290, statement by the authors.)
81. *DM*, Vol. 3, p. 292.
82. *Le Monde*, July 8–9, 1990, p. 5.
83. Attali, *Verbatim III*, p. 526.
84. See p. 29.

85. Doise and Vaïsse, *Diplomatie et outil militaire*, p. 649.
86. Interview with Jacques Andréani, June 26, 1992.
87. ⟨http://www.nato.int/docu/comm/49–95/c900706a.htm⟩, p. 1.
88. Védrine, *Les mondes de François Mitterrand*, p. 459.

CHAPTER 2

From the Gulf War to the New Strategic Concept (July 1990– December 1991)

INTRODUCTION: THE FIVE NATO SUMMITS OF THE DECADE

Five NATO summits were held in the decade of the 1990s or, to put it another way, in the period since the fall of the Berlin Wall. These were at London in July 1990, at Rome in November 1991, at Brussels in January 1994, at Madrid in July 1997, and at Washington, D.C., in April 1999. At the first of these, in London, the NATO Heads of State and Government called for the elaboration of a New Strategic Concept, which was promulgated at the next summit, in Rome at the end of 1991, and which moved NATO strategically outside the confines of its member states and into a new role as a democratizing and stabilizing element in the European region as a whole. The Concept also prescribed new military roles for NATO beyond the traditional one of collective defense. As Lawrence R. Kaplan put it, the Rome Summit put NATO into the crisis management business.[1]

As we have seen in the previous chapter, it was also at the London Summit in July 1990 that NATO for the first time recognized "the move within the European Community toward political union" and the "development of a European identity in the domain of security."[2] This "identity" was to become a leitmotif in the four summits that followed to the point where, at the Washington Summit of April 1999, NATO declared that, "We acknowledge the resolve of the European Union to have the capacity for autonomous action so that it can take decisions and approve military action where the Alliance as a whole is not engaged."[3]

In this and following chapters we will trace the evolution of this "identity in the domain of security" toward "autonomy" as it transpired through the succeeding summits, not only of NATO but of the EU as well, and the effect that events external to Western Europe had on this process.

As we have also seen in the previous chapter, François Mitterrand at the London Summit sought to preserve the credibility of the French nuclear deterrent in the face of a newly emerging strategy envisaging the use of nuclear weapons only as a last resort. He pronounced the latter idea as "antinomic" to the French strategic doctrine of deterrence ("a war is not to be fought but to be prevented"). In spite of this reservation, however, France subscribed to the communiqué of the London Summit, and this was to have an effect on the eventual rapprochement of France with NATO later in the decade.

OUTBREAK OF WAR IN THE GULF

Hardly was the ink dry on Mitterrand's strong demurrer in London on NATO's nuclear policy when, with the Iraqi invasion of Kuwait on August 2, 1990, France was forced, to some degree against its basic inclination, into siding with the Anglo-Americans against Saddam Hussein. François Mitterrand, who had been working to keep NATO "on the reservation," that is, confined to Western Europe, found himself propelled into taking part in an out-of-area military operation that, at its core, was a NATO one in all but the name. As Gülnur Aybet put it, "[The Gulf War was] an operation planned by the U.S., and largely implemented with the aid of its European allies, using the nuts and bolts of NATO command and communications."[4]

Saddam Hussein's attack on Kuwait took nearly everyone by surprise. Though the Iraqi troop buildup was readily observed through U.S. technical intelligence means, Washington appeared to believe that Saddam was only posturing in order to wring concessions from Kuwait. Moreover, moderate Arab leaders assured the United States that the issue would be settled "in the Arab way," through extensive palaver at the conference table.

But there was another reason for the surprise. The West was distracted, as noted by a number of observers, including Hubert Védrine and U.S. Secretary of State James Baker, by the supreme efforts being made at the time to convince Mikhail Gorbachev to accept German reunification on U.S. terms. Indeed, Gorbachev, whose focus was on obtaining increased Western aid to the USSR,[5] reversed his position between mid-March and mid-July 1990. What Moscow refused on March 19, it accepted on July 16: a reunified Germany within NATO.[6] This was less than two weeks after the London NATO Summit and the image it projected of a more benign and more politically oriented Atlantic Alliance. In addition, Gorbachev promised to withdraw all Soviet troops from East Germany by the end of 1994.[7]

In the immediate aftermath of the Iraqi attack, the Soviets went even further. Exploiting his personal relationship with Foreign Minister Eduard Shevardnadze, Secretary of State James Baker persuaded him to issue a joint statement in Moscow on August 3, 1990, condemning the Iraqi invasion and calling for an arms embargo. On the latter issue, Shevardnadze did not consult Gorbachev but agreed to it because he thought it was right.⁸

France surprised some observers in immediately denouncing Saddam's actions and in going along with its Anglo-American allies in proposing stiff sanctions against him in the UN Security Council, starting with a condemnation on the day of the invasion itself (Resolution 660) and through a string of subsequent resolutions culminating with the application of a blockade against Iraq (Resolution 670 of September 25, 1990). This interventionist stance was not without its incongruities, as France had long espoused a pro-Arab policy and had favored Iraq in particular as a special client for arms sales and as a special trading partner whose oil output was of major importance. This policy, in place since Charles de Gaulle's denunciation of Israel's preemptive attack in the June 1967 war, was put to its most difficult test in the conflict with Saddam Hussein.

There were reasons behind this apparent tilt away from France's long-standing pro-Arab policy: in part it was due to French historical tradition, and in part it was due to France's position in the UN Security Council. France's tradition as an ex-colonial power and as the most ancient nation-state in Europe was such that, together with Great Britain, these were the only European powers who were willing, even eager, to undertake armed interventions abroad. As Margaret Thatcher asserted in her memoirs, "As was the case at the time of the Falklands War, France adopted a firm position; in spite of a speech in September at the UN that was out of place, and in which he tried to link a solution of the Gulf conflict with that of the Middle East, President Mitterrand and France showed throughout the crisis that the French were, apart from us, the only Europeans with the guts for fighting."⁹

Second, France's position on the UN Security Council, where it held the power of the veto, made it necessary to live up to the image that this status provided. France, one of only two West European countries in this position on the Security Council, had to weigh its votes very carefully and take European considerations as a whole into account.

A veto by France of a resolution sponsored by the Anglo-Americans was not something to be done lightly, especially if France were to find itself on the same side of a vote as the USSR or China. At a restricted Cabinet meeting on August 9, 1990, shortly after the Gulf crisis began, Mitterrand was categoric on this point: "If we have to choose, I believe we must join the struggle against [Saddam] Hussein, no matter what the consequences. If we don't do it, we will be the false friends ['les faux frères'] of the West."¹⁰

The French president was acutely aware that France was compelled to demonstrate its importance and said so publicly: "France is present. It must remain present. France is not a small country. It has a say . . . France must be present before as well as in the aftermath of this conflict."¹¹

Though France frequently had played the role of spoiler in the Alliance, the history of the Cold War showed that when a war crisis threatened, France was generally among the firmest in its support of the Alliance. This was most notably evident in the Berlin dispute (1958–1961) and in the Cuban Missile Crisis (1962). This pattern was to hold true also in the Gulf crisis, although as hostilities loomed, France did its best to prevent war by offering face-saving proposals to Saddam Hussein—the object being, in addition to attempting to avoid war, that of preserving France's image before Arab public opinion. At the same time, there was never any question in Mitterrand's mind that Saddam Hussein had committed an unpardonable aggression against Kuwait: "France has decided to associate its efforts with those countries who have committed themselves to the reestablishment of international law violated by Iraq," Mitterrand declared in a public statement at the end of the restricted Cabinet meeting of August 9, 1990.[12]

In the meeting of August 9, 1990, the chief dissenter was Jean-Pierre Chevènement, who, besides being an outspoken nationalist by political temperament, was in the doubly delicate position of being defense minister and of having been an active member in the France-Iraq Friendship Group: "What is at stake is our Arab policy. The game of the Americans is dangerous. If Saddam Hussein wins, it is obvious [what will happen]. If he loses, who will oppose anti-Western fundamentalism? If the Iraqi regime is swept away, with it will be swept away the sole obstacle to Iranian fundamentalism. We should emphasize economic means and a dialogue with the Arabs. We should explore the possibility of talking with Iraq."[13]

Though Chevènement agreed with the Cabinet consensus that Saudi Arabia should be aided if attacked, he pleaded against an automatic intervention on the part of France against Iraq and advocated an autonomy of command for French military elements deploying to the Gulf.

Lionel Jospin, who was later to become prime minister (and Chevènement his interior minister), disagreed on the issue of Islamic fundamentalism: "I do not believe in the thesis of the 'barrier against fundamentalism' put forward by Chevènement. A secular dictatorship can be just as dangerous as revolutionary fundamentalism. In no way should we find ourselves on the side of Iraq. If we let this fait accompli stand it will be catastrophic."[14]

Mitterrand, obviously irritated with the stubborn opposition of Chevènement, arrived at the bottom line:

Of course we should think about the future of our relations with Iraq and with the Arabs. But the problem is this: are we going to let the Americans act alone with the British? ... [The Americans] know that the other Europeans—Italy, Spain, Portugal—do not have much desire to get involved in this affair, [and] that the French and the British are the only ones who are able to act. If we don't respond to them, that means that we are remaining on the sidelines.[15]

Under discussion at the August 9 meeting was the issuance of a communiqué in which the government would explain the actions it had taken so far, including voting for Resolutions 660 and 661 of the UN Security Council, respectively condemning the invasion and instituting an embargo. The communiqué also stated that the French government was sending "materiel" and "technicians" to Saudi Arabia in response to requests from that government. Finally, the government announced that it was sending naval and air reinforcements to the Gulf to intervene should the need arise.[16] Mitterrand, who had prepared personally the final version of the communiqué, next read it at what was to be the first of fifteen press conferences he held on the Gulf crisis.

Mitterrand had already decided on August 7 to send the French aircraft carrier *Clemenceau* to the Gulf, though not with Super-Étendard attack aircraft but, instead, with largely symbolic Gazelle helicopters.[17] (These were from the 5th Combat Helicopter Regiment[18].) Still, the dispatch of the *Clemenceau*, which also had on board 800 men of the French Rapid Action Force (FAR),[19] was important and visible because, for one thing, the British did not possess an aircraft carrier.

THE DECISION TO SEND FRENCH TROOPS TO SAUDI ARABIA

On September 14, 1990, Iraqi forces took over five Western embassies in Kuwait City, including the French but excluding the British and American. Four French diplomats were arrested, including the military attaché. Mitterrand told his military chief of staff, Admiral Jacques Lanxade, "Saddam has stepped over the line. This is a provocation. We cannot back away."[20] (In the event, Palestinian leader Yasir Arafat, who had taken the side of Saddam in the crisis, was instrumental in helping arrange the release of French hostages in Kuwait,[21] including those from the French Embassy. On October 30, the 253 French hostages held in Kuwait were returned to France. Another 3,700 Westerners remained behind[22].)

Saddam's action on September 15 against the French embassy in Kuwait led to the dispatch of French troops to the theater. The 6th Light Armored Division, which would be the core of the French military effort in the war, known under the name of Operation Daguet (Stag), was sent to the Gulf starting on September 20.[23] The Division comprised the 4th Regiment of Dragoons and the 1st Combat Helicopter Regiment.[24] It was agreed at the outset that though the division would be under French command, its actions would be coordinated with the Allies.[25] General Maurice Schmitt, chief of staff of the French Armed Forces, explained the nuances of the French situation in an interview with *Terre Magazine*:

It is not so much a question of autonomy of forces but autonomy of decision . . . when forces belonging to several nations take part in a common mission, it is necessary to have structures of coordination. These exist and we are part of them. It would be stupid, in the name of a desire for autonomy, not to have recourse to local facilities—for example, logistics. . . . We must retain absolute mastery over our participation in this crisis. This does not exclude, quite the contrary, military cooperation, first of all with the host countries, and subsequently with the allied forces.[26]

General Schmitt and his military colleagues came to the conclusion that the French ground forces should be concentrated in the western sector in Saudi Arabia. "Such a deployment would not get us mixed in with the American forces and thus was in keeping with our military interests and our concern for independence or autonomy which was bound to come up here or there," he recounted.[27] Another reason, which General Schmitt evokes in his memoir, was that, while French forces were suited for a wide end run by mobile units in the extreme western sector, they were not tailored, with the light AMX-10 tank, to take on Iraqi forces dug in with T-72 tanks. Even if the French had a medium tank division instead of a light armored division, the French medium tank, the AMX-30 B2, was not a match for the T-72.[28] By the time the hostilities began, the French had put together a regiment of AMX-30 tanks within the Daguet Division.[29]

Lieutenant General (Ret.) Bernard E. Trainor, co-author of *The Generals' War*,[30] gave an account of the role of the French forces that does not differ materially from that of General Schmitt:

As usual, Franco-American relations on the military level were good. Also as usual, the rub came on the political level. The French had a light division in the Gulf (the 6th). Originally they refused to put it under American operational command. Rather, the division became part of the Arab command. It became clear that the arrangement was not going to work very well, so the French reluctantly turned to the Americans. They became part of the American XVIII Airborne Corps. They were put way out on the left flank to screen the rest of the corps. As a sweetener, a brigade of the U.S. 82nd Airborne Division was put under the operational command of the French 6th Division. Neither unit had the muscle to do much serious fighting in an armored environment. Both did a credible job, but saw little action.[31]

Thus, for reasons of prestige and rank, centered on France's position as a permanent member of the UN Security Council, and for reasons of Western solidarity, Paris was forced into going against the grain of its pro-Arab policy and into supporting the Anglo-American position, even to the extent of sending troops into the battle. And finally, and ultimately, French ground forces, though assigned to the far western sector of the front and not in the midst of the other troops of the coalition, were placed under the orders of the coalition commander, General Norman Schwarzkopf. French air elements, however, operated on an independent basis.[32]

According to the memoirs of General Schmitt, his relations with General Schwarzkopf and with General John Galvin, the Supreme Commander Allied Forces Europe (SACEUR), were excellent throughout the campaign, and following the conclusion of it, General Schwarzkopf was given a French Legion white képi as a gesture of esteem. As noted by General Trainor, relations of the French military with their American counterparts are traditionally better than those at the political level. Indeed it was the French effort to mediate in the situation and, in the process, to propitiate Saddam Hussein that was the principal cause of friction between Paris and Washington during the Gulf crisis.

FRENCH MEDIATION EFFORTS

Though Mitterrand believed that war was the most likely outcome ("We are in a logic of war," he said to the press on August 21[33]), he sought to bring Saddam around to a peaceful solution of the crisis, partly to maintain French credibility in Arab public opinion and partly to "show the French difference" politically, which essentially meant not appearing to tail after the Anglo-Americans. In a speech before the UN General Assembly on September 24, he held out an olive branch to Saddam, which was not to the liking of his Western allies. As noted previously,[34] he linked a solution of the Gulf crisis to the larger Arab-Israeli problem, thereby appearing to espouse Saddam's spurious propaganda point that the two situations were connected.[35] Moreover, he held out the possibility that Kuwait might be returned to democratic rule via "the democratic expression of the choices of the Kuwaiti people," thereby undermining the credibility of the Kuwaiti ruler, Shayk Jabar al-Sabah, who had fled to Saudi Arabia in the face of the Iraqi invasion.[36] For this he received a low-key admonition from President Bush to the effect that democracy could not be imposed from outside of Kuwait.[37]

Mitterrand's most urgent priority was to try to prevent war from breaking out and, thereby, to demonstrate that France was not only for peace but also against Arabs being killed in a one-sided war. Any gesture by Saddam Hussein that would indicate his intention to withdraw from Kuwait would be sufficient, Mitterrand declared in public and in private, for the Allies to call off an attack. To help bring this about, Mitterrand on several occasions sent emissaries on special missions to meet with Iraqi officials in Europe and in Baghdad. However, as Mitterrand was to find out to his chagrin, Saddam Hussein, while making certain cosmetic adjustments, remained unbudgeable on the core of the proposals being made variously by France and the USSR as the crisis reached its height: he would not withdraw from Kuwait.

Mitterrand's efforts dovetailed largely with those of the Soviets, in particular with that of Mikhail Gorbachev's special representative for Iraq, Yevgeniy Primakov. Mitterrand supported the Soviet initiatives because they were in line with his own attempts to prevent hostilities and also because he was anxious to help shore up Gorbachev's position internally in the Soviet Union. Gorbachev and Mitterrand met on October 29, 1990, at Rambouillet and were in general accord on what might be offered to Saddam as an excuse for him to pull his troops out of Kuwait without losing face (the prospect of an international conference to settle the larger Middle East issue and the possibility of negotiations with Kuwait under a new Kuwaiti regime, all under the rubric of an "Arab solution"), but at the same time, both leaders realized that there was little chance of such initiatives being approved by the Anglo-Americans. While Gorbachev did not want to break the solidarity of the five permanent members of the Security Council in the Gulf crisis, neither did he want a military action against Iraq to take place.[38]

In the climactic vote (Resolution 678 of November 29, 1990, which set a date of February 15, 1991, for Iraqi compliance), Gorbachev did not break ranks with the Western coalition but went along with the use of force against Iraq, under the euphemistic formula of using "all necessary means" to compel it to withdraw from Kuwait. Nor did France break ranks, although three weeks earlier, Secretary of State James Baker, under a thin veneer of anonymity, had doubted the full commitment of Syria and France to the coalition's military effort.[39]

On two further occasions, tension rose on the diplomatic level between the United States and France. The first was in December 1990 over a resolution in the Security Council advocating a settlement of the Arab-Israeli problem on the basis of long-existing UN Resolutions (242 and 338). After exchanges between Washington and Paris, including between President Bush and President Mitterrand, a compromise was finally achieved whereby the possibility of holding an international conference on the issue was mentioned not in the text of the resolution but only in the annex. Thus a U.S. veto of Resolution 681 (of December 20) was avoided.

The second occasion was a unilateral French initiative through the Security Council, hours before the deadline for Iraqi compliance was to end on January 15, 1991, and six days after a meeting in Geneva between James Baker and Foreign Minister Tariq Aziz had ended in a total standoff. The French proposal was that Iraq commit to a withdrawal and begin it immediately, as a means of avoiding hostilities. Both the British and the Americans were hostile to the proposed resolution, and France withdrew it. British Prime Minister John Major publicly reproached Mitterrand for not having informed him of the initiative when they met at the Élysée Palace on January 14. Mitterrand let it be known that at that time the text was not ready.[40]

Throughout the latter part of the Gulf crisis, the French government's tendency to send its own emissaries in parallel démarches to the Iraqis or to intermediaries was a chronic source of concern to Washington, which, as the leader of the coalition and having by far the most troops in the field, wanted to control the diplomatic game as much as possible by itself. President Bush wrote directly to President Mitterrand on this, on December 7, 1990: "Dear François . . . we think that official parallel discussions between other members of the coalition and Iraq are not very judicious, and that the creation of parallel channels only offers to Saddam Hussein the occasion for an attempt to weaken the coalition. . . . I hope you will discourage such initiatives."[41]

All in all, Mitterrand's initiatives provoked considerable annoyance in the Bush administration, which in the final analysis preferred a military showdown to an extended stalemate with a highly unreliable interlocutor—Saddam.

THE BALANCE SHEET OF THE WAR

This was France's first external war since the Suez operation of 1956. Paradoxically, in this case it was necessary for France, in order to demonstrate its status as a world power, to go along with and participate in the American-led military coalition instead of contesting, as was so often the case during the Cold War, American military moves. Though Paris sought to demonstrate the French "specificity" ("la spécificité française") in other ways, as in passably disruptive initiatives to win concessions from Saddam and, particularly, as in Mitterrand's last-minute proposal to the UN Security Council, France never shrank from its strategic "duty." Once having entered into the "logic of war," as Mitterrand himself put it, it was unthinkable that France could be other than on the side of its principal Western allies. This also had something to do with France's changed position due to the ending of the Cold War. As French Foreign Minister Hubert Védrine put it, "Our unique position [as] a Western country [being a] pivot between East and West disappeared with [the end of] the bipolar world."[42]

The Gulf War was also the first occasion since World War II that French forces had been placed under American command. This was not to the liking of the paleo-Gaullists and the Left in France, including and most notably Defense Minister Jean-Pierre Chevènement. In two letters to President Mitterrand in which he offered his resignation, on December 7, 1990, and January 1, 1991, Chevènement made known his objections to the American plan of attack, particularly the length and destructiveness of the projected air campaign, which he saw as reflecting typical U.S. concerns about its own casualties and disregard for those of others, in this case in particular, Iraqi civilians. In the two letters he also voiced his concerns about the autonomy of the French forces, which he described as "very relative," while conceding that the war plan submitted by General Schmitt (of which he attached a copy to Mitterrand in the January 1 letter) was the best the French could have in terms of freedom of action within the coalition and of preventing excessive casualties among the French forces. Chevènement also pressed for French air attacks to be limited to Kuwaiti territory.

Above all, Chevènement was concerned for the image of France: "Between the objective officially sought and the means employed there is a disproportion which is contrary to the very idea of justice. Such a war, if it takes place, risks discrediting for a long time the actions of the United Nations and the image of France in the world. How can the people of the Third World be made to understand that an American life is worth tens or even a hundred Iraqi lives?"[43] In public statements and in obstructive actions as Defense Minister, Chevènement did his best to undermine France's participation in the coalition, until ultimately Mitterrand had to force his resignation and replace him with Pierre Joxe at the end of January 1991.

All in all, the French military performance suffered in comparison with the British, though the British effort was the yardstick that the French used in deciding what their own contribution should be.[44] The British, unlike the French, had a full-blown armored division (the 1st Armored Division), which, by General Schmitt's own reckoning, destroyed 300 Iraqi tanks and armored vehicles.[45] This is confirmed by the following breakdown of what the 1st Armored Division destroyed, according to British records: some 200 tanks, 100 armored personnel carriers, and 100 artillery pieces. The British Division, with its two armored brigades (the 4th and the 7th), was equipped principally with the Challenger 1 Main Battle Tank (221 of them) and the Warrior Armored Infantry Fighting Vehicle (327 of them).[46]

In the air operations the French Jaguar attack aircraft did not have night-flying capability,[47] unlike the British. And the British commitment of personnel was more than two times that of the French.[48] All in all, the commitment of French personnel at the time the land fighting began was 14,000.[49] The British Army alone counted 28,000 personnel in the 1st Armored Division plus another 5,000 in support units. Together with maritime and air units and other support units, this was the largest U.K. overseas military operation mounted since World War II.[50]

In the military campaign against Saddam, the French felt keenly their technological deficiencies—in intelligence, in communications, and in logistics, as well as in the lack of the most modern equipment for its aircraft, including a night-flying capability. Some of these military deficiencies were a reflection of its nearly thirty years of isolation from the NATO integrated command. As a pseudonymous French general commented after the fact, "How was it, with one of the highest [relative] budgets in the world, and [representing] an important levy on the national wealth, the French Army was so badly organized, equipped and trained, and showed an incapacity to stand comparison with our partners, particularly the British?"[51]

The facts that, in the Gulf War, France endorsed an out-of-zone role for the NATO powers, that its forces were placed under American command, and that it participated in a military operation under the sanction of the UN, all served to call into question the very bases of French strategic doctrine. France's twin emphases on the early use, or rather the threatened use, of nuclear weapons, plus the maintenance of light intervention forces to uphold French interests abroad, particularly in Africa, were unsuitable for large-scale military operations outside the zone of NATO, such as was the case in the Gulf War. The same unnamed French general cited previously emphasized this shortcoming: "The relative success of the Gulf War should not create illusions. It revealed the obsolescence of the French armed services [and] their lack of adaptation for conventional warfare in force in a theater of operations."[52] France turned to the principle of "force projection" and a smaller, professional army as a result of the Gulf War (in which Paris sent no draftees to the front).

Although France's military contribution was limited and not on the same technical level as that of the United States, what took place in the Gulf War in geopolitical terms, if not in real power terms, was the first application, posthumously, of what Charles de Gaulle had unsuccessfully proposed in 1958: a "tridominium" of the United States, Great Britain, and France to run the strategic problems of the world.

However, although the "tridominium" was functional during the war against Saddam Hussein, it fell apart in the incomplete peace that followed. Once again, the French found themselves shut out of U.S. plans and intentions in the aftermath of the conflict. Manifestations of U.S. triumphalism, coinciding with a blunt letter of February 23, 1991, from U.S. Undersecretary of State for Security Affairs Reginald Bartholomew, warning European governments not to disrupt the role of NATO,[53] served to increase the sense of bitterness and distrust in Paris. Frédéric Bozo evoked this postwar atmosphere: "Seen from Paris, American precipitousness in pushing through a reform of NATO which offered only a façade of europeanization could only be interpreted as a will to 'preempt' the European objectives of France. Moreover, the Gulf War and the postwar context . . . without doubt strengthened a certain French suspicion with regard to a rapprochement with NATO which might well, in these conditions, develop into a one-way street."[54]

Fortunately, another summit between Bush and Mitterrand, this time at Martinique in March 1991, served to calm the atmosphere. But only for a time.

In fact, the "tridominium" of the Gulf War operated under the umbrella of a United Nations Resolution that made no mention of either NATO or the European Community (EC) or the Western European Union (WEU). Nevertheless, on the operational level, NATO was extremely important in the conduct of the Gulf War, as its troop assets in Europe were brought into play in the Middle Eastern theater. Also, the WEU's planning mechanisms were activated during the crisis: on August 21, 1990, the WEU's Foreign and Defense Ministers met in Paris to work out guidelines for cooperation in the Gulf, and a week later, the WEU's Chiefs of Defense Staff began to meet for the first time.[55] The WEU action was aided by the fact that the WEU had conducted a minesweeping operation in the Gulf in 1987 during the Iran-Iraq War.[56] American military planners, however, generally considered these WEU activities as an unhelpful and unnecessary complication that only served to muddle things.

NATO'S NEW STRATEGIC CONCEPT

Though Mitterrand had registered strong opposition to the strategic line that the July 1990 London Summit had taken, and perhaps because of it, the French asked to be included in the ad hoc Strategy Review Group (SRG) formed by NATO later in July 1990 to elaborate the line laid out in the London Summit and, thus, develop a so-called New Strategic Concept. With France included, the SRG became a meeting of sixteen NATO nations and not fifteen.

However, the French did not participate in the first three drafting sessions of the SRG, which lasted from August 1990 to March 1991, at which time Ambassador Gabriel Robin, the French Permanent Ambassador to NATO, announced that France would participate in future deliberations of the group. On March 15, 1991, the French joined in the debate on the proposed fourth draft and became major players in the remaining drafting sessions leading to the presentation of the New Strategic Concept at the next NATO Summit at Rome on November 7–8, 1991.

Although the French participation in the SRG led to immediate hopes that France was in the process of returning to the NATO fold, Ambassador Robin made clear at the time he announced his country's participation that under no circumstances would France consider returning to the NATO military structure. This position was confirmed by Foreign Minister Roland Dumas in a public statement in late March 1991.[57]

During those SRG meetings in which the French participated, major concessions were wrung from the United States, according to American officials familiar with the talks who became dismayed with what they saw as the French and, to some extent, the Germans carving out a new role for Europe and, in the process, downgrading the importance of NATO. Initially, as these officials related it, the United States had considered that an enhanced European identity and defense role would be welcome, as it would mean that Europe would pay relatively more (the familiar "burden-sharing" theme)—just as long as it remained clear that the strengthened "European pillar" would be locked firmly into NATO.

By the time of the ministerial meeting of the North Atlantic Council (NAC) at Copenhagen on June 6–7, 1991, attended by the Foreign Ministers of the Alliance,[58] the presence of the French in strategic deliberations already could be felt. As *Le Monde* commented, "The Atlantic Council at Copenhagen will ... remain in the annals as the one in which NATO explicitly recognized in the Europe of the Twelve the right to look after its security."[59] The Copenhagen communiqué specifically stated, "We welcome efforts further to strengthen the security dimension in the process of European integration and recognize the significance of the progress made by the countries of the European Community towards the goal of political union, including the development of a common foreign and security policy."[60]

But the communiqué also stated that the adaptation of NATO and the development of a European security identity were "mutually reinforcing," to wit:

The development of a European security identity and defense role, reflected in the strengthening of the European pillar within the Alliance, will reinforce the integrity and effectiveness of the Atlantic Alliance.... The Alliance is the essential forum for consultation among its members and the venue for agreement on policies bearing on the security and defense commitments of its Allies under the Washington Treaty.... We all agree that the military dispositions necessary to ensure the collective defense of the Allies must be maintained. This applies particularly to the integrated military structure for the Allied countries that participate in it.[61]

The Rome NATO Summit Declaration of November 8, 1991, reaffirmed what it termed "the consensus in Copenhagen," endorsing the development of a European security and defense role while also reaffirming the Alliance as the essential forum for consultations of the Allies on defense matters under the Washington Treaty. At the same time, and perhaps reflecting the influence of the "Europeanists" anxious to establish a double vocation for the WEU, the Rome communiqué also stated, "We welcome the perspective of a reinforcement of the role of the WEU, both as the defense component of the process of European unification and as a means of strengthening the European pillar of the Alliance, bearing in mind the different nature of its relations with the Alliance and with the European Political Union."[62]

The Rome Declaration also noted that the Alliance's New Strategic Concept, published the day before at Rome on November 7, 1991, "reaffirms NATO's core functions and allows us, within the radically changed situation in Europe, to realize in full our broad approach to stability and security encompassing political, economic, social and environmental aspects, along with the indispensable defense dimension."[63]

The "core functions" of NATO, as set forth in a communiqué of June 1991, can be summed up as follows: (1) to provide a stable security environment in Europe based on democratic institutions; (2) to serve as a transatlantic forum for allied consultations; (3) to deter and defend against any threat of aggression against a NATO state; and (4) to preserve the strategic balance within Europe.[64] The New Strategic Concept document of November 7, 1991, projected these "core functions" onto a somewhat wider screen, mandating that in peacetime the Atlantic Alliance could "contribute to the maintenance of the stability and equilibrium in Europe . . . bring a contribution to dialogue and cooperation in Europe as a whole, in participating in confidence-building measures, including those which increase transparency and improve communication, as well as the verification of arms control agreements . . . [and] be called upon to contribute to peace and stability in the world by furnishing forces for missions of the United Nations."[65]

While not modifying the language of the Washington Treaty regarding the mission of collective defense (Article 5) and the territory of the member countries to which it applied (Article 6), the New Strategic Concept fell back on a rather liberal interpretation of Article 4 as a catchall for other missions:

Any armed attack on the territory of the Allies, from whatever direction, would be covered by Articles 5 and 6 of the Washington Treaty. However, Alliance security must also take account of the global context. Alliance security interests can be affected by other risks of a wider nature, including proliferation of weapons of mass destruction, disruption of the flow of vital resources and actions of terrorism and sabotage. Arrangements exist within the Alliance for consultation among the Allies under Article 4 of the Washington Treaty and, where appropriate, coordination of their efforts including their responses to such risks.[66]

What Article 4 of the Washington Treaty states is as follows: "The parties will consult together whenever, in the opinion of any of them, the territorial integrity, political independence or security of any of the parties is threatened."

As for the "democratizing" role of NATO, it should be noted that Article 2 of the Washington Treaty had mentioned the "development of peaceful and friendly international relations" as well as the strengthening of "free institutions" and the promoting of "conditions of stability." The New Strategic Concept reaffirmed these principles while giving a proactive emphasis to NATO's pan-European vocation: "Based on common values of democracy, human rights and the rule of law, the Alliance has worked since its inception for the establishment of a just and lasting peaceful order in Europe."[67]

Thus the "widening" of NATO had been decreed, and the new attributions of the Alliance were certainly not to the liking of the "Europeanists"—particularly the establishment of defense liaison arrangements with some of the former Eastern bloc countries, with implied guarantees of security; the environmental and nuclear security initiatives in the east; and the possibility of peacekeeping missions outside the zone of the Washington Treaty.

However, though the "widening" of the Atlantic Alliance had been set in train, the "zone" of NATO military operations remained unchanged from that originally laid out in Article 6 of the Washington Treaty: the defense of the territory of Alliance members.

Although, technically, the French did not disturb the consensus around the New Strategic Concept, they made plain through public statements at the time of the Rome Summit that they disagreed with aspects of it, particularly the "widening" of NATO and the use of nuclear weapons only as a last resort, which, as noted earlier, had the effect of undermining the French nuclear doctrine. However, and most importantly for the "Europeanists," the principle of a defense and security role for Europe had been recognized by NATO at the summit level at the Rome meeting.

THE REORGANIZATION OF NATO: THE MILITARY DIALOGUE

Parallel to the SRG meetings, which had resulted in NATO's New Strategic Concept, presented at Rome on November 7, 1991, informal meetings were held in Brussels among the sixteen ambassadors of the Alliance. These were termed "brainstorming meetings." One of the items on the "informal" or "private" agenda of these meetings was a proposal for a European SACEUR.[68]

American officials familiar with the ambassadorial talks were disappointed that the United States did not scotch this idea immediately, because from their point of view, it spread confusion among the smaller powers who were anxious to preserve the U.S. anchor in Europe represented by an American SACEUR. Eventually the United States stated that it would not consider a change from an American SACEUR, and the matter was dropped from the agenda. At the end of May 1991, Secretary of Defense Dick Cheney reaffirmed this decision publicly.[69] The issue was to emerge again later in the decade.

While discussions were continuing at the SRG level and in the "brainstorming meetings," the Defense Planning Committee (DPC)[70] was proceeding with its own planning for a restructuring of NATO based on the principle, enunciated at the July 1990 London Summit, of multinational forces. Part of the developing problem was structural, and here France was at a disadvantage: though France was part of the ad hoc SRG, it did not belong to the military organs of NATO (the DPC, the DPC's Nuclear Planning Group, the Military Committee, and the Chiefs of Staff Committee), which continued on with a life of their own. Part of the problem was also one of approach. The French arguably could claim that military planning should take place only as a follow-up to a reconceptualization of the Alliance. As French Foreign Minister Roland Dumas observed in June 1991, "It would seem logical that the political objectives should be defined first, that next a strategy should be made clear, and that finally the forces should be restructured. . . . It seems that in this instance it was done the other way around."[71]

By contrast, the American approach, decidedly pragmatic, was to develop a military structure based on an approximation of scenarios that were deemed likely to happen. Behind this genuine difference of approach was a leaven of opportunism and cynicism on both sides: the Americans, in seeking to lock in quickly a readapted NATO military structure still under the integrated NATO command; and the French, in not letting the opportunity pass to get Europe out from under the American yoke in matters of defense—an opportunity that had not been there as long as the potential of nuclear conflict posed by the Cold War was real.

It soon became apparent to the French that, on the military level, the swiftly engaged reform of NATO was not going in the direction of less integration. Furthermore, the military restructuring was focussing on the creation of a Rapid Reaction Corps with implied future missions outside the NATO zone.

Eventually, the DPC came around to presenting its recommendations. As announced following a meeting of the DPC and the Nuclear Planning Group on May 27–28, 1991, the core of the proposals was as follows:

We have agreed the basis of a new force structure consisting of Main Defense Forces, Reaction Forces and Augmentation Forces, including multinational forces of all types: land, air and maritime. In particular we have agreed various national contributions to the multinational corps of Main Defense Forces for which detailed planning will now proceed. With regard to Reaction Forces, we have agreed that these should consist of immediate and rapid reaction forces, comprising contributions from most NATO nations and including national as well as multinational formations. As part of the rapid reaction forces, we have agreed the creation of a Rapid Reaction Corps for Allied Command Europe, under United Kingdom command with a multinational headquarters.[72]

The chief innovations in the DPC proposals were the multinational formations which were to be created and the fact that the Allied Rapid Reaction Corps (ARRC) would be essentially a European force. Specifically, it was planned that this force would comprise some 70,000 men, made up of two British divisions, one mixed division (German-Dutch–Belgian–British), and one Italian division (with Turkish and Greek supporting elements). The Main Defense Forces would be made up of seven army corps, six of which would be multinational (the seventh being a German corps based in the former East Germany).[73]

THE "OCTOBER SURPRISE" OF MITTERRAND AND KOHL

The announcement on May 29, 1991, of the plan for the ARRC to be functioning by 1995[74] caused a reaction of consternation and near-panic in the Élysée. The French had made clear all along in the SRG meetings that they did not accept the multinational concept for NATO. There soon followed another burst of activism by the French, this time aided and abetted by the Germans, who were not pleased at the idea of a British commander at the head of the ARRC. By the autumn of 1991, under the particular impulsion of Chancellor Helmut Kohl, the French and German answer to the ARRC, elaborated with great secrecy, was ready: there was to be a "European Corps," or "Euro-Corps," with the 4,200-man Franco-German brigade, created in 1987, serving as its nucleus. This brigade had been placed under the orders of the Franco-German Defense Council, created in 1988 under the rubric of the Élysée Treaty of 1963. The Euro-Corps, when constituted, would comprise some 35,000 men—hardly a negligible force.

The presentation of this "fait accompli" was made on October 14, 1991, in a joint statement by President Mitterrand and Chancellor Kohl on foreign policy and European defense, to which they attached proposed texts for a common foreign and security policy for the European Union, to be considered by the Maastricht EC Summit on December 9–10. Describing the WEU as "an integral part of the process of European union," the two leaders called for a clear organic relationship between the WEU and the [European] Union, plus the operational development of the WEU acting in conformity with the directives of the Union.[75]

At the end of the proposed texts, tacked on almost as an afterthought, was the following "petite surprise": "Pour mémoire: French-German military cooperation will be strengthened beyond the existing brigade. The augmented Franco-German units could thus become the nucleus of a European Corps which could include forces from other members states of the WEU. This new structure could also become the model for closer military cooperation between member states of the WEU."[76]

Earlier, on October 4, 1991, an Anglo-Italian initiative, presented as a compromise proposal but likely intended, at least by the British, as a preemptive move, suggested that a European rapid reaction force could be created to act where NATO could not go. The Anglo-Italian text recommended over the long term "a common defense policy compatible with the common defense policy which we already have with our Allies in NATO."[77]

Mitterrand and Kohl had gone ahead and presented their "October Surprise" without a discussion of the merits of the Anglo-Italian proposal, except to pay perfunctory tribute in their October 14 statement to "various contributions, of which the latest is the Anglo-Italian joint declaration."[78]

According to U.S. officials, the German rationale for this development, seemingly in contradiction with NATO's ARRC, was that both they and the French needed the European Corps as a justification for keeping French forces in Germany. The Germans also claimed to see the corps as a way of drawing the French closer to NATO.

The position of U.S. officials, on the other hand, was that for the first time the "leak-proof vessel"—Germany's undivided participation in NATO—was beginning to malfunction. As they saw it, there were two problems: unless the French-German proposed corps were clearly linked to NATO, and unless the first priority of the German troops assigned therein was to NATO, this arrangement would be unacceptable because it would not be in keeping with the spirit of NATO and WEU declarations. (The German element in the Franco-German Brigade was composed of German territorial troops not part of the NATO force structure. Hence this problem had not arisen prior to the announcement of the Franco-German Corps.)

THE CREATION OF EUROPEAN DEFENSE: MAASTRICHT

The European defense identity was made explicit, albeit in a conditional fashion, at the Maastricht Summit on December 9–10, 1991, at which time the European Community became the European Union. In instituting a common foreign and security policy for the Twelve, the Maastricht Treaty language noted the following: "The common foreign and security policy shall include all questions related to the security of the European Union, including the eventual framing of a common defense policy, which might in time lead to a common defense."[79]

The question of the autonomy of this European defense entity was left vague, largely due to the fact that the authority that would direct it, the WEU, was in a form of dependent relationship with NATO, as we have noted earlier.[80]

Thus, on the one hand, the Maastricht Treaty language stated that the WEU should become the defense arm of the European Union: "The [European] Union requests the Western European Union, which is an integral part of the development of the European Union, to elaborate and implement decisions and actions of the Union which have defense implications."[81]

But, on the other hand, the Maastricht Treaty stated that those members of the European Union who were also members of NATO would not have a changed relationship with NATO: "The policy of the [European] Union . . . shall not prejudice the specific character of the security and defense policy of certain member states and shall respect the obligations of certain member states under the North Atlantic Treaty and be compatible with the common security and defense policy established under that framework."[82]

In a still further refinement, the Maastricht Treaty mandated that the article on common foreign and security policy "shall not prevent development of closer cooperation between two or more member states on a bilateral level, in the framework of the WEU and the Atlantic Alliance, provided that such cooperation does not run counter to or impede that provided for in this title."[83]

Despite all the studied ambiguities and compromises in the process that had led to the paired declarations of the Rome Summit (NATO) and the Maastricht Summit (EU), the terrain was decidedly different than before: a defense identity for Europe *qua* Europe had been recognized by NATO, meaning in the first instance by the United States, and at the summit level. At Rome, this identity was "reflected in the further strengthening of the European pillar within the Alliance."[84] At Maastricht the formulation was nuanced further into Europe eventually framing a "common defense policy."[85] Fundamentally, a "common defense policy" could only imply greater autonomy for Europe in the area of defense.

For the "Europeanists," it had been an effort stretching back into the 1980s to gain acceptance of the principle of a European defense identity, centered around a reactivated WEU, described by the WEU Ministerial Council on June 12, 1984, as "the only European organization which is by treaty competent in defense and security matters."[86]

This action was reinforced three years later, in the light of the intervening signature of the Single European Act and the intention to create a European Union, by the so-called "platform statement" of the WEU Council at The Hague on October 27, 1987. The following were among the principal points in this statement:

the construction of an integrated Europe will remain incomplete as long as this construction does not extend to security and defense.

A major instrument for attaining this objective is the modified Brussels Treaty [of 1954]. The WEU is indeed the only European authority competent in matters of defense. The point on which a consensus should be made clear relates to the exact place of the WEU with respect to the future political union and with respect to the Atlantic Alliance. The French positions, which have been expressed in common with Germany . . . are well known. They are aimed at making the WEU an organ of the [European] political Union.[87]

French (and to a lesser extent German) intentions, even at that early date, could not have been clearer. Five years later, at Rome and Maastricht, ended the first chapter in a subtle struggle of the "Europeanists" to get out from under American tutelage in matters of defense.

The dialectic went on, as was evident in the declaration of the subsequent NATO ministerial meeting at Oslo (June 4, 1992), in which the U.S. effort to nail down the status of German forces—the heretofore "leak-proof vessel"[88]—was clearly apparent: "as the transformation of the Alliance proceeds, we intend to preserve the operational coherence we now have and on which our defense depends. We stress the importance of maintaining Allies' existing obligations and commitments of forces to NATO, and we emphasize in this regard that the primary responsibility of forces answerable to the WEU will remain NATO's collective defense under the Washington Treaty."[89]

Although the French, in press statements, made known their reserves on the strategy of the use of nuclear weapons only as a last resort, they had subscribed to and, indeed, participated in the elaboration of NATO's New Strategic Concept. As Diego Ruiz-Palmer noted, "once France had subscribed in 1991 to the same Strategic Concept of the Alliance as its allies, and once the distinction between integrated forces and nonintegrated forces no longer covered either a political need or a tangible military reality, it became less and less conceivable that France could continue to remain apart from the decision-making bodies of the Alliance."[90]

NOTES

1. Lawrence S. Kaplan, "Globalization, Regionalization and the Military: The Evolution of NATO as a Military Organization," paper presented to the 19th International Congress of Historical Sciences, University of Oslo, August 6–13, 2000, and published in the proceedings of the conference, p. 168.

2. See p. 34.

3. ⟨http://www.nato.int/docu/pr/1999/p99–064e.htm⟩, p. 6.

4. Gülnur Aybet, *A European Security Architecture after the Cold War: Questions of Legitimacy* (London: Macmillan, 2000), p. 100.

5. Hubert Védrine, *Les mondes de François Mitterrand. À l'Élysée, 1981–1995* (Paris: Fayard, 1996), p. 523. ("As for Mikhail Gorbachev, in the summer of 1990, he was focused on a single idea: obtain from the West a more substantial and less conditional aid than that promised [at the G7 summit of the major industrial powers] at Houston. As a consequence, he would not refuse the West anything with regard to Saddam Hussein.")

6. Pierre Favier and Michel Martin-Roland, *La Décennie Mitterrand, Vol. 3, Les défis (1988–1991)* (Paris: Seuil, 1996), p. 281 (hereafter cited as *DM*).

7. Catherine Guicherd, *A European Defense Identity: Challenge and Opportunity for NATO* (Congressional Research Service Report for Congress, June 12, 1991), pp. 7–8.

8. James A. Baker III with Thomas M. DeFrank, *The Politics of Diplomacy: Revolution, War and Peace, 1989–1992* (New York: G. P. Putnam's Sons, 1995), p. 15.

9. Margaret Thatcher, *The Downing Street Years* (London: HarperCollins, 1993), p. 819. (Cited in *DM*, Vol. 3, p. 508.)

10. Jacques Attali, *Verbatim III, 1988–1991* (Paris: Fayard, 1995), p. 560; *DM*, Vol. 3, p. 511.

11. *Le Monde*, December 21, 1990, p. 2. (Press conference of François Mitterrand, December 19, 1990.)

12. Attali, *Verbatim III*, p. 561.

13. Ibid., p. 558.
14. Ibid., p. 560.
15. Ibid., pp. 559–60.
16. Ibid., p. 561.
17. Ibid., p. 555.
18. Frédéric Guelton, *La guerre américaine du Golfe* (Lyon: Presses Universitaires de Lyon, 1996), p. 100.
19. *DM*, Vol. 3, p. 512.
20. Ibid., p. 516.
21. Ibid., p. 528.
22. Guelton, *Guerre du Golfe*, p. 255.
23. General Maurice Schmitt, *De Diên Biên Phu à Koweït City* (Paris: Grasset, 1992), p. 191.
24. A British military source on the basis of records held in the British Army's Historical Branch.
25. *DM*, Vol. 3, p. 518.
26. Guelton, *Guerre du Golfe*, p. 121. Reference is to *Terre Magazine*, No. 19 (1990): 8–9.
27. Schmitt, *Koweït City*, p. 181.
28. Ibid., p. 215.
29. Ibid., p. 251.
30. Michael R. Gordon and General Bernard E. Trainor, *The Generals' War: The Inside Story of the Conflict in the Gulf* (Boston: Little Brown and Company, 1995).
31. Interview with Bernard E. Trainor, October 2, 2000.
32. *DM*, Vol. 3, p. 565.
33. Ibid., p. 514.
34. See p. 41.
35. *DM*, Vol. 3. p. 520.
36. Ibid., p. 519.
37. Ibid., p. 523.
38. Ibid., p. 531.
39. Ibid., p. 534.
40. Ibid., p. 561 n.2.
41. Ibid., p. 546.
42. Hubert Védrine, dialogue avec Dominique Moïsi, *Les cartes de la France à l'heure de la mondialisation* (Paris: Fayard, 2000), p. 31.
43. Jean-Pierre Chevènement, *Une certaine idée de la République m'amène à...* (Paris: Albin Michel, 1992), pp. 302–3.
44. Guelton, *Guerre du Golfe*, p. 104.
45. Schmitt, *Koweït City*, p. 245.
46. A British military source.
47. Schmitt, *Koweït City*, p. 229.
48. Guelton, *Guerre du Golfe*, p. 142.
49. Ibid., p. 143.
50. A British military source. N.B. According to this source, British military records show that the total deployment in Desert Storm of the three French branches of service amounted to 16,400 personnel.
51. "Nomion," "François Mitterrand et le système militaire français," in Samy Cohen,

ed., *Mitterrand et la sortie de la guerre froide* (Paris: Presses Universitaires de France, 1998), p. 450.

52. Ibid.

53. Guicherd, *A European Security Identity*, p. 58.

54. Frédéric Bozo, *La France et l'OTAN: de la guerre froide au nouvel ordre européén*, (Paris: Masson, 1991), p. 188.

55. Guicherd, *A European Defense Identity*, p. 14.

56. Ibid. Also see p. 3.

57. Ibid., p. 54.

58. N.D.L.R. The North Atlantic Council (NAC) meets either as a summit or as a ministerial (foreign ministers).

59. *Le Monde*, June 9–10, 1991, p. 3.

60. American Embassy Copenhagen telegram to State, No. 4244, June 7, 1991, p. 1. N.B. Official English-language texts of NATO documents carry British-English spellings. In this case they have been Americanized.

61. Ibid., pp. 1–2.

62. "Rome Declaration on Peace and Cooperation," NATO Press Service, November 8, 1991, p. 3.

63. Ibid., p. 2.

64. NATO Press Communiqué M-1(91)44, June 7, 1991.

65. Bernadette d'Armaillé, *L'Architecture européenne de sécurité* (Paris: CREST, 1991), p. 114. (Translation by the author.)

66. ⟨http://www.nato.int/docu/comm/49–95/c911107a.htm⟩, pp. 4–5.

67. Ibid., p. 5.

68. SACEUR is the acronym for Supreme Allied Commander Europe.

69. Bozo, *La France et l'OTAN*, p.185.

70. N.D.L.R. The Defense Ministers of the Alliance make up the Defense Planning Committee.

71. Reply by Dumas to questions by members of the Western European Union (WEU) Assembly in Paris on June 4, 1991. Quoted in Bozo, *La France et l'OTAN*, p. 183.

72. NATO Press Service, Press Communiqué M-DPC/NPG-1(91) 38, p. 3. N.B. The core element in the "immediate" reaction force is the 5,000-man Allied Command Europe (ACE) Mobile Force, which has been in existence since the 1960s but which was used operationally for the first time in the Gulf War, when it was deployed to Turkey. This is not to be confused with the Allied Rapid Reaction Corps (ARRC) described earlier. See also Bozo, *La France et l'OTAN*, p. 182.

73. *Le Monde*, May 30, 1991, p. 6.

74. Bozo, *La France et l'OTAN*, p. 182.

75. *Le Monde*, October 17, 1991, p. 4.

76. Ibid.

77. *Le Monde*, October 6–7, 1991, p. 5.

78. *Financial Times*, October 17, 1991, p. 5.

79. Maastricht Treaty text published by the European Community, Article D, paragraph 1.

80. See p. 3.

81. Maastricht Treaty text, Article D, paragraph 2.

82. Ibid., Article D, paragraph 4.

83. Ibid., paragraph 5.

84. ⟨http://www.nato.int/docu/comm/49–95/c91108a.htm⟩, "Rome Declaration on Peace and Cooperation," November 8, 1991, p. 3.

85. Maastricht Treaty, Article D, paragraph 1.

86. Dominique David, ed., *La Politique de Défense de la France: textes et documents* (Paris: Fondation pour les études de Défense Nationale, 1989), p. 120.

87. D'Armaillé, *Architecture européenne*, pp. 47, 54.

88. See p. 55.

89. NATO Press Service, Press Communiqué M-NAC-1(92) 51, pp. 2–3.

90. Diego A. Ruiz-Palmer, "La coopération militaire entre la France et ses alliés, 1966–1991: entre le poids de l'héritage et les défis de l'après-guerre froide," in Maurice Vaïsse, Pierre Mélandri, and Frédéric Bozo, eds., *La France et l'OTAN, 1949–1996* (Brussels: Editions Complexe, 1996), p. 598.

CHAPTER 3

From the Bosnian War to France's Move Toward NATO (1992–December 1995)

INTRODUCTION

During the forty-odd years of the Cold War, the United States can be said to have created a hegemonic power in Europe through the integrated military command of NATO. It was a counterpart of the command system that the Soviets had in the East, but it was based on consent rather than coercion. In this perspective, what took place in 1989–1991 was the dissolution of the Eastern command system and the calling into question of the Western one.

The period of European "revolutions" stretched from the fall of the Berlin Wall in November 1989 to the failed *putsch* in Moscow in August 1991 and its aftermath. It was precisely in this period that a related *aggiornamento* took place in the world of NATO and European defense, culminating in the NATO Summit in Rome on November 7–8, 1991, and the Maastricht Summit of the newly named European Union (EU) on December 9–10, 1991. As a result of these two meetings, an eventual defense vocation for Europe, as such, was recognized at the summit level by all the Western powers concerned, including the United States. The ambiguities and tensions that have resulted from this "*aggiornamento* in the West" embodied first in the Euro-Corps and later in the decade in the autonomous European defense force, form the core of this and the following chapters.

France, which had long considered itself the "keeper of the temple" of the EU, both as the instrument of a strategy of peace in Europe and as a means of keeping a leading voice in European affairs, had through the Maastricht Treaty, signed on February 7, 1992, and ratified a year later, helped to anchor Germany to the West through the European Monetary Union (EMU). It had managed further to temper Germany's ardor for an expansion of the EU into central

Europe, invoking the principle that the EU had to be "deepened" before enlargement could be considered.

At the other end of the dialectic, NATO witnessed a change of roles for itself out of the two summits of London (July 1990) and Rome (November 1991). It became a stabilizing and democratizing force for Europe as a whole and not just a collective defense organization for Western Europe. Nevertheless, the enlargement of NATO was not on the agenda at this point. Potential opposition to it was not confined to Russia; there was also some objection within Western Europe to an expansion of NATO's roles. This sentiment was expressed most prominently in France, which had accepted NATO's New Strategic Concept with some reluctance and which has traditionally regarded itself as the conscience of a Europe desirous of not being overwhelmed by the United States' economic and military superiority.

Although making some concessions to NATO because of the imperatives for Western cooperation in the wars that broke out in the Gulf and the former Yugoslavia in the 1990s, François Mitterrand remained until the end of his presidency (in May 1995) a firm advocate of keeping NATO (and thus the United States) "on the reservation." Mitterrand's view was that NATO ought to be confined to the original zone of the countries of Western Europe and to its original mission of collective defense, as called for respectively in Articles 6 and 5 of the Washington Treaty of 1949. For France, extending the zone of NATO's competence for intervention meant extending the zone of American domination, via NATO's integrated command, to other areas besides Western Europe.

Perhaps Mitterrand's sharpest criticism of the attempt to extend NATO's role came in a speech on the occasion of "National Meetings for Europe" on January 10, 1992, at which time the French president registered his satisfaction at the Maastricht Declaration of the previous month but noted that the EU largely had lacked a common approach to foreign policy in the past:

the countries of the [European] Community appeared [to feel] they had to accept without batting an eyelid the proposals of M. Reagan suggesting consideration . . . of Japan's entry into the Atlantic Alliance, and a whole series of ludicrous proposals concerning which one did not see the countries of the Community put up a common front against such shocking propositions. It was also a question, regarding the concept of the Atlantic Pact, and its geographical area, of the possibility of being drawn into a series of common actions well beyond what had been foreseen, and of being used as an auxiliary in many political actions bearing no relationship to our interests. And on that too, it must be said that a unified foreign policy of the Twelve was far from being achieved.[1]

It was the aim of Mitterrand not only to limit the role of NATO in the wake of the end of the Cold War but also to give impetus to a political and security identity that would be Europe's own. As Louis Gautier has pointed out, French initiatives in the period after the fall of the Berlin Wall, from 1990 to the end of Mitterrand's presidency in 1995, were not just reactive: "the underlying design remained constant and determined: a push for greater European integration."[2]

Over time, however, the successive wars in the Gulf and in the disintegrating Yugoslav federation made moot the issue of NATO involvement in interventions outside its collective defense zone. Moreover, the attempted rapprochement of France with NATO in the mid-1990s, initiated by Mitterrand's successor, Jacques Chirac, as a means of lessening France's strategic isolation evident in the Gulf and Yugoslav wars—a rapprochement which did not come to fruition—was an additional reason for France revising its objections to an expanded role for NATO.

INSTABILITY OUTSIDE THE ALLIANCE, DISUNITY WITHIN THE ALLIANCE

By the time of the next NATO summit, in Brussels in January 1994, the moment had arrived for NATO to make a clearer statement concerning its future relationship with Russia and Eastern Europe on the one hand and with the European Union and its putative defense wing, the Western European Union (WEU), on the other. The threat of a Russian attack into Western Europe was no more, yet civil war had been going on for nearly three years at the doorstep of Europe, first in Slovenia and Croatia and then in Bosnia, provoking severe strains in the Western Alliance: the Europeans were proving incapable of mastering the situation in the Balkans as they had earlier set out confidently to do, while the United States, with its casualty-averse philosophy stemming from the Vietnam War, and fresh off the miraculous success of the Gulf War, was unwilling to help with ground troops.

In the face of this new instability in southeastern Europe, there was a clear recognition on both sides of the Atlantic that new arrangements and new structures had to be developed if the West was going to assure order at its frontiers and in the wider world. Bosnia and the former Yugoslavia as a whole were seen primarily as Europe's problem and only secondarily as America's. Yet the European Union had been unable to stop the fighting in the former Yugoslavia while the United States stood apart.

From Washington's point of view, the chief obstacle in the Euro-American relationship was disunity within the Atlantic Alliance, which generally meant the problem of dealing with France. From the European point of view, most often and most insistently expressed by France, the problem was getting out from under the abnormal rigidity of the Cold War period, represented in the concept of the indivisible defense of Europe through the means of the NATO integrated command, and in so doing, allowing Europe to have a certain autonomy in matters of defense. Washington, not having grasped fully what Nicole Gnesotto has described as "the extraordinary permanence of French ambitions,"[3] was inclined to believe that with certain concessions, which would not change the fundamental nature of the Alliance, the French could be brought around to ending their thirty-year isolation from the military structures of NATO. Although the French continued to be disadvantaged by not being within the NATO military structure, time would prove this assumption to be overoptimistic.

THE EMERGENCE OF THE EUROPEAN SECURITY AND DEFENSE IDENTITY

As the Brussels NATO Summit opened in January 1994, a certain amount of progress had been made in harmonizing the European and American viewpoints. The tentatively worded Common Foreign and Security Policy (CFSP) enshrined in the European Union's Maastricht Treaty, signed on February 7, 1992, had evolved into something more concrete with the Petersberg Declaration of the WEU four months later, on June 19, 1992. In this declaration, the WEU assigned to itself the less militarily onerous tasks of peacekeeping and crisis management, thus implicitly leaving the "heavy lifting"—collective defense—to NATO. Something still more concrete was to emerge from the January 1994 Brussels Summit: the European Security and Defense Identity (ESDI), which was officialized as a sort of institutional expression of the CFSP.

THE CREATION OF THE PARTNERSHIP FOR PEACE

As noted in the previous chapter, France, following its participation in the Gulf War alongside the United States and Great Britain, had signed on with some reluctance to NATO's New Strategic Concept at the Rome NATO Summit in November 1991. Once this had been done, as Diego Ruiz-Palmer pointed out, France's remaining aloof from operational decision-making in the Alliance was becoming more and more anomalous.[4] More significantly still, France, with encouragement from Germany, agreed on January 21, 1993, that the Euro-Corps would be placed under NATO's command in a time of military emergency in Europe. The Euro-Corps, formerly known as the French-German Corps, had been officially established at a bilateral summit at La Rochelle on May 21–22, 1992. This creation had been mainly at French instigation, and, as noted in the previous chapter, was intended in part as a counterweight to the new ARRC of NATO, headed by a British general.

As the Brussels Summit approached, NATO's strategic objectives were twofold. The first was that of reaching out to the east to fill the vacuum created by the collapse of the Soviet Union at the end of 1991 and, thereby, provide security to the existentially threatened states of Central Europe. This led to the idea of the Partnership for Peace (PfP), which was put together in a meeting of senior U.S. officials at the home of U.S. ambassador to NATO Robert Hunter in the fall of 1993. The North Atlantic Cooperation Council (NACC), which had been created in 1991 as part of NATO's outreach toward Eastern Europe, was considered "broken" and ineffective. It was only a talking organization of the member countries. The Supreme Allied Commander Europe (SACEUR), General John Shalikashvili, sought interaction with these countries' militaries. What Shalikashvili wanted, in his own words, was "to get NATO dirt under their fingernails."[5]

The PfP was presented at a press conference on October 20, 1993, by Secretary of Defense[6] Les Aspin at a meeting of NATO defense ministers at Travemünde, Germany. According to General George Joulwan, who took over as SACEUR immediately after the meeting, the PfP idea was the brainchild essentially of two people: General Shalikashvili, the outgoing SACEUR, who was returning to Washington to become Chairman of the Joint Chiefs of Staff, and Ambassador Hunter.[7] The PfP was officially announced at the Brussels NATO Summit in January 1994 and was described as a "major initiative . . . in which we invite Partners to join us in new political and military efforts to work alongside the Alliance."[8] According to a senior U.S. defense official, the concept behind the PfP was to slow down the growing impulse toward NATO enlargement by giving the governments in Eastern and Central Europe something concrete, but it turned out to have the opposite effect. It only whetted the appetites of these governments for joining NATO.[9]

THE COMBINED JOINT TASK FORCES (CJTFs)

The second strategic objective of NATO as the Brussels Summit approached was to create a power projection capability that would enable NATO to go beyond its traditional mission of collective defense of the member states, a mission that is spelled out in Article 5 of the Washington Treaty. With a series of local wars having broken out in the former Yugoslavia in 1991, the idea here was to achieve the flexibility that would enable NATO to conduct a variety of operations that were not subsumed under Article 5. These would be operations not encompassing total war but including the halting of hostilities between warring parties, euphemistically called "peace enforcement" operations, and other less demanding actions down to humanitarian interventions—in essence the "Petersberg tasks" mentioned previously.[10] This perceived need led to the Combined Joint Task Force (CJTF) concept, which, like the PfP, and also a commitment in principle to enlarge NATO at some point in the future, were all unveiled at the January 1994 Brussels Summit.

The CJTFs, as the name suggests, were to be "combined" (comprising armed forces from different allied countries) and "joint" (made up of different arms of service—land, sea, and air forces). They would be "separable but not separate" from NATO and would be set up to run crises under WEU auspices, or under NATO, including operations with other "partner" nations (those of the PfP) outside Western Europe.

Though Nicole Gnesotto has written that the French may have suggested the CJTF idea,[11] it seems clear, as noted previously, that it was of American origin. According to what General Shalikashvili recounted to author James Goldgeier, he had been seeking a more flexible command arrangement that would allow NATO forces to deploy externally and to use, as necessary, units not formally connected to the integrated command structure. These would include not just the French but also other European countries outside NATO whose participation might be useful in a particular situation. As Goldgeier wrote, referring to Shalikashvili and on the basis of talks with him and other U.S. government officials, "As he looked at Bosnia, [Shalikashvili] was ... concerned that there was no command structure for out-of-area operations that would have a headquarters flexible enough to absorb non-NATO members as well as the French, who had left NATO's integrated command in 1966. In response to this ... problem, his staff would develop the Combined Joint Task Forces (CJTF) which would be unveiled at the NATO summit [in Brussels] in January [1994]."[12]

As mentioned earlier, both the CJTF concept and the Partnership for Peace were launched at the same time, at the Brussels NATO Summit of January 10–11, 1994. The summit's communiqué not only supported "the development of the emerging European Security and Defense Identity and endorse[d] the concept of Combined Joint Task Forces" but at the same time announced NATO's intention to launch the "major initiative" of the Partnership for Peace. The two concepts, PfP and CJTF, were interrelated. As the new SACEUR, General Joulwan, was later to describe it, "My role was to take [the PfP] initiative and make it into an operational concept and link it with CJTF."[13]

Thus it could be said that, on the European Union side, ESDI was the operationalization of the Common Foreign and Security Policy, and the CJTFs were the tactical instrumentalization of ESDI. In a parallel way, the PfP was the operationalization of the NACC, which had been created in 1991 as part of NATO's outreach toward Eastern Europe, and the CJTFs could be considered, at the same time, as the tactical instrumentalization of the PfP.[14] This parallelism was reflected in the Brussels Summit communiqué, which described the CJTFs "as a means to facilitate contingency operations, including operations with participating nations outside the Alliance."[15]

Implementation of the CJTF concept could be done by NATO or by the WEU.[16] In the latter case, this would be for the purpose of carrying out "Petersberg-type" missions in which NATO would not be involved—although most American military officials have had difficulty visualizing when NATO would not be involved in a contingency operation of any significance. Nevertheless, in theory at any rate, it would be essentially NATO capabilities and personnel that would be loaned out to the WEU (and therefore would be "separate"), but then these assets would have to be returned after the operation (and therefore would not be "separable"). As James Goldgeier wrote, on the basis of interviews with Shalikashvili and other U.S. government officials,

The Combined Joint Task Forces proposal would allow the Europeans to develop their own capacities to use NATO to act in cases in which the United States declined to send troops, and it made acting out of area a real possibility. "Separable but not separate" forces would give NATO a flexibility it did not possess before. It would also head off any effort by the French to turn the Western European Union (the European Union's defense arm) into a competitor to NATO in the European security environment.[17]

Notwithstanding General Shalikashvili's intention to keep the French down, to paraphrase Lord Ismay's famous dictum in a different context,[18] American defense officials viewed the CJTF concept as an enticement to the French with the intention of convincing them to come closer to NATO.[19] In truth, the CJTF concept was useful to the French, because it was a way—at least theoretically—of getting around the fact that France was not a member of NATO's integrated command structure. If a force could be deployed externally that included the NATO Allies as well as the French, and also selected Partner countries, this could provide the much-needed flexibility called for in the New Strategic Concept promulgated at the Rome NATO Summit in November 1991: "To ensure that . . . Allies' forces can play an effective role both in managing crises and countering aggression against any Ally, they will require enhanced flexibility and mobility and an assured capacity for augmentation when necessary."[20]

Thus the French emerged from the Brussels Summit relatively pleased, especially in contrast to the previous summit in Rome at the end of 1991. François Mitterrand, severe judge that he was of American policy, had this to say in the Brussels Summit's aftermath: "Between Rome and Brussels, there was a considerable difference in tone. What had to be forced out of the Americans at Rome, in terms of recognition of a European defense identity, appeared perfectly natural at Brussels."[21]

According to a senior U.S. defense official, there was a confluence of interest that made both the United States and France satisfied with the outcome of the Brussels Summit in general and the CJTF concept in particular. Both saw an advantage with this concept: the United States, for power projection to enable the carrying out of non–Article 5 operations; and France, for the promise it held that changes in the NATO structure away from the rigidities of the Cold War would be forthcoming.

But the CJTF concept remained curiously in abeyance, with the Americans regarding it as essentially a European problem, leaving it to the latter to come up with suggestions but then showing little enthusiasm for the suggestions when they were made. According to Colonel S. Nelson Drew, who was later to be killed along with two prominent American diplomats in a vehicular accident in Bosnia, "Underlying this Washington approach was also a subtle suspicion among many on both sides of the Atlantic that, left to their own devices, the European Allies would never be able to agree on any alternative to acting within NATO."[22]

THE BALKAN IMBROGLIO

When the hostilities in the Yugoslav Federation broke out in July 1991,[23] first in Slovenia and then in Croatia, following their successive declarations of independence, it generally was regarded as Europe's problem to solve. It was also, to some degree, Europe's responsibility. Goaded by Germany, the EU had recognized Slovenia and Croatia as independent states, and later, in April 1992, it had proceeded to recognize Bosnia as well, following an overwhelmingly favorable referendum that the Bosnian Serbs, however, boycotted.[24] Luxembourg's Prime Minister Jacques Poos, exercising the rotating presidency of the European Council, declared that "the hour of Europe has arrived."[25] The Bush administration agreed, in the form of Secretary of State Baker's famous dictum, "We don't have a dog in this fight."[26] This formula became increasingly hollow, however, in the first months of 1992, when the Bosnian war erupted and 750,000 Muslims were driven out by attacking Serb forces.[27]

Though Mitterrand correctly sensed that the incoming Clinton administration, which took office in January 1993, was more flexible on the subject of a European defense identity than its predecessor had been, the prospects for inter-Allied harmony on the former Yugoslavia were going in the opposite direction: they were diminishing. This was chiefly because President Clinton was under pressure from his own earlier campaign statements to undertake a more activist policy in Bosnia.

The type of action that the Europeans undertook in Bosnia, a so-called "humanitarian intervention" in the form of the United Nations Protection Force (UNPROFOR) contingent, proved powerless to stop the Bosnian Serb atrocities. UNPROFOR's mission was solely to protect humanitarian convoys. The UN soldiers, led by Britain and France, did not arrive en masse in Bosnia until the summer of 1992, by which time Bosnian Serb forces had overrun two-thirds of the country.[28]

At the same time, European plans for a settlement of the political future of Bosnia floundered. Diplomacy was to be the other part of Europe's strategy, in addition to its humanitarian mission with its troops in the former Yugoslavia. The international community's first mediator, Lord Carrington, was replaced by a team of co-presidents, David Owen and Cyrus Vance, named at a peace conference in London in August 1992. The conference was held under the auspices of Great Britain, which held the rotating presidency of the EU at that time. A follow-up conference was held in January 1993 at Geneva. The Vance-Owen peace plan that emerged, and its variant, a plan put together by Owen and UN diplomat Thorvald Stoltenberg following the departure of Vance, failed to gain the adherence of the contesting forces in Bosnia.

The Clinton administration's first major initiative was the "lift and strike" proposal. This involved, on the one hand, lifting the embargo, which had favored Serbia as the inheritor of the Yugoslav Army, and, on the other, conducting air raids against Bosnian Serb positions. The plan failed to gain the support of the Western Allies, as the lamentable mission of Secretary of State Warren Christopher to Europe in May 1993 testified.

President Mitterrand turned down the "lift and strike" proposal (as did the British) because he considered that lifting the embargo would impel the Bosnian

Serbs to act preemptively, and the Bosnian Muslims would not be able to rearm in time to prevent themselves from being crushed.[29] As far as the French president was concerned, Bosnia never should have been recognized as a country in the first place.[30] The Serbians had essentially won the war in Bosnia,[31] and their gains there could not be reversed. Therefore the best that could be hoped for was a negotiated settlement (which, however, had constantly eluded the EU and UN negotiators). Above all, said Mitterrand in his famous dictum, "One must not add war to war."[32]

As 1994 began, pressure on the West to do something to stop the slaughter in Bosnia increased. On March 2, 1994, the Clinton administration obtained signature on a pact to create a Muslim-Croat federation in Bosnia.[33] On April 25, 1994, a "Contact Group" of the principal interested foreign parties was created and included the United States, Britain, France, Germany, Russia, and Italy.[34]

The gradually developing activism of the Clinton administration on Bosnia was disturbing to the British and the French in one sense, as both of them had troops on the ground in what was essentially a humanitarian mission and were relatively easy targets for Bosnian Serb attacks. This policy difference led to considerable friction between the United States and the Europeans. The latter, with their vulnerable UNPROFOR troops, were ill-disposed to take criticism from an American government unwilling to commit forces of its own.

Shortly after the Brussels NATO Summit in January 1994, Hubert Védrine, then secretary-general of the Elysée, wrote the following note to Mitterrand:

I fear that the United States has no vision of the future and no idea as to the way of bringing these unfortunate peoples [in ex-Yugoslavia] to coexist peacefully and reconstruct their country. They are encouraging the Bosnians to fight to the last Bosnian, just as they incited the Hungarians to rise up against the Soviets and armed the Afghan guerrillas against the same Soviets—which has not prevented them from being totally indifferent to the chaos that has befallen Afghanistan.[35]

Védrine went on to describe the American policy as the secondary cause for the perpetuation of the war, the primary one being the fanaticism of the warring parties themselves. Referring to a "Euro-American malaise" over Yugoslavia, Védrine wondered whether it would not be useful to force things to a crisis in order to get the Americans to change their attitude.[36]

A year after the Brussels NATO Summit of January 1994, the allied position in Bosnia seemed as mired down as ever. Although in April 1994 the Contact Group of the major concerned outside powers had been formed[37] and though it was the embryo of a concert of powers that would arrive eventually at a settlement, such a settlement could not be imposed on the warring parties at that time. For their part, the Russians complained about NATO's ultimatums and its sporadic use of air power without direct reference to members of the UN Security Council, such as was the case after the Markale marketplace explosion on February 5, 1994. At that moment, NATO threatened to attack unless the Bosnian Serbs withdrew their heavy weapons from the vicinity of Sarajevo, which the Bosnian Serbs proceeded to do. But the stalemate continued, as the Russians were unable to induce Yugoslav President Slobodan Milosevic to accept the Contact Group's peace plan.

The pressures on the Clinton administration to intervene in the former Yugoslavia increased further with the emergence of an aggressive Republican Party majority in Congress in the midterm elections of November 1994. To stave off congressional plans for a unilateral lifting of the embargo for the Bosnians, the Clinton administration committed itself to provide 15,000 American troops to cover the withdrawal of the UNPROFOR contingent, should that prove necessary.

The continuing failure of the UN and the European Union to stop the Serb aggression in Bosnia, as well as the steadily mounting criticism of Serbia in Western European opinion, led to a turn toward NATO as a more effective instrument of coercion. As the Western attempt to end the fighting in Bosnia intensified, Allied command arrangements in the theater were both awkward and inconsistent. The Americans had no troops on the ground, yet they held the power to coerce the Bosnian Serbs through the use of largely U.S. airpower under NATO's command. The French were punctilious about not using NATO airpower except under strict UN control, whether by the Security Council or the secretary-general. As Hubert Védrine described it,

There were two opposing conceptions. One, mainly American, preferred that the chain of decision for possible military actions come out of NATO, in other words in fact the Pentagon and the White House. The other, and which was ours . . . considered NATO as an efficient military organism, but [one of] execution, and which should not act except on the basis of a political decision taken by the Security Council . . . or by the Secretary General, or by his representative for Bosnia.[38]

The French wanted the operational command in the former Yugoslavia not to be in the hands of NATO, since it was not an Article 5 operation,[39] but rather to be run as an ad hoc command arrangement dependent on the number of peacekeeping forces each nation committed.[40] This meant that it would essentially be run by Britain and France. Though it was hard to gainsay the French on this, since it was they and the British who had troops in the theater, the Americans sought to prevent such arrangements. The Americans "were determined," according to Védrine, "to prevent . . . the Europeans from mounting an ad hoc system of intervention in Yugoslavia run by them which would allow them to do without NATO or use it only as a service provider."[41]

The fact was that, although the UN had asked for NATO's help in the wake of the Sarajevo bombing in February 1994, NATO did not have a free hand to act. Under what General Joulwan described as the "dual key operational decision," a second "key" was held by UNPROFOR on the ground.[42] Although this later was to be corrected when an intervention force went into Bosnia in a unified command arrangement under General Joulwan as SACEUR, it would not be for nearly another two years.

The impasse over Bosnia was a source of severe transatlantic tensions. As Richard Holbrooke was later to write, "By the spring of 1995 it had become commonplace to say that Washington's relations with our European allies were worse than at any time since the 1956 Suez crisis.... Bosnia ... had defined the first phase of the post–Cold War relationship between Europe and the United States and seriously damaged the Atlantic relationship."[43]

In May 1995, Jacques Chirac succeeded François Mitterrand as head of the French state. The newly elected French president, with his hussar's temperament, wasted no time in making himself felt in the military domain. Decrying the humiliating treatment meted out by the Bosnian Serbs to United Nations, and particularly French, soldiers who were taken as hostages and then released, Chirac prodded Britain and the Netherlands to join with France in creating a Rapid Reaction Force in Bosnia.[44] This move, announced on June 3, 1995, was aimed at strengthening the hand of the UNPROFOR there. Later that month, Chirac made his first visit as president to Washington, where his blunt warnings about Western drift in Yugoslavia contributed to a reevaluation of U.S. policy and a more interventionist orientation.[45]

In the summer of 1995, partly due to Chirac's more muscled approach, partly due to a new activism in U.S. policy with the arrival on scene of Richard Holbrooke as the American negotiator in the Bosnian crisis,[46] and partly due to the galvanizing effect produced by the accidental deaths of three senior U.S. officials on Mt. Igman,[47] the Bosnian stalemate showed signs of ending. The defining moment came when one of the Muslim enclaves designated by the UN as safe havens, Srebrenica, was attacked by the Bosnian Serbs on July 11, 1995. The massacre that took place there, which a lightly armed Dutch UNPROFOR force proved helpless to prevent, galvanized the United States, Britain, and France into action. The subsequent NATO air strikes against Bosnian Serb positions, coupled with a decisive Croatian offensive that drove the Serbs out of the Krajina, led Slobodan Milosevic to the bargaining table, and the American-engineered Dayton accords were signed on November 20, 1995.

In what has been described as a CJTF in concept, if not in name, an Implementation Force (IFOR) was created for Bosnia, with NATO (including the French) and PfP participation. It was NATO's first out-of-area deployment in its history.[48] The head of IFOR was not a ground force commander but a U.S. admiral, Leighton Smith, who was chosen, according to Richard Holbrooke, in order to prevent having a French general in charge, which would have been "politically impossible for the United States."[49] As General Joulwan described the evolution of the process which led to IFOR, the "PfP/CJTF operational concept was essential in getting both NATO and partner nations ready two years in advance for successful deployments to Bosnia. It also convinced the Russians to join Operation Joint Endeavor [in Bosnia] under SACEUR command."[50]

The eventual use of force by NATO in the summer of 1995, under a thin UN cover, put an end to the argument against the use of NATO outside its original defensive zone. Furthermore, as in the Gulf War, Bosnia found the French again compelled to join in coalition warfare with other NATO forces, and under American command. This once more exposed French deficiencies in equipment, but it also enhanced military-to-military cooperation between the French and Americans, opening the way for further rapprochement of France with NATO. In the words of General Christian Quesnot, chief of President Mitterrand's military staff at the Élysée, "certain rapprochements with NATO were undergone rather than desired, because of the Yugoslav conflict."[51]

At the diplomatic level, the American takeover of the peacemaking process in Bosnia in 1995 produced considerable annoyance among European officials. The Dayton accords, managed almost exclusively by the Americans, turned out to be not much different from what had been proposed earlier by the Contact Group for the former Yugoslavia. The fact that the accords were subsequently signed in a formal ceremony in Paris served to paper over some of these differences.

JACQUES CHIRAC'S RAPPROCHEMENT WITH NATO

With the advent of the presidency of Jacques Chirac in May 1995, the tentative rapprochement between France and the military structure of NATO gained significant momentum. As noted earlier, some, notably Védrine, the departing secretary-general of the Elysée who was later to become foreign minister, saw a deviation from the traditional Gaullist consensus on defense.[52] The senior military figure at the Elysée under Mitterrand, General Christian Quesnot (1991–1995),[53] echoed this view: "I remained chief of the military staff under Jacques Chirac for several months. There was a real break with the Gaullist-Mitterrandian heritage with regard to NATO. I am not making a judgment on it; it was a political act."[54]

By this time France, with a new activist and conservative president, was now perceived as a "willing ally," who, together with Britain, was disposed to intervene abroad militarily along with the United States. This had been the case during the Gulf War. It had also been the case in Yugoslavia with the French participation in Operation Deny Flight,[55] which had been launched in April 1993 with the purpose of closing off Bosnian air space to Serbian planes. As the 1990s went on, the French were becoming acquainted with NATO operationally on the ground and in combat zones. As Nicole Gnesotto has observed about French rhetoric, "The discourses of autonomy often contradict the practice of cooperation."[56] And this cooperation on the ground, though not without friction, was a progressive one.

With peace finally having been established in Bosnia, NATO could turn in earnest to its problems of institutional adaptation. On December 5, 1995, less than a month after the Dayton accords, Chirac made a major gesture: the French government announced that it was returning to the NATO Military Committee (made up of the Chiefs of Defense Staffs of the member countries) and would also attend sessions of NATO Ministers of Defense when those meetings were considered North Atlantic Council meetings. France did not return, however, to the integrated command itself, pending the introduction of reforms in the NATO structure.

The return of France to the Military Committee of NATO and its associated bodies was a very significant symbolic step. However, there long since had been a series of agreements that, though not formally linking France to NATO's integrated command, provided for cooperation between the two parties in various areas and in different sorts of emergencies.

THE INTEGRATED COMMAND

NATO's integrated command had started to function at the beginning of 1951. What seemed so tentative in 1949, so problematic—a credible defense of Western Europe in the face of a huge Soviet Army—had become effortlessly efficient, though unused, by the time the Berlin Wall came down forty years later. At that moment, the NATO instrument—the unified command—had become more important than the purpose for which it was created: though the threat had gone, the instrument remained as a testimony to the unity of Europe—under American aegis.

The NATO organization had been fashioned to defend against the threat of a massive attack from the East. This required a highly centralized command for the use of both conventional and nuclear weapons. The imperative of the integrated command was that of maximum efficiency. It was not an instrument to be thrown away easily, although it had been created at a time when the West faced mortal danger from the East, and that time was no more.

In France, the unreconstructed school of thought was that the integrated command should go. In the words of Gabriel Robin, former French ambassador to NATO: "Integration *is* the SHAPE and the SACEUR. [The latter's] role is predominant, his prerogatives are exorbitant. [The SHAPE/SACEUR system] is anachronistic. It is not necessary to defend Europe at present. We have a completely changed universe. . . . There is only one real reform [of NATO] that has a basis in reality, and that has to do with who commands."[57]

Although the integrated command theoretically was an anomaly with the end of the Cold War, it nevertheless turned out in Bosnia that nothing was possible until the Americans intervened and exercised the facilities of this command. The virtue of this system—American participation and know-how—was seen once again as crucially important, despite its vice—the increasingly anachronistic deficit of sovereignty for the Western European countries in an era when the Cold War was over.

As Diego Ruiz-Palmer has pointed out, the relationship between France and NATO after the caesura of 1966 had been based in part "on joint military action, but at the same time . . . on the mutual recognition of a strategic disagreement in the nuclear area and on the non-participation of an ally in an integrated military structure considered by the other members of NATO as the keystone of [a] common defense."[58]

It is also worth noting in this regard that, of the many agreements concluded between France and NATO since 1966, from the Ailleret-Lemnitzer accords of 1967 on operations in the central zone of Europe through the Lanxade-Naumann-Shalikashvili agreement of January 1993 on placing the Euro-Corps under NATO in a time of emergency, none touched on the use of France's nuclear deterrent. According to the chief of staff of the French armed forces, writing in 1981, "The cooperation [between France and NATO] concerns only conventional forces and excludes, therefore, any planning for the utilization of nuclear forces."[59] France's *force de frappe*, consequently, has remained for the last thirty years the wild card, so to speak, in the defense of Western Europe.

With the end of the Cold War, however, nuclear deterrence has taken on a lesser importance, a fact that has been acknowledged by Jacques Chirac himself: "In the new international context, nuclear deterrence will not occupy the same place as during the Cold War. It was then the keystone arch of our defense, in the sense that our whole military apparatus was subordinated to it."[60]

Nevertheless, the French nuclear deterrent, which was never palpably operational during the Cold War anyway, lives on—albeit in a reduced status and in the background. In the words of President Chirac, "Deterrence still constitutes the ultimate assurance of our security and the guarantee of our independence."[61] In a related sense, it can be said that the French nuclear deterrent overhangs the European scene as a sort of existential threat: France can obliterate Germany, but the reverse is not true. Still, the threat is not real; this very expensive instrument is not to be used, according to Chirac: "the nuclear strategy of France will of course remain [that of] deterrence and therefore defensive, excluding—it goes without saying—all idea of battle."[62]

France and Great Britain—the only nuclear powers in Western Europe—have been engaged in regular discussions on nuclear strategy since 1993.[63] French officials, up to and including President Chirac, have described these discussions as fruitful and important without being much more specific than that. Chirac has said only that the French and British deterrent forces have a role to play in the common security policy of the European Union. At the same time he assured audiences that there was no intention to come up with a French or Anglo-French nuclear guarantee as a substitute for the American deterrent in Europe. The intention was to reinforce deterrence globally.[64]

It is with continental Western Europe that the problem of the French nuclear deterrent becomes contentious. The French-German imbalance in the nuclear weapons area, which had been a larval issue for some time, rose to the fore in the 1990s. A major point of contention, aside from the fact that the French nuclear "umbrella" has never been extended explicitly beyond the "sanctuary" of French Metropolitan territory, were the stocks of Hadès missiles (and also the older Pluton variety)—those tactical weapons of short and medium range ("prestrategic" weapons, in French terminology), which were supposed to serve as a final nuclear warning shot but of which France possesses hundreds.

The sudden uselessness of these weapons, which could only land in Central or Eastern Europe, became evident with the end of the Cold War. Taking the new situation into account, President Mitterrand announced unilaterally in September 1991 the nondeployment of French prestrategic weapons.[65] On April 12, 1992, he announced on television the suspension of nuclear testing in the Pacific.[66]

What is more, Mitterrand seemed also to recognize the problem that the French strategic nuclear deterrent was posing for a European defense identity: he opened the debate on this hitherto taboo subject, although in characteristically vague terms, in the wake of the Maastricht Summit, on the occasion of "National Meetings for Europe."[67] Mitterrand stated: "Is it possible to conceive of a European [nuclear] doctrine? This question will rapidly become one of the major issues in the construction of a common European defense."[68]

Jacques Delors, then president of the European Commission, went even further when he said, on the same occasion, "I cannot prevent myself from thinking that if, one day, the European Community has a very strong political union, then why not transfer the nuclear weapon to this political authority?"[69]

Tensions within Europe, particularly in Germany, arose again during the brief period of French resumption of nuclear testing in the Pacific in the summer of 1995. That September, and obviously partly as a palliative, Prime Minister Alain Juppé raised the notion of "concerted deterrence" between France and its European neighbors—again without further specifics. It was not clear what "concerted deterrence" involved, but the new French president, Jacques Chirac, made clear what it did not involve: "It is not a question of enlarging our deterrence or of imposing on our partners a new contract. It is [rather] a question of taking into account the consequences of a community of destiny, of an increasing intertwining of our vital interests."[70]

With the French nuclear deterrent now of reduced importance, the French desire to draw apart from NATO as a means of retaining the independence of the *force de frappe* lost much of its intensity. In 1966 this was a very real consideration, as France was still struggling to make its nuclear weapons capability operational and, since the beginning of the decade, had fended off American pressures to accept a system—the Multilateral Force—that would have, at most, eliminated and, at least, diminished the French independent deterrent.

The softening of this negative constraint on France being linked to NATO's military organization was accompanied by new, positive incentives for France to draw closer to NATO: the end of the Cold War unleashed the West's potential to intervene more freely in areas of crisis, and France, along with Britain, was traditionally the leading interventionist power in Europe. As for Russia, not only was its capacity to oppose such interventions much reduced, but it also occasionally was disposed to join in such ventures, as was demonstrated in its participation in the Implementation Force (IFOR) operation in Bosnia-Herzegovina.

For France, the end of the Cold War has meant that intervention capability, rather than nuclear deterrence, has been given pride of place. As Jacques Chirac put it, "the strategy of action, which lies with conventional forces that are autonomous and projectable, with reliable command capabilities, and with diversified means of intelligence, has developed a new importance."[71]

This "strategy of action by projectable forces" impelled France to draw closer to NATO, where the know-how and the capability for such action exists. But in addition to the lessening importance of nuclear weapons and the newly favorable climate for intervention, there was another reason for France's rapprochement with NATO in the middle of the 1990s: the diminished American military presence—and therefore influence—in Europe following the end of the Cold War.

An alliance reflects the relative political weight of its members and, accordingly, as time goes on, changes in these relative weights. During the Cold War, the weight of the United States vis-à-vis its European partners was overwhelming. The survival of Europe and the Western world depended on the efficiency of the U.S. nuclear deterrent force. The defense of Europe, in order to be at a top level of performance, both nuclear and conventional, had to be under American control. The presence of some 350,000 U.S. military personnel in Europe was not only a guarantee of the U.S. commitment to defend the Continent; it was a reinforcement of the American predominance in NATO. The American military presence in Europe is now roughly 100,000, less than a third of what it was at the height of the Cold War. Western Europe does not need the U.S. nuclear umbrella at present, and it no longer needs the United States to defend itself.

With the relative political weight of the United States within NATO clearly reduced as a result of the end of the Cold War (1989) and the breakup of the Soviet Union (1991), two major developments took place within NATO. First, there was a perceived need to adapt NATO's rigid chain of command now that the "indivisible" defense of Europe was no longer required. Second, with the relative weight of the United States within NATO reduced, France not only could feel freer to challenge existing NATO doctrines and procedures; it also could move closer to the NATO structures without the same fear of loss of sovereignty that existed during the Cold War. Indeed, the ease with which France was able to effect changes—at least in theory—in NATO's defense outlook was a reflection of these changing political weights. The United States for its part, given its loss of relative weight within NATO, also felt disposed to show greater flexibility and a greater sense of accommodation.

As Diego Ruiz-Palmer has noted, one of the paradoxes of the France-NATO relationship following 1966 was that "of an ally who, while accepting the hypothesis of joint military action and the necessity of preparing it and of devoting effective military means to it when the time came, placed itself, by its own volition, outside the political-military and military bodies of the Alliance, in which were decided the strategic principles and the operational modalities which would govern, on the ground, this joint action."[72]

This *outsider* situation, difficult for France operationally after the caesura of 1966, became more and more onerous as the Cold War wore off. As the only major power in Europe, other than Britain, able to join in foreign interventions in the free atmosphere of the post–Cold War, France was impelled to take steps to overcome the disadvantages of its isolation from the NATO military bodies.

The process was slow and halting under the long presidency of François Mitterrand. As noted earlier,[73] Mitterrand restrained Jacques Chirac during the first "cohabitation" government (1986–1988) from drawing close to NATO. When Chirac returned to the scene as president in May 1995, he wasted little time in initiating a rapprochement with NATO, and as noted previously, the change in atmosphere soon was felt within the French military.[74]

The new French president, having spent some time in his formative years in the United States, was perceived to be free of the traditional French reservations about American culture. By the end of the year, France had rejoined the Military Committee of NATO, and shortly thereafter, Jacques Chirac explained publicly the rationale behind this change:

Before you, I reaffirm the position of France: the political commitment of the United States in Europe and its military presence on European soil remain an essential factor in the stability and security of the Continent—and also of the world. France is ready to assume its full share in this renovation process. She demonstrated this in announcing a few weeks ago her rapprochement with the military structures of the organization. And I wish to confirm today the spirit of open-mindedness and availability with which France approaches this adaptation of NATO, including the military side, as long as the European identity can assert itself fully therein.[75]

NATO ENLARGEMENT

Starting informally in the fall of 1993 but officially at the time of the Brussels NATO Summit in January 1994, an oscillation away from the EU, preoccupied with its own "deepening," and towards NATO took place. It was a process that would culminate in the admission to NATO of Poland, the Czech Republic, and Hungary at the Washington NATO Summit five years later, in April 1999.

The signal for this significant change was given in a seminal article, entitled "Building a New NATO," published in *Foreign Affairs* in the fall of 1993.[76] This was the public version of a study that had been done for the RAND Corporation by three experts on NATO and Europe, Ronald D. Asmus, Richard L. Kugler, and F. Stephen Larrabee.[77] The article called for a new "grand strategy for the West" to handle challenges in two "arcs of crisis": one, an eastern arc running from north Central Europe down through Turkey, the Caucasus, and Central Asia, and the other running from the Maghreb through the Middle East and Southwest Asia. Wrote the authors: "Such a strategy must be, first and foremost, political and economic. But the West must also establish a stable security framework for these regions. The obvious tool for this new strategy is NATO. The Persian Gulf War and the ongoing Yugoslav crisis have shown the European Community incapable of taking on such a task. Achieving consensus among the 12 EC members, especially when military action is required, is nearly impossible."[78]

Significantly, the RAND trio did not advocate a "unilateral" extension of NATO. They emphasized the need for "a coherent and coordinated Western strategy for the integration of Poland, Hungary, the Czech Republic and possibly Slovakia into both the EC and NATO."[79] This new strategy of integration to the East was vitally essential for NATO, which would have to "go out of area or go out of business."[80]

The European Union logically should have been the institution that reached out to Central and Eastern Europe at the end of the Cold War. But this was not to be the case. As Michel Tatu pointed out, the EU "limited itself to establishing a space of prosperity and liberty in the face of the Communist Bloc. It neither could, nor would export its order beyond the borders of its member states."[81]

This reticence on the part of the EU was not foreordained. Indeed, in the Treaty of Rome of 1957, which created the European Economic Community, it is explicitly stated that all countries of Europe are eligible to join. However, the dialectic of deepening and enlargement, particularly the uncertainty over anchoring Germany to Western Europe through the Euro, was a factor in play in the EU in a way that it was not in NATO. As Jacques Delors, the president of the European Commission from 1985 to 1995, put it in an interview in *Le Monde*: "the dilemma between enlargement and deepening is real. Our historic duty is to reunify Europe and thus open our arms to those countries which are just as European as us, but we know, in the light of previous enlargements, that we risk diluting the enterprise."[82]

In retrospect, it is not difficult to see how NATO stepped into a vacuum created by the reluctance of the EU to move eastward. Though a similar perspective of dilution of the institution by expansion eastward existed both for the EU and NATO, moving to the east as a structural problem was much less severe for NATO than for the EU, NATO being only a military organization. Conversely, the issue of "deepening," that is, strengthening the institution as a first requirement before enlargement, did not arise with NATO as it did for the EU. NATO did not need to be strengthened as a defensive organization: the threat of a massive Russian attack into Western Europe was *dépassé*. As pointed out earlier, NATO enlargements are much easier to carry out structurally than are those of the EU, where the candidate countries have to satisfy the requirements contained in the 80,000 pages of the *acquis communautaires*.[83]

In the period from the early to mid-1990s, NATO sought on occasion to coordinate its own ideas on enlargement with the plans of the EU in this domain but was told, in the words of a knowledgeable senior American official, that this was none of NATO's business. According to a French NATO specialist, a joint effort was undertaken in 1994 to see if the two processes could be coordinated. The effort was abandoned as unworkable.

NATO expansion did not become officialized as an aim of the Alliance until the January 1994 Brussels Summit. It was then that a commitment to enlarge NATO at some point in the future was made ("We expect and would welcome NATO expansion that would reach to democratic states to our East, as part of an evolutionary process"[84]). By the time of the next summit, in July 1997 in Madrid, NATO had precipitated itself into inviting three former satellite countries to join: Poland, the Czech Republic, and Hungary.

NOTES

1. French Embassy Press Service, Washington, D.C. Text of speech of President Mitterrand, p. 6.
2. Louis Gautier, "L'Europe de la défense au portant," *Politique Étrangère*, vol. 2 (1999), p. 235.
3. Nicole Gnesotto, *La puissance et l'Europe* (Paris: Presses de Science Po, 1998), p. 61.
4. Diego A. Ruiz-Palmer, "La coopération militaire entre la France et ses alliés, 1966–1991: entre le poids de l'héritage et les défis de l'après-guerre froide," in Maurice Vaïsse, Pierre Mélandri, and Frédéric Bozo, eds., *La France et l'OTAN, 1949–1996* (Brussels: Editions Complexe, 1996), p. 598. Also see pp. 100–101.
5. Interview with a senior U.S. defense official.
6. James M. Goldgeier, *Not Whether But When: The U.S. Decision to Enlarge NATO* (Washington, D.C.: Brookings Institution, 1999), p. 42.
7. Interview with General Joulwan, March 27, 2000.
8. ⟨http://www.nato.int.docu/pr/1994/p94–003.htm⟩, p. 1.
9. Interview with a senior U.S. defense official.
10. See p. 64.
11. Gnesotto, *La puissance et l'Europe*, p. 55.
12. Goldgeier, *Not Whether But When*, p. 26.
13. Interview with General Joulwan.
14. It is noteworthy in this respect that a study that was part of a working group effort to prepare for the Brussels Summit was entitled "Operationalizing NACC and a Draft NACC Charter." (Goldgeier, *Not Whether But When*, p. 24.)
15. ⟨http://www.nato.int/docu/pr/1994/p94–003.htm⟩, p. 3.
16. Ibid.
17. Goldgeier, *Not Whether But When*, p. 57.
18. Lord Ismay, the first secretary-general of NATO, is reported to have said that NATO was there for the purpose of keeping the Russians out, the Americans in, and the Germans down.
19. Interview with a senior U.S. defense official.
20. ⟨http://www.nato.int/docu/comm/49–95/c911107a.htm⟩, paragraph 46.
21. Pascal Boniface, "Révolution stratégique mondiale, continuité et inflexions de la politique française de sécurité," in Samy Cohen, ed., *Mitterrand et la sortie de la guerre froide* (Paris: Presses Universitaires de France, 1998), p. 180.

22. S. Nelson Drew, *NATO from Berlin to Bosnia* (Washington, D.C.: Institute for National Strategic Studies, National Defense University, McNair Paper 35, January 1995), p. 21.

23. Pierre Favier and Michel Martin-Roland, *La Décennie Mitterrand, Vol.4, Les déchirements (1991–1995)* (Paris: Seuil, 1999), p. 183 (hereafter cited as *DM*).

24. Ibid., p. 296.

25. Pascal Boniface, ed., *L'Année Stratégique 2001* (Paris: Éditions Michalon, 2000), p. 20.

26. Richard Holbrooke, *To End a War* (New York: Random House/Modern Library, 1999), p. 27 n.8. Reference is to Laura Silber and Allan Little, *Yugoslavia: Death of a Nation* (London: Penguin Books/BBC Books, 1996), p. 201.

27. Roger Cohen, "Eyewitness Account," review of Timothy Garton Ash, *History of the Present* (New York: Random House, 2000), in *New York Times Book Review*, October 29, 2000, p. 13.

28. *DM*, Vol. 4, p. 294 n.1. In early 1992, 14,000 blue-helmeted UN troops had been placed in Croatia to protect the Serb minorities in the Krajina and Slavonia. (Ibid., p. 295.)

29. Hubert Védrine, *Les mondes de François Mitterrand: A l'Elysée, 1981–1995* (Paris: Fayard, 1996), p. 654.

30. *DM*, Vol. 4, p. 508.

31. Ibid., p. 525.

32. Védrine, *Les mondes de François Mitterrand*, p. 638. Even Védrine, who was closely linked to Mitterrand as the secretary-general of the presidency, considers the use of this phrase unfortunate: "the President, in spite of himself, sent a bad signal to the protagonists, and especially to the Serbian leaders, which doubtless contributed to making them think they could persist in their actions." (Ibid.)

33. *DM*, Vol. 4, p. 518.

34. Ibid., p. 521.

35. Ibid., p. 512. The note was dated January 25, 1994.

36. Ibid.

37. See above this page.

38. Védrine, *Les mondes de François Mitterrand*, p. 652.

39. Drew, *NATO from Berlin to Bosnia*, p. 15.

40. Ibid., p. 18.

41. Védrine, *Les mondes de François Mitterrand*, p. 657.

42. Interview with General Joulwan.

43. Holbrooke, *To End a War*, p. 361.

44. Ibid., p. 65.

45. Ibid., p. 330.

46. Ibid., p. 74.

47. See also p. 119. According to a U.S. defense official, after this accident word came down from higher authorities to the effect that, "we want this thing [Bosnia] fixed."

48. Holbrooke, *To End a War*, p. 361.

49. Ibid., p. 328.

50. Interview with General Joulwan. N.B. A year later IFOR was renewed under a new name, SFOR (Stabilization Force).

51. Cohen, ed., *Mitterrand et la sortie de la guerre froide*, p. 186.

52. See p. 13.

53. See above this page.
54. Cohen, ed., *Mitterrand et la sortie de la guerre froide*, p. 180.
55. Ibid., p. 179.
56. Gnesotto, *La puissance et l'Europe*, p. 113.
57. Remarks made by Ambassador Robin on February 10, 1996, at a conference entitled "France and NATO" held under the auspices of the Center for Defense History Studies in Paris. (N.B. SHAPE is now located in Mons, Belgium.)
58. Ruiz-Palmer, "La coopération militaire entre la France et ses alliés," p. 569.
59. Ibid., p. 578.
60. Press Service of the Presidency, Speech of Jacques Chirac to the Institute of Higher Studies of National Defense (IHEDN), June 8, 1996, p. 5.
61. Ibid.
62. Ibid., p. 3.
63. Daniel Vernet, "La révolution stratégique chiraquienne," *Le Monde*, June 8, 1996, p. 12.
64. Speech of Jacques Chirac speech to IHEDN, p. 6.
65. *Le Monde*, September 13, 1991, p. 3. (Press conference of François Mitterrand.)
66. Antoine Sanguinetti, "French military equipment, too expensive and outmoded," *Le Monde diplomatique*, July 1992, p. 10.
67. See also p. 62.
68. *Le Monde*, January 12–13, 1992, p. 1.
69. Ibid.
70. Speech of Jacques Chirac to IHEDN, pp. 6–7.
71. Ibid., p. 5.
72. Ruiz-Palmer, "La coopération militaire entre la France et ses alliés," p. 569.
73. See p. 13. N.D.L.R. "Cohabitation" meant that one party controlled the presidency and another the National Assembly and, therefore, the Prime Ministership. In that period, Jacques Chirac was Prime Minister.
74. See p. 72.
75. "France and NATO," *Radio France Inter*, "Le téléphone sonne," February 8, 1996. (Voices of Charles de Gaulle and Jacques Chirac. The latter's statement was made on February 1, 1996.)
76. Ronald D. Asmus, Richard L. Kugler, and F. Stephen Larrabee, "Building a New NATO," *Foreign Affairs*, September/October 1993, pp. 28–40.
77. Goldgeier, *Not Whether But When*, pp. 32–33.
78. Asmus, Kugler, and Larrabee, "Building a New NATO," p. 31.
79. Ibid., p. 35.
80. Ibid., p. 31.
81. Michel Tatu, "Kosovo: une chance pour l'Europe," *Politique Internationale*, no. 85 (autumn 1999): 196.
82. *Le Monde*, January 19, 2000, p. 2.
83. See p. 6.
84. Brussels Summit Declaration ⟨http://www.nato.int/docu/pr/1994/p94-003.htm⟩, p. 3.

CHAPTER 4

From the AFSOUTH Imbroglio to the Madrid Summit (1996–July 1997)

THE HIGH POINT OF THE BERLIN MINISTERIAL MEETING

By the mid-1990s, the French had begun to shift tactics. Rather than trying to create a separate European defense identity around the WEU, with all that implied in terms of cost and redundancy of effort, and given the lukewarm reaction of many of the Western European countries toward the Euro-Corps,[1] the French announced their readiness to create a distinctly European defense "pillar" within NATO. In return they would expect a "reform" of NATO that would take on the character, though not stated so outright, of a modification of the SACEUR system.

This change in outlook, spurred on by France's participation in a series of coalition operations in the Gulf and in the former Yugoslavia, caused a rethinking of the foundations of French defense policy that had been put in place by General de Gaulle during his years in power (1958–1969) and had remained the subject of a national consensus since. The bedrock of this "Gaullist consensus" can be summed up as follows: national independence for France and an autonomy of decision in defense matters—both of which being related to and backed up by France's nuclear deterrent, the centrality and sacrosanct nature of which were beyond discussion. Such a policy, by definition, was accompanied by a certain distance from NATO. Hubert Védrine described this Gaullist consensus as having lasted until 1995.[2] What undermined this consensus, in part, was the lessening significance of nuclear weapons with the ending of the Cold War, as Jacques Chirac himself acknowledged in a speech in June 1996.[3]

Two and a half years after the Brussels Summit, a new political-military framework for NATO was endorsed at the North Atlantic Council Ministerial meeting of June 3–4, 1996, at Berlin. In the communiqué of this meeting, three broad objectives for NATO were set out:

- Build[ing] a European Security and Defense Identity [ESDI] within NATO,
- [Undertaking] new roles and missions relating to conflict prevention and crisis management and . . . against the proliferation of weapons of mass destruction . . . while maintaining [the] capability for collective defense, and
- Broadening and deepening [the] dialogue and cooperation with Partners, notably through the Partnership for Peace and the North Atlantic Cooperation Council.[4]

ESDI, evoked at the Brussels Summit, was, in the words of Nicole Gnesotto, "duly crowned" at the Berlin Ministerial.[5] Emphasis was given to the key role of the CJTFs (Combined Joint Task Forces), which were the operational expression of ESDI and which permitted "the use of separable but not separate military capabilities [of NATO] in operations led by the WEU, and the participation of nations outside the Alliance."[6] This "separable but not separate" formula had first been evoked at the Brussels Summit, and the CJTF concept also had been agreed to in principle at that time.

The Military Committee of NATO, with France now participating as of December 1995, was charged with making recommendations to the Council at its next meeting in December 1996 on how the implementation of the CJTF concept was to be worked out. The Berlin communiqué also underlined the importance of the creation of "a military command structure better suited to current and future Euro-Atlantic security."[7] Recommendations as to a new command structure were also to be made by the Military Committee through the vehicle of what was referred to as the Long-Term Study.

The Berlin Ministerial Meeting of NATO seemed to satisfy the French both in terms of the ESDI and in terms of the internal reform of NATO. In the French view, the reform of NATO structures necessarily had to be accomplished before the anticipated enlargement of NATO to the East, the principle of which had been accepted at the January 1994 Brussels Summit.

The Berlin Ministerial was the high point in the rationalization of U.S. and European (mainly French) concerns. French officials were content at the conclusion of this meeting, feeling that NATO at last was moving in the right direction. Though little in substance had changed as to France's position vis-à-vis NATO, the public perception was otherwise in the wake of the Berlin meeting, as Louis Gautier has noted: "this rapprochement, variously appreciated and commented upon, was perceived as a very significant reorientation in French defense policy."[8]

On the occasion of the Berlin Ministerial Meeting, President Chirac announced that France was resuming its full place at meetings of NATO Defense Ministers whenever they were held, and this was followed by France's attendance at such a meeting on June 14, 1996. However, France did not return to the integrated military structure of NATO, nor did it join the Defense Planning

Committee and its Nuclear Planning Group—both created around the time of the French departure from the NATO military structure and both considered by the French to be part of the integrated command. Nevertheless, though not joining in the sessions of the Nuclear Planning Group, France announced its willingness to discuss nuclear matters with the United States. This was declared by President Chirac during a visit to the United States on February 1, 1996.

At the time of the Berlin Ministerial, France led its partners to believe that its further return to NATO would depend on whether the reform process proceeded satisfactorily. This meant mainly the elaboration of a revised integrated command structure. It was following this moment, a moment of French euphoria at the end of the Berlin ministerial, that things seemed to go off, both in terms of ESDI and in terms of the internal reform of NATO. It is not difficult to see why, for one can find in the Berlin communiqué words that anticipated the problems that would ensue when one entered into the details of the negotiations. Nicole Gnesotto has described this moment of apogee and its rapid dissipation:

The [meeting] of NATO at Berlin, in June 1996, marked the apogee of that reconciliation—[which seemed] finally possible—of the Alliance, Europe and France: the reform of NATO was supposed to permit the enrolling of European defense into the Atlantic organization and to construct, between America and Europe, a strategic partnership that would both reinforce the Euro-American Alliance and assure the increase in strategic power of the European partners. However, very rapidly this hope was to appear for what it was: an umpteenth disappointment.[9]

Overall, one can summarize the American approach in the following formula: flexible on principles, firm on details. The French, on the other hand, focus more towards abstraction: once the principle has been agreed upon, the details can be put into place in a more or less logical manner. This difference in approach is one means of understanding the disappointment that followed the Berlin Ministerial Meeting of June 1996. The French appeared to have thought that a real turning point had taken place with the communiqué of this meeting. It was not just a question of the reaffirmation of the ESDI, but it also was acknowledged that the Western European Union (WEU) could take charge of purely European operations, including the planning of them, in borrowing NATO assets for these purposes, including communications, intelligence, and airlift.

It is noteworthy that the Berlin communiqué is studded with the phrase "within the Alliance" and, like a mantra, is repeatedly invoked, explicitly or implicitly, in juxtaposition with the term "European Security and Defense Identity." The same is the case for the formula of "capabilities that are separable but not separate."

Equally important in the Berlin communiqué was the mention of several organizational principles that could be said to add up to the "fencing in" of the WEU, perhaps reflecting the Shalikashvili aim, cited earlier, of not allowing the French to use the WEU as a competitor to NATO.[10] First, NATO itself could conduct non–Article 5 operations, that is, operations other than collective defense.[11] These equated with the so-called "Petersberg tasks" self-assigned to the WEU in June 1992. Second, the release of NATO assets for WEU-led operations was to be approved by the North Atlantic Council (NAC).[12] And third, "appropriate personnel within the NATO command structure" would be double-hatted to enable them to conduct WEU-led operations.[13]

THE FATE OF THE CJTFs

As noted previously,[14] according to the decisions of the NATO ministerial meeting in Berlin, the CJTFs were supposed to be the operational expression of the ESDI. They were to be the instrument whereby NATO could put its assets of communications, intelligence, airlift, etc. at the disposition of the Western European Union (WEU). These assets of NATO were to serve in support of operations under the rubric of "crisis management," or "Petersberg tasks."

From the NATO point of view, the making available of NATO assets involved two important operational conditions. First, NATO would monitor the use of these assets and, if necessary, call them back into NATO if a higher priority arose. (In any case they would be called back after the termination of a "Petersberg-type" operation.) Second, the deputy to the SACEUR, who is a European and who would direct an operation of "crisis management" under the aegis of the WEU, would still retain his responsibilities toward his chief, the SACEUR, who has always been an American.

Subsequent negotiations foundered over the issue of how much freedom of action the Europeans would have in bringing into being an ESDI. In the beginning of the consideration of the CJTF concept, the United States was receptive to the idea of establishing the CJTFs in so-called "national nuclei," that is, in centers outside the regional commands of NATO, provided these "nuclei" could be brought up to the level of NATO standards. In the view of American officials, these "national nuclei" would be skeletal only and would not come up to strength until and unless an operation was envisaged.[15]

After France's thirty years of self-isolation from the military structures of NATO, the Chirac government, in pressing for "national nuclei" for the CJTFs, seemed to aim at creating purely European organs of defense within the NATO organization. Eventually, however, U.S. military planners rejected the idea of "national nuclei" and instead pressed successfully for embedding the CJTFs in the various NATO commands.

The differences over the location of the CJTFs were a reflection of the larger issue of how much autonomy the Europeans were going to have in carrying out "crisis management" operations on their own but with the use of NATO assets. From the point of view of the "autonomists" in Europe and especially, one could say, the French, the arrangements insisted upon by NATO (read the United States) had to do not with autonomy but rather with dependence.

THE DISPUTE OVER NATO'S SOUTHERN COMMAND (AFSOUTH)

When the other major issue, the internal reform of NATO, was evoked at the Berlin Ministerial, it was logical to assume, at least from the European point of view, including and especially that of the French, that *a priori* a reform was considered necessary. Apparently acting from that assumption, the French began to take a number of initiatives concerning structural reform.

According to a press article, which has not been confirmed, it was a question of a request on the part of the French that a supercommand be created for NATO. The officer holding this position would be over both the ACLANT (Atlantic Command) and ACE (European Command). The proposal was made to the American Secretary of Defense, William Perry, by the French Defense Minister, Charles Millon, during a meeting in the summer of 1996. The idea was that this supercommand would be held by an American, but the strategic command for Europe (that of the SACEUR) would be given to a European. The reaction from the American side in the first instance was not negative but, rather, the contrary. However, in the final analysis, and there is some doubt that the suggestion was taken seriously, the proposition was turned down and Secretary Perry so notified Defense Minister Millon in August 1996.[16] What is clear in all this, and according to a knowledgeable French source, Millon did propose that the SACEUR be a European officer. According to this source, Millon went to London to meet Perry, who was on an official visit.[17]

Following the U.S. turndown, President Chirac may have decided that he was aiming too high and would adjust his sights accordingly. In a letter to President Clinton, to which there was also a follow-up letter, Chirac proposed something that was less far-reaching than the supercommand proposal. What he proposed, in substance, was that since the Americans held the two strategic commands, the SACLANT in Norfolk, Virginia, and the SACEUR in Mons, Belgium, one of the regional commands in Europe (which were being consolidated from three to two—north and south) be given to a European, specifically that of the Southern Command at Naples. And he wrote by hand at the bottom of the letter, "Bill, this is very important to me."

It turned out that what may have seemed reasonable to the French was totally unacceptable to the Americans, who had the impression, rightly or wrongly, that the French were overreaching. In Washington, it was thought that significant concessions had been made to the French at the Berlin meeting, in terms of attempting to persuade them to return to full partnership in NATO, and suddenly the United States was confronted with the disagreeable surprise of a seemingly new "condition." The public rejection of Chirac's request by the new secretary of Defense, William Cohen, and press leaks about the French president's letters, only served to raise the temperature between Washington and Paris in the fall of 1996.

The letter from Chirac specified that an arrangement would have to be found that would preserve American command of the U.S. Sixth Fleet. The U.S. position was that in the event of any military action, the Sixth Fleet would be a part of it and, also, that any separation from the Southern Command would violate the principle of the indivisible defense of the countries of NATO, a principle that is rooted in NATO doctrine.

It should be noted that there is a long history concerning the Southern Command, which has been held by an American admiral located in Naples since NATO's inception, in particular. In 1950–1951, at the time of the creation of the NATO commands, the British wanted to have the leading post in the Atlantic Command. This was refused by the Americans, but the British were offered the compensation of a minor command over the English Channel, which was called the Channel Command. Later, the British were given charge of what was called the Middle East Command in the eastern Mediterranean (which no longer exists), but the head of this command had to report back through the SACEUR.

As for the French, they wanted at the onset of NATO to have charge of a separate command in the western Mediterranean because of their interests in North Africa. This was rejected categorically by the Anglo-Americans. It should be noted that, at the time, the French were in an extremely weak position vis-à-vis the Anglo-Americans, and there was also the factor, which may have been only subliminal, that the French navy did not participate much in the war against the Germans. According to a document of the Joint Chiefs of Staff at the time, "Any change to the Strategic Defense Concept [of NATO] which would impair the recognition and responsibility of the U.S. and the U.K. for organization and control of the sea lanes or constitute a basis for the designation of a French commander in any theater command arrangements which might develop within NATO would . . . be unacceptable."[18]

The upshot was that the French, who at the time were supposed to provide the bulk of the troops for the defense of Western Europe, did not receive any of the principal NATO commands. General Alphonse Juin was named deputy for the Central NATO Command (General Eisenhower, as the SACEUR, kept the top Central Command position for himself). It is true that General Juin later acceded to the top post in the Central Command but without having charge of the air forces in the command, these being placed directly under the SACEUR. Already, in July 1951, General Juin described the central sector command he was about to take over as "too subjugated to SHAPE."[19]

There is another point about the early years, which is just as important. At the beginning, the Military Committee of NATO had the mission of serving as the link between the political authority of NATO, the North Atlantic Council, and the SACEUR. This Military Committee had an inner core, which was called the Standing Group, composed of representatives of the United States, the U.K., and France. In the NATO hierarchy, the Standing Group, which sat in Washington, was above the SACEUR. But Eisenhower, who was located in Europe, obtained from the Standing Group a derogation that allowed him, as SACEUR, to have direct contact with the political and military authorities in Western Europe.

In February 1951, there was a proposal by the State and Defense Departments to move the Standing Group to Paris, but the Joint Chiefs of Staff turned this aside on the grounds that it would "subject SACEUR to direct political pressure which might be detrimental to him militarily."[20] (!) Thus the Standing Group was marginalized little by little, and in 1966 it ceased to exist altogether, because the French quit the integrated military command at that time.

It is also worth noting in this context that at the Berlin meeting in 1996 a Policy Coordination Group was created to "meet the need, especially in NATO's new missions, for closer coordination of political and military viewpoints."[21] This political-military group was to a great extent brought about by the insistence of the French that there be a body in which they could participate that would not be tied to the NATO defense planning structures.

Notwithstanding the disputes, both recent and ancient, over the regional commands, it is an undeniable fact that during the Cold War, the integrated command of NATO and the concept of the indivisible defense of Europe functioned very well and served admirably the interests of the West. Thus one could summarize the American attitude in the phrase, "If it ain't broke, don't fix it."

According to Pentagon officials, a compromise was being worked out in the spring of 1997 that might have been acceptable to Chirac, had his party coalition been returned to power in the elections. The compromise was focused on satisfying French demands regarding the Southern Command by creating a regional CJTF at Naples that would be commanded by a European and would conduct operations in the Mediterranean region. According to one State Department official intimately connected with the NATO process, Chirac's government held out the possibility that France might rejoin the NATO military structure at the time of the Madrid Summit in July 1997.

Pentagon officials claim to this day that what halted the French move back toward NATO more than anything else was the imprudent decision of Chirac to schedule the snap legislative election of May 1997, which upset this final attempt at a rapprochement between France and NATO. Perhaps such a rapprochement was only a vain hope, considering the personal disappointment that Chirac underwent when his letters to Clinton were rejected.

Chirac long had signaled his intention to revise the standoffish French position toward NATO that Mitterrand had maintained, as in these remarks attributed to him in 1993:

[He] conclud[ed] that if France want[ed] to play a determining role in the creation of a European defense identity, it must take into account [the] state of mind of its partners, and reconsider to a large degree the form of its relations with NATO. It [was] clear, in effect, that the necessary rebalancing of relations within the Atlantic Alliance, relying on existing European institutions such as the WEU, [could] only take place from the inside, not against the United States but in agreement with it.[22]

Following his accession to the presidency in June 1995, Chirac had clearly worked toward an accommodation with NATO, as France joined the Military Committee in December 1995 and the regular meetings of the Defense Ministers (as of the Berlin Ministerial of June 1996). He seemingly needed something to show for this forthcomingness but unfortunately picked an issue on which the United States was simply not prepared to budge. The fact that he put his request in writing, a move that not everyone around him thought was wise, not only raised the stakes but certainly wound up deepening his own disappointment.

Chirac's failure of political judgment in scheduling an early election while still enjoying a parliamentary majority ushered in a third period of "cohabitation" in France in the space of a dozen years. The arrival of the new socialist coalition government, led by Prime Minister Lionel Jospin and Foreign Minister Hubert Védrine, both of whom (especially Védrine) had systematically criticized Chirac's rapprochement with NATO, meant that no further movement in the direction of NATO was possible. Jospin, in a statement to Agence France Presse on February 4, 1996, had aligned himself with the positions previously taken by former President Mitterrand. Jospin said he was "not favorable" to the rapprochement of France with NATO and hoped that France's "autonomy of decision" would be oriented toward the construction of a European defense system.[23]

According to the same State Department official cited earlier,[24] "There was no way that a cohabitation government could have secured a return [to the integrated command]."[25] However, while the prospective French "return" to NATO remained stalemated, the French retained their "acquis": membership on the Military Committee and attendance at Defense Ministers' meetings.

BLOCKAGE CONFIRMED: THE MADRID NATO SUMMIT (JULY 1997)

By the time of the next NATO Summit, held in Madrid on July 7–8, 1997, progress on achieving a greater equilibrium in NATO between Americans and Europeans through the CJTF concept and related proposals had stalled. The blockage was patent, even though the summit declaration contained soothing language to the effect that "substantial progress has been achieved in the internal adaptation of the Alliance,"[26] The communiqué exhorted the members to "work on the resolution of outstanding issues" with the aim of reaching agreement by the next NATO Ministerial in December 1997.[27]

On July 2, 1997, just prior to the Madrid Summit, the French announced that the internal reform of NATO had not proceeded far enough for them to undertake a further rapprochement with the Alliance's military structure. By this time, however, the United States had other preoccupations. In a sort of inverse parallel to the EU, the United States had put aside the "deepening" of NATO (i.e., its internal reform) in favor of the enlargement of NATO.

The movement in favor of an enlargement of NATO had been gaining steam since the time of the publication of the article in the fall 1993 issue of *Foreign Affairs*, as mentioned in the previous chapter.[28] In the fall of 1994, NATO enlargement was included in the Republican Party's election platform, the "Contract with America."[29] On November 4, 1994, the NATO Participation Act, aimed at getting new candidate members ready for membership,[30] became law, and in the text four prospective members were named: Poland, the Czech Republic, Hungary, and Slovakia.[31] The latter country was subsequently dropped from consideration because of the undemocratic nature of its government.

Further steps in the process were taken as Congress, on February 16, 1995, passed the NATO Expansion Act by a 241–181 vote.[32] The NATO Enlargement Facilitation Act was passed in July 1996 and provided funds to the three candidate countries—Poland, the Czech Republic, and Hungary—to enable them to achieve membership in NATO.[33] In November 1996, a private organization, the United States Committee to expand NATO, was formed.[34]

Although enlargement of NATO "to any other European state" was contained in Article 10 of the 1949 North Atlantic Treaty, the extension of this provision as a declaratory policy of the U.S. administration began to quicken as the Bosnian war was being brought to a close in late 1995. In a speech at Prague in March 1996, President Clinton left no doubt that NATO enlargement was a clear aim of U.S. policy.[35] In a speech at Stuttgart in September 1996, Warren Christopher announced that there would be a summit in 1997 to consider the admittance of new members as well as a plan for a charter between Russia and NATO.[36] In the following month, October 1996, President Clinton, in a speech in Detroit, set a deadline of 1999 for the admission of the new members of NATO.[37]

Although a majority of Americans favored NATO enlargement,[38] a number of prominent individuals outside the government were vocal in their opposition to this enlargement, among them the former SACEUR, retired General John Galvin, and George Kennan.[39] The latter was later to describe NATO enlargement as "the most fateful error of American policy in the entire post–cold-war era."[40]

Those in the United States who objected to NATO enlargement were concerned chiefly that it would harm the West's relationship with Russia and weaken U.S. security cooperation with the Russians.[41] Others, including Senator Sam Nunn, General (Ret.) Brent Scowcroft, and Senator Patrick Moynihan, thought that EU expansion should precede that of NATO.[42] Still others, chiefly those in the Pentagon, were content to remain with the Partnership for Peace instead of going for NATO expansion, because the PfP did not carry with it the security guarantee that full membership in NATO would involve.[43]

But within the administration itself, there was a gathering momentum for NATO enlargement, led conceptually by National Security Adviser Anthony Lake and operationally by Richard Holbrooke, who had returned from the ambassadorship in Germany to become Assistant Secretary of State for European Affairs.[44] Holbrooke, who initially had taken the view that EU expansion should come first, had become a vigorous proponent of going ahead with NATO expansion instead.[45]

As far back as December 1994, the administration had set for itself a two-track policy that would eventually end up in NATO enlargement:[46] first, there would be an effort to coopt or propitiate Russia into accepting a NATO move to the east. This would be done by associating Russia as much as possible with NATO decisions without, however, offering Russia membership in NATO. Second, NATO would facilitate entry into membership of the three selected central European countries.[47]

The first part of the two-track policy was to culminate in the NATO Russia Founding Act of May 27, 1997, which would pave the way for the creation of the Permanent Joint Council, which in turn was to be the forum for strategic discussions between NATO and Russia.[48] Accompanying this part of the policy was an effort to ease Russian fears concerning NATO's boundaries being moved to the east. At the NATO Foreign Ministers' meeting in Brussels in December 1996, Secretary of State Warren Christopher pledged that there would be no nuclear weapons installed on the territories of new NATO members.[49] This commitment was reaffirmed in a NATO "unilateral statement" of March 14, 1997.[50]

The move toward NATO enlargement was crowned at the Madrid NATO Summit, with invitations being issued to three Central European countries—Poland, the Czech Republic, and Hungary[51]—and with the further statement that "no European democratic country whose admission would fulfill the objectives of the Treaty will be excluded from consideration."[52] At the NATO ministerial meeting at Sintra, Portugal, a month earlier, only the United States and Iceland proposed limiting the new entrants to three, as against five. Of the other two Slovenia, supported by Italy, made more sense geographically, as a bridge to Hungary. However, to include Slovenia and exclude Romania would have been too much of an affront to the French, so the U.S. position remained at three.[53]

To ease the feelings of those allies disappointed in the choice of only three new member countries and in the highhanded way this was brought about, NATO issued a statement at the Madrid Summit that included the following: "With regard to the aspiring members, we recognize with great interest and take account of the positive development toward democracy and the rule of law in a number of southeastern European countries, especially Romania and Slovenia. . . . At the same time, we recognize the progress achieved toward greater stability and cooperation by the states in the Baltic region who are also aspiring members."[54]

Whether consciously or not, the United States was putting itself in the position of being able to use the three prospective new members as a counterweight to the "autonomists" within NATO led by France. This was particularly true as regards Poland, which dwarfs the other Eastern European countries in population and has strong ties to the United States through its large immigration there. As Nicole Gnesotto has pointed out, public opinion in these Central European countries regards the United States as an equalizing force vis-à-vis the Western European powers, in particular the French-German "couple."[55] This power balance, if it can be called such, is one that has persisted to this day.

THE NASCENT DEFENSE ROLE OF THE EU

With the United States preoccupied with the enlargement of NATO, a nascent trend toward a defense role for Europe began to develop within the EU. In June 1997, the Amsterdam Treaty, the sequel to the Maastricht Treaty, had gone into effect, incorporating into the legal corpus of the EU the rather meager results of the EU's Intergovernmental Conference (IGC) (March 1996-May-1997). Four issues were left in suspense by the IGC, and all were related to the EU's ability to take on new members while avoiding institutional paralysis. These were adjustment of voting weights within the European Council, the number of commissioners, the extension of qualified majority voting to a greater number of issues, and the issue of "enhanced cooperation."[56] The latter, which would permit countries who so chose to move toward greater integration in various areas, was evoked as a possibility in the Amsterdam Treaty, but only for Community matters (First Pillar) and Police and Judicial Cooperation in Criminal Matters (Third Pillar)—not for the intergovernmental Common Foreign and Security Policy (Second Pillar).[57] Presumably, "enhanced cooperation" could be extended to the CFSP at some point in the future.

The incompleteness of the Amsterdam Treaty meant that, effectively, the expansion of the EU into Eastern Europe would have to be put off, as the institutional mechanisms were too unwieldy for a larger organization. The membership of the EU stood at fifteen, with the last three countries—Finland, Sweden, and Austria—having been admitted without difficulty on January 1, 1995.

In the matter of European defense, however, the Amsterdam Treaty contained certain new provisions. First, it created the post of a High Representative to preside over the EU's Common Foreign and Security Policy (CFSP). Second, it strengthened slightly the highly conditional language of the preceding Maastricht Summit by referring to "the *progressive* definition of a common defense policy."[58] (Italics added.) Maastricht had merely stated that the common foreign and security policy *could* lead eventually to a common defense. Third, the so-called "Petersberg tasks," which the WEU had assigned to itself in 1992,[59] were incorporated into the treaty, thus reinforcing the legitimacy of the EU's political-military role.[60] These Petersberg tasks were specified in the Amsterdam Treaty language as follows: "humanitarian and evacuation missions, missions for maintaining peace and missions using combat forces in crisis management, including missions for the establishment of peace."[61]

One major issue in the defense area was left unresolved at Amsterdam. This was the question of the WEU's relationship to the EU. The treaty merely stated that the WEU could be incorporated into the EU, should the European Council so decide. The vague conditionality of this language masked the fact that at Amsterdam, as Jolyon Howorth noted, "Tony Blair opposed his veto, in the name of the primacy of NATO, to [a] French-German plan for [an] EU-WEU merger."[62] How and why the British position changed in the course of the next year and a half is the subject of the next chapter.

NOTES

1. R. E. Utley, *The French Defence Debate: Consensus and Continuity in the Mitterrand Era* (London: Macmillan, 2000), p. 170.
2. See p. 13.
3. See p. 130.
4. NATO Press Communiqué M-NAC-1 (96) 63, p. 2.
5. Nicole Gnesotto, *La Puissance et l'Europe* (Paris: Presses de Sciences Po, 1998), p. 39.
6. ⟨http://www.nato.int/docu/pr/1996/p96–063e.htm⟩, p. 3.
7. Ibid.
8. Louis Gautier, *Mitterrand et son armée, 1990–1995* (Paris: Grasset, 1999), p. 436, n.93.
9. Gnesotto, *La Puissance et l'Europe*, p. 42.
10. See p. 67.
11. ⟨http://www.nato.int/docu/pr/1996/p96–063e.htm⟩, p. 4.
12. Ibid., p. 6.
13. Ibid., p. 5.
14. See p. 147.
15. Charles G. Cogan, *Force to Choose: France, the Atlantic Alliance and NATO—Then and Now* (Westport, Conn.: Praeger, 1997), p. 133.
16. *International Herald Tribune*, July 3, 1998, p. 8.
17. Interview with a senior French diplomtic official.
18. National Archives II (NA II), Records Group 218, 1948–1959 Geographic Files, Box 97, Section 44, JCS Document 81212 (in reference to a request by the French representative on the Standing Group for a modification of the Defense Plan with regard to the lines of communication linking France with North Africa).
19. Vincent Auriol, *Mon septennat 1947–1954* (Paris: Gallimard, 1970), p. 354. (Letter from Juin to President Auriol, July 10, 1951.) N.B. SHAPE stands for Supreme Headquarters Allied Powers Europe and was then located at Rocquencourt, outside Paris.
20. NA II, Walter Poole, *The History of the Joint Chiefs of Staff: The Joint Chiefs of Staff and National Policy*, vol. IV, 1950–1952, p. 226.
21. ⟨http://www.nato.int/docu/pr/1996/p96–063e.htm⟩, p. 3.
22. Utley, *The French Defence Debate*, p. 173. (Jacques Chirac to a reception in honor of reserve officers in Paris, February 8, 1993. Cited in R. P. Grant, "France's New Relationship with NATO," *Survival*, vol. 38, no. 1 (spring 1996): 63.)
23. Gautier, *Mitterrand et son armée*, p. 436, n.92.
24. See p. 89.
25. Interview with a State Department official.
26. ⟨http://www.nato.int/docu/pr/1997/p97–081e.htm⟩, p. 1.
27. Ibid., p. 7.

28. See p. 77.
29. James M. Goldgeier, *Not Whether But When: The United States Decision to Enlarge NATO* (Washington, D.C.: Brookings Institution, 1999), p. 78.
30. Ibid.
31. Ibid., p. 82.
32. Ibid., p. 83.
33. Ibid., p. 79.
34. Ibid., p. 137.
35. Ibid., p. 102.
36. Ibid.
37. Ibid., p. 105.
38. Ibid., p. 139.
39. Ibid., p. 141.
40. George Kennan, "A Fateful Error," *New York Times*, February 5, 1997, p. A23. (Cited in Goldgeier, *Not Whether But When*, p. 142.)
41. Goldgeier, *Not Whether But When*, p. 140.
42. Ibid., p. 142.
43. Ibid., p. 107.
44. Ibid., p. 152.
45. See pp. 6–7.
46. Goldgeier, *Not Whether But When*, p. 74.
47. Ibid.
48. Ibid., p. 129.
49. Ibid., p. 112.
50. Ibid., p. 113.
51. Gnesotto, *La Puissance et l'Europe*, p. 36.
52. ⟨http://www.nato.int/docu/pr/1997/p97–081e.htm⟩, p. 3.
53. Goldgeier, *Not Whether But When*, p. 120. N.B. Whether France's sponsorship of its East European "Latin" protégé, Romania, was in part a ploy to muddy up a measured NATO enlargement cannot be judged with certainty. However, it should be noted that, though the United States and Germany were the main sponsors of NATO enlargement, it was the former French president, the late François Mitterrand, who left office in 1995, who was the most persistent opponent of it.
54. Ibid., p. 121.
55. Gnesotto, *La Puissance et l'Europe*, p. 102.
56. *Le Monde*, November 29, 2000, p. 2.
57. ⟨http://www.ireland.com/special/treaty/treaty/chap17.htm⟩, p. 3. However, the treaty did provide for "constructive abstention" in the CFSP, whereby a member state may allow a decision to be adopted as a decision of the EU without being bound to apply it or pay for it. (Ibid.)
58. Gnesotto, *La Puissance et l'Europe*, p. 82.
59. See p. 64.
60. Gnesotto, *La Puissance et l'Europe*, p. 82.
61. *Bulletin d'Etudes de la Marine*, no. 16, November 1999, pp. 4–5.
62. Jolyon Howorth, "Défense européenne: entre atlantisme et européisme," in Thierry de Montbrial and Pierre Jacquet, eds., *Ramses 2001* (Paris: Dunod for the Institut Français des Relations Internationales, 2000), p. 244.

CHAPTER 5

The Turn Toward Autonomy: St. Malo to Kosovo to Cologne (July 1997–June 1999)

THE ST. MALO DECLARATION

By the time of the Madrid NATO Summit (July 1997), the United States had become fully preoccupied with the enlargement of NATO. In the period leading up to the summit, the United States had laid carefully in place a system for dealing with Russia's opposition to it. On May 27, 1997, the NATO-Russia Founding Act, setting the basis for their mutual relations and cooperation, was signed. At the Madrid Summit itself, Poland, the Czech Republic, and Hungary were invited to begin accession talks with NATO. The announced goal in the Madrid communiqué was that ratification would take place in time for membership to be effective by the time of the fiftieth anniversary of the Washington Treaty in April 1999.[1] This did not come as a surprise, as President Clinton had already mentioned the fiftieth anniversary as the goal for the entry of the first group of new NATO members in a speech at Detroit in October 1996.[2]

As noted in the previous chapter,[3] in the margins of the Madrid Summit, the rupture in the French rapprochement with NATO was consummated: the French announced that this process was now halted, as the progress in the reform of NATO had not gone far enough. It was clear that, in the period 1994–1996, one had missed the boat, both in terms of the reform of NATO and in terms of the development of a European Security and Defense Identity (ESDI) within the Alliance. In turn, this provoked a move toward autonomy in defense on the part of the more independent elements within the European Union. On both sides, as between the "Atlanticists" and the "Europeanists," or put more narrowly, as between the Americans and the French, there was a consensus at least on one point, although each side put its own interpretation on it. And that point is, had the conditions spelled out in the Berlin communiqué of 1996 been implemented, there would have been no need for a move toward autonomy in defense for the EU. There would have been no need for the process that was to lead, a year later, to the Anglo-French declaration at St. Malo in December 1998.

It was the Amsterdam Summit and Treaty (May 1997) that provided the basis for this turn toward autonomy. While it did not bring defense into the EU, it paved the way. As we have seen in the previous chapter, it introduced certain innovations into the EU treaty corpus. It endorsed crisis management ("Petersberg tasks") as an EU function, and it provided for a person to direct the EU's Common Foreign and Security Policy (CFSP). Although the new British prime minister, Tony Blair, turned down treaty language that would have merged the WEU with the EU, the Amsterdam Treaty held out this possibility for the future, should the European Council so decide.

Even though Amsterdam opened the way toward autonomy, without a meeting of the minds between Britain and France on European defense, no movement toward a tangible CFSP and a tangible ESDI was possible, as Jolyon Howorth has pointed out.[4] Britain had rejected persistently and for decades a defense role for the EU. Even though Tony Blair continued this refusal at Amsterdam, the brand new British prime minister, elected in May 1997 under the banner of "New Labor," was clearly more innovative and less anti-European than his Conservative predecessors. Slowly, the British position began to change. At no point, however, did the British project this change as a move away from NATO. In an interview published in the summer of 2000, George Robertson, who was defense minister in the Blair government and later became secretary-general of NATO, alluded to this change in policy: "As one of the principal architects of this [new] policy . . . I can tell you that it was a carefully thought out one. I [long] had pleaded the cause of a reinforcement of the European dimension within the [NATO] organization. This did not prevent me from being intimately persuaded of the importance of the transatlantic relationship, both for the Europeans and the Americans."[5]

According to a senior British defense official, Blair and his team were taken aback on coming into office as they discovered the lack of military self-sufficiency among Europe's major powers. As the Kosovo crisis developed in 1998, the continued reluctance of the Clinton administration to contemplate the use of American ground troops there prior to a settlement stood in contrast to the British (and to a lesser extent the French) willingness to entertain a ground intervention. Another factor that played in here, perhaps even crucially, was that Tony Blair, blocked by his own public opinion from joining the European Monetary Union, could demonstrate his European credentials by moving closer to the French position on European defense.

Thus the stage was set for a major sea change in British policy, which became evident in late 1998, first with the informal EU summit at Pörtschach, Austria (October 24–25), then in a speech by Prime Minister Blair in Edinburgh in November, and finally with the Anglo-French summit at St. Malo (December 3–4, 1998). As Peter Rodman observed, Blair "invoked Kosovo in his seminal

Edinburgh speech: Europe had been 'hesitant and disunited' over Kosovo, he complained; it was time for Europe to develop a capacity for autonomous action so that it would not always be so completely dependent on the United States."[6]

The Anglo-French declaration at St. Malo on December 4, 1998, made clear that Prime Minister Blair was ending Britain's long-standing proscription against the European Union becoming involved in defense matters. The declaration stated in part:

> The European Union needs to be in a position to play its full role on the international stage. This means making a reality of the Treaty of Amsterdam . . . [by a] full and rapid implementation [of] the Amsterdam provisions on the Common Foreign and Security Policy (CFSP). This includes the responsibility of the European Council to decide on the framing of a common defense policy of CFSP. . . . To this end, the Union must have the capacity for autonomous action, backed up by credible military forces [and] the means to decide to use them . . . in order to respond to international crises.[7]

Although the St. Malo declaration did not state so outright, it prefigured the absorption of the WEU into the EU, a possibility that had been evoked in the Amsterdam Treaty. The St. Malo declaration stated that the EU would take "account of the existing assets of the WEU and the evolution of its relations with the EU."[8] With the WEU out of the way, this would mean that the EU would become the European defense counterpart of NATO—thus adding coherence and balance to the Euro-American equation. The WEU had remained in an emasculated state vis-à-vis NATO since 1954, when the European Defense Community project died in the French parliament, and it was then agreed as an alternative that Germany would enter NATO (and also the WEU). This effectively left the WEU without a role, since NATO was the much stronger organization and the Germans were in it. Despite French efforts to revive the WEU starting in the 1980s, this situation persisted until the eventual absorption of the WEU by the EU in November 2000. Furthermore, the subordinate position of the WEU had been institutionalized from the very beginning: according to the Modified Brussels Treaty, which created the WEU in 1954, the latter was supposed to "rely on the appropriate Military Authorities of NATO for information and advice on military matters."[9]

Certain residues of the WEU remain, notably the Brussels Treaty itself, which in its Article V guarantees an automatic military response from the other members of the treaty if one of them is attacked. Also, two remnants of the WEU are expected to remain for the foreseeable future: the WEU Assembly and the Armaments Group associated with the WEU.[10]

The St. Malo Declaration also heralded a new "bicephalic" role for a European defense capability, one that could be inside or outside NATO: "the European Union will also need to have recourse to suitable military means (European capabilities pre-designated within NATO's European pillar or national or multinational means outside the NATO framework)."[11] Thus St. Malo, which was the first of several not wholly welcome surprises for the Americans, subtly shifted the emphasis on ESDI toward autonomy and away from integration in the Alliance.

The declaration that emerged from the St. Malo Summit marked a significant departure from previous British positions: not only did Britain endorse an autonomous role for Europe in defense matters (while remaining "in conformity with . . . [existing] obligations in NATO"), but it also, for the first time, agreed to a defense role for the European Union: "the Union must have the capacity for autonomous action, backed up by credible military forces."

The St. Malo accords, which had followed a precursor statement by Tony Blair at the Pörtschach meeting in October 1998,[12] constituted the first sign of concrete steps toward the abandonment of the WEU and its absorption into the EU. This change eventually was to provide a degree of coherence that heretofore had been lacking. Obviously, it would be easier to sort out transatlantic defense roles between two organizations (NATO and EU) rather than have a third, the WEU, in the middle as a "bridge" between the two, as it was often described. While the WEU's role was left ambiguous in the St. Malo declaration, it was clear that from then on the EU would be at the forefront of a European defense identity. It was entirely logical and coherent for the main European institution, the European Union, to take over the role of Europe's security and defense. In the words of Jacques Chirac, "Our goal must be to make the European Council [of the European Union] the supreme body of orientation and decision in this domain [of our European policy of joint defense], particularly vis-à-vis the WEU. It is thus, and only thus, that we can make a coherent and overall plan based on what we have accomplished so far in our different projects of bilateral cooperation."[13]

The St. Malo declaration was met with surprise and some chagrin in Washington. Immediately after the declaration, Secretary of State Madeleine Albright issued a cautionary statement:

What we do not want is that this European defense identity sap the vitality of NATO. We want to avoid decoupling [between Europe and America]. NATO should remain an organization of sovereign allies, in which the European decision process is not separated from the wider decision of the Alliance. Secondly, we also want to avoid duplication. Resources are too scarce for the allies to do force planning, operate command structures and buy equipment twice: firstly in NATO and secondly in the EU. Finally we should avoid any discrimination regarding a member of NATO who is not a member of the EU.[14]

Albright's speech was referred to as that of the "three D's": no decoupling, no duplication, and no discrimination, to which Lord George Robertson, the incoming secretary-general of NATO, subsequently offered a counter formula dubbed the "three I's: *Indivisibility* of the Alliance, *Improved* European capabilities, and *Inclusiveness* of all partners."[15]

St. Malo did not become a serious issue between London and Washington, in part because the latter was dependent on British support in actions against Saddam Hussein (Operation Desert Fox, the Anglo-American punitive air action in Iraq, was only days away), and the American administration had a high degree of confidence in Tony Blair.

Though Germany was not made a party to the St. Malo declaration before the fact, Bonn had the experience of years of strategic cooperation with Paris and the two countries' close relationship in defense matters had been reaffirmed in the Mitterrand-Kohl declaration of December 1, 1998. The Germans subsequently went along with the St. Malo declaration. Later, in a summit meeting at Cologne on June 3, 1999, the remainder of the countries of the EU, including the neutrals, gave their approval also.

THE KOSOVO CAMPAIGN

Though trouble in Kosovo long had been predicted, even before the end of the war in Bosnia, the Western powers were unable to develop a strategy to head it off. In a sense, revolt had been brewing ever since Slobodan Milosevic took away the autonomous status of the province in 1989. In February–March 1998, Serb special forces began conducting raids against villages thought to be supporting the newly formed Kosovo Liberation Army (KLA), resulting in some 2,000 killed and 250,000 Kosovar refugees fleeing into Albania.[16] In March, United Nations Security Council Resolution 1160 imposed an arms embargo that applied equally to Serbia and the KLA.

In the summer of 1998, Britain and France, whose long experience in having troops on the ground in the former Yugoslavia had drawn them into closer consultations, began pushing for stronger measures to be taken to halt the atrocities in Kosovo. On June 8, 1998, the United States and the European Union imposed economic sanctions on Serbia, and four days later the Defense Ministers of the EU threatened Serbia with reprisals if the repression continued in Kosovo.[17] United Nations Resolution 1199 of September 23 called for a cease-fire and the withdrawal of Serbian forces from Kosovo and declared that "additional measures" would be taken in the event of noncompliance, which was taken by the West (but not the Russians) as authorizing the use of force. There followed the mission of Richard Holbrooke to Milosevic, resulting in an agreement on October 14, 1998, on Kosovo, including a partial Serbian withdrawal, aerial surveillance, and the arrival of an observer group under the auspices of the Organization for Security and Cooperation in Europe (OSCE). Soon thereafter, Milosevic proceeded to violate the agreement repeatedly. This led to the positioning of a French-led NATO extraction force in Macedonia, in case the OSCE observers had to be withdrawn.

Throughout the period, the Clinton administration refused to countenance the sending of American ground troops to Kosovo. But following the massacre of forty-five civilians by Serb forces in the village of Racak on January 15, 1999,

Jacques Chirac and Tony Blair announced that they were prepared to send ground troops into Kosovo. Then, with Britain and France in the lead, a conference was organized at Rambouillet between the Serbs and the Kosovars. The conference, co-chaired by the U.K. and France, lasted from February 6–23 and ended in failure, with Milosevic rejecting a clause calling for a referendum in three years' time on the ultimate status of Kosovo. A second conference was convened in Paris on March 15 but ended without resolution three days later. Although the KLA, under American pressure, accepted the proposals, the Serbs rejected them and, in particular, the following military clause (appendix B, paragraph 8), added at Paris, which would have given NATO forces freedom of movement into Kosovo via Serbia: "NATO personnel shall enjoy, together with their vehicles, vessels, aircraft and equipment, free and unrestricted passage and unimpeded access throughout the FRY [Federal Republic of Yugoslavia] including associated airspace and territorial waters. This shall include, but not be limited to, the right of bivouac, maneuver, billet and utilization of any areas of facilities as required for support, training and operations."[18]

Whether, at the Rambouillet summit itself, Britain and France were overtaken by a harsher U.S. position vis-à-vis the Serbs is not clear. As Barry Posen has pointed out, with reference to the military clause cited above, "The clause is to say the least undiplomatic, and its introduction into the accords raises questions about either the wisdom or the motives of whoever introduced it."[19] What is clear is that the United States had a particular role in shepherding the Kosovar delegation at the talks and, specifically, in including Kosovo Liberation Army Chief Hashim Thaçi in the delegation. This surprised and disconcerted the French, who had been considering Ibrahim Rugova as the sole political interlocutor on the Kosovar side.[20]

As Pascal Boniface has pointed out, it was a mistaken assumption that the Kosovo intervention was engineered by the Americans, with the Europeans only playing the role of auxiliaries. The political role of the Europeans was stronger than it was in Bosnia, in part because Britain and France, in the fall of 1998, were coming together to develop concerted policies in defense, culminating in the St. Malo declaration of December 1998. Also, although Richard Holbrooke was brought into play episodically to try to convince Slobodan Milosevic to change his policy toward the Kosovars, he was not exercising continual political direction as he had done during the Bosnian war. Wrote Boniface: "After St. Malo, the Europeans were caught up in a dynamic whose consequences turned out to be quite positive. The escalation of events in Kosovo were a challenge to the British and French to act or else be accused of making symbolic démarches. The specter of European impotence in Bosnia reemerged. At that point France and Great Britain undertook an initiative which led to the Rambouillet summit."[21]

And having been a major actor in convening the summit, France had to ensure that it played a key role in whatever developments ensued. According to the French Defense Ministry, "France having played a galvanizing role in the most recent diplomatic phases ([conferences of] Rambouillet [and] Paris), it was a question of confirming that, in the operational phase, Paris continued to weigh in on the decisions [to be] taken and contribute concretely to their execution."[22]

With the Serb refusal of the Rambouillet terms, the NATO bombing campaign swiftly followed. It was initiated on March 24 and lasted seventy-eight days, during which the number of Kosovar Albanians fleeing from their homes climbed to some 800,000.[23] At the outset of the campaign, President Clinton announced that the use of American forces for an invasion of Kosovo was not contemplated.

In the air campaign, the Europeans brought to bear a political weight that was considerably in excess of their military contribution. This influence was exercised through the foreign ministers of the five most concerned powers—the United States, France, Great Britain, Germany, and Italy—usually through the medium of a daily telephone conference among them.[24] This was not wholly to the liking of the American military engaged in the conflict. One American general stated openly that, "a country that furnished eight per cent of the overall [air] effort over the Balkans should not be in a position to restrain American pilots who were carrying 70 per cent of the load."[25]

Russian and EU mediation, encouraged particularly by Germany, led finally to Milosevic's acceptance of terms on June 3. An occupation force for Kosovo (KFOR) was put in place, with Britain, France, the United States, Germany, and Italy as leading participants.[26] The return of the role of the UN in Kosovo was effected with the end of the air campaign, in part due to French pressure. UN Resolution 1244, which set the terms of the arrangements, did not call for a referendum on the status of Kosovo, as was stated in the Rambouillet proposals, but rather kept Kosovo within the Yugoslav Federation with, however, a large measure of autonomy to be accorded to the province.

This was the first war of NATO in its fifty years of existence, with the exception of some limited air operations conducted against Bosnian Serb forces in 1994 and 1995. Unlike the Bosnian operation, the intervention in Kosovo was conducted without a specific mandate from the United Nations. But according to NATO Secretary-General Lord Robertson:

Even in the case of Kosovo, I believe that we acted in conformity with the Charter of the United Nations. We applied the principle of the preeminence of international law in the face of a humanitarian catastrophe. If we did not obtain a green light from the Security Council before intervening in Kosovo, it was because we knew full well that Russia would oppose it [with the] veto. Remember, incidentally, that this same country had cosigned, in the fall of 1998, a resolution expressly calling for the reduction of the repressive Serbian apparatus in Kosovo, the halting of violence against civilians, and the application of a political strategy in favor of the autonomy of the province. And it was precisely in the name of these objectives that the Kosovo intervention was decided upon.[27]

In any event, the Kosovo campaign terminated with the reinsertion of the UN into the settlement, a development that had originated with a set of German proposals for settling the conflict. These proposals, aired on April 14, included "some kind of major UN role in the administration of Kosovo."[28]

The dominant impression left with the Europeans as a result of the air campaign in Kosovo was that of their appalling weakness compared to that of the Americans in the conduct of modern warfare. This set off a debate within the major countries of Western Europe over their continent's military inadequacy, a debate that has continued ever since. In the Kosovo operation, according to NATO's secretary-general, Lord George Robertson:

The Americans had to furnish 80 percent of the aircraft and 90 percent of the equipment and specialized munitions in the course of this operation. Even if the Europeans constituted the bulk of the troops that were mobilized, they were not more than 20 percent among the forces effectively engaged in the air attack operations. Isn't this a dramatic avowal of weakness? The Europeans imperatively have to give themselves the capability for conducting such operations by themselves when the [Atlantic] Alliance, as such, is not involved.[29]

BRITISH AND FRENCH "LESSONS LEARNED" FROM KOSOVO

Both the British and the French Ministries of Defense drew up "lessons learned"[30] documents in the aftermath of the Kosovo air campaign. The British document was entitled, "Kosovo—Lessons from the Crisis," and the French one, "The Lessons of Kosovo" ("Les enseignements du Kosovo"). The difference between them was characteristic. As Jolyon Howorth noted:

Whereas the British document concentrates on building up troop levels, the French document stresses, systematically, that in every area where Europe lags behind the U.S., a special effort needs to be made to close that gap.... London's preferred scenario would be one in which the EU acts as an "intelligent consumer of NATO's military services." ... Between the French maximalist quest for "autonomy" and the UK reliance on NATO for strategic assets, there is currently a gulf which words alone are unlikely to be able to continue to bridge.[31]

Part of the reason for the difference in approach between the British and the French was that the former had the benefit of more recent strategic guidance. This was the Strategic Defense Review (SDR), published in July 1998 as a government White Paper, and, as such, constituted a policy document. The SDR clearly set Britain on a course of expeditionary warfare with the goal of "projecting power in support of national foreign policy. That requirement implies an expeditionary capability that must not be at the mercy of host-nation support."[32] To accomplish this would require the construction of two new aircraft carriers (CVFs) with Short Takeoff and Vertical Landing (STOVL) aircraft—

projected to be the United States' Joint Strike Fighter (JSF)—plus supporting strategic air and sealift.[33] "The STOVL-equipped CVF would allow simultaneous aircraft landings and takeoffs—a fundamental advantage. These decisions lie at the heart of the expeditionary equipment developments proposed in the Strategic Defense Review."[34]

Expeditionary operations—the "core requirement" of the SDR—were to be carried out by "Joint Rapid Reaction Forces (JRRF) operating under the aegis of a coalition or treaty structure."[35] Such a requirement necessitated radical organizational and personnel changes: "The United Kingdom will now operate a pool of joint forces capable of mounting expeditionary operations in cooperation with the United States and other principal allies."[36] This transformation of the U.K. force structure and the full manning to accompany it had not been accomplished by the time of the Kosovo air campaign: "Consequently, operations in Kosovo . . . led to overstretch which would not have occurred had the SDR been fully implemented. This is regrettable and placed additional strain on our forces."[37]

The Kosovo air campaign, according to the British "lessons learned" report, vindicated the planning assumptions of the SDR: "Our programme to adjust the structure, equipment and capabilities of the forces has been validated. The importance of taking forward the [Strategic Defense] Review cannot be overstated. It is essential to building armed forces that are capable of serving the U.K.'s interests for the next fifteen to twenty years."[38]

The British report acknowledged the "reliance of European Allies on the ability of the United States to provide military capability quickly and effectively in large-scale operations such as the Kosovo conflict."[39] Areas in which the Europeans were obviously deficient were the following:

- Precision all-weather strike;
- Strategic lift;
- Intelligence, surveillance, and reconaissance;
- Suppression of enemy air defense/electronic warfare;
- Air to air refueling.[40]

Nevertheless, the British report added, European air forces played a significant part in the air campaign: They "were able in particular to provide a number of the scarce force multipliers such as Air to Air Refueling aircraft and intelligence gathering assets—both areas where the U.K. was able to play a major role."[41] The report's statement that "we look to a joint all-weather precision attack capability"[42] clearly refers to the anticipated acquisition of the Joint Strike Fighter.[43]

The British report had nothing but praise for the role of NATO in the Kosovo crisis and its importance for the future:

NATO played a fundamental role in underpinning the diplomatic attempts to find a resolution in the period leading up to the air campaign, in leading the air campaign and other military operations in support, including a major humanitarian effort, and in leading KFOR since the end of the conflict. NATO will remain the organization of choice for operations of a similar scale and complexity in the future, and certainly for operations where the Europeans and the U.S. wish to act together. NATO remains the cornerstone of our security and defense policy.[44]

Other than the assertions that "NATO proved itself to be a capable and effective crisis management organization" and that the U.K. crisis management structures worked well, the lead finding of the British report on Kosovo stressed that "NATO Allies and EU partners must work together to improve their capabilities."[45] In a likely reference to the U.S. reluctance to get involved in a ground war—a possibility that President Clinton did not suggest as an option until May 23, two months into the air campaign—the British report stated that "To maintain our flexibility of action and the highest possible level of uncertainty in the minds of our adversaries, we should plan for as many military options as necessary."[46]

The value of the Alliance's solidarity was stressed in the British report as a "crucial consideration in planning and executing the NATO campaign."[47] Special mention was made of the fact that "interoperability with French maritime units was successfully achieved, with Royal Navy ships operating under French command for the first time."[48]

The French "Lessons of Kosovo" was quite different from the British one, as Jolyon Howorth has pointed out.[49] In part this was because, as noted above, the French did not have a recent strategic charter, as did the British in their "Strategic Defense Review" of July 1998. The French overall strategic guidance was contained in the "White Paper" ("Livre Blanc") of 1994, the first such document since 1972. It was a document of compromises that in part reflected the existence of a "cohabitation" government at the time, the president being a Socialist (François Mitterrand) and the prime minister being a Gaullist (Edouard Balladur). As Rachel Utley observed:

While the government of the day had an ideal opportunity to give France a defense mechanism for the twenty-first century through [the Livre Blanc of 1994], the first such document for over twenty years, that opportunity was largely missed. Although it attempted to set priorities for France's future defense missions, it failed to make the decisive choices necessary to implement those missions. The nuclear force retained the same deterrence doctrine it had gained in the 1960s; conscription remained; and the strains on equipment were aggravated by the extension of the armed forces' roles.[50]

Utley's contention is that France, "contrary to other states, who seized the opportunity for a fundamental reassessment of their defense and security provisions," was unable to do so, in part due to constraints on resources:[51] "France's inadequate force projection capabilities, condemned at the beginning of the

1980s, remained in the 1990s. Such factors did not augur well for France's future capacity to participate in international military actions relying increasingly on airpower, or in distant missions requiring a troop presence on the ground."[52]

Though the Livre Blanc signalled a transition from a defense of France's borders to a wider concept of defense focused on international stability and cooperative military efforts with allies,[53] it maintained the primacy of France's nuclear deterrent and did not constitute an enabling document for a new era of "high-end" expeditionary warfare. Nevertheless, the subsequent military program law of 1997–2000, while at a lower level of strategic conception than that of the Livre Blanc, did signal a transition toward expeditionary warfare. The French "Lessons of Kosovo" noted with satisfaction how the 1997–2002 program law had set France on a new route in terms of "professionalization of our forces; the effort devoted to intelligence; [and] the emphasis placed on capabilities and means of projection, particularly in terms of command."[54]

Yet only in one major respect did French military procurement get out ahead of the British in the 1990s. It projected a new, nuclear-powered aircraft carrier, the *Charles-de-Gaulle*, to be ready at the end of the century. The two British carriers cited above will not be ready until the 2010–2015 time frame. Until that time, Britain will be without an aircraft carrier. However, though the *Charles-de-Gaulle* made its first test cruise in January 1999, it is still not operational as of early 2001, because of a serious problem of a broken propellor. Having sold its earlier generation aircraft carrier, the *Foch*, to Brazil and having authorized the latter to use spare parts from its other one, the *Clemenceau*, France, too, found itself without an aircraft carrier.[55] Nevertheless, in its military program law for 2003–2008, France's procurement goals included the construction of a second nuclear aircraft carrier and the acquisition of the Airbus military transport plane (A400 M).[56]

As Jolyon Howorth has noted, the French "Lessons of Kosovo" was intent on bridging the capabilities gap that separates it from the United States.[57] This gap, according to the French Defense Ministry study, was notable in the following areas: acquisition, integration, and exploitation of intelligence on a real-time basis; tactical air transport; aircraft identification; satellite guidance systems; precision weapons; penetration of enemy air defenses; and bomb damage evaluation.[58]

In his introduction to the French "Lessons of Kosovo," Defense Minister Alain Richard set the tone: "The crisis of Kosovo was a determining factor in heightening Europe's awareness. The lessons drawn from it will be incorporated in the dossier of European defense which will be one of the primary axes of the French Presidency of the European Union in the second half of 2000."[59]

The "Lessons of Kosovo" spelled out the contribution of the French forces to the Kosovo air campaign as follows:

- In the air campaign, France deployed 100 aircraft (ten of which were refueling planes), which was about 10 percent of the coalition's contribution. The French contribution amounted to 20 percent of the offensive missions, 21 percent of the reconnaissance missions, and 12 percent of the transport and support missions.

- On the ground, France participated in all the operations in the area: the extraction force (KVM) placed in Macedonia; operation Allied Shelter for aiding the Kosovar refugees coming into Albania; and the Kosovo Force (KFOR) in Kosovo itself and in Macedonia. At the height of the Kosovo operation France had 7,000 troops in the area plus another 3,000 in Bosnia.

- France's naval contribution included the aircraft carrier group Foch, from which air operations were conducted, plus a nuclear attack submarine and antiaircraft frigates. Of the Europeans, only Britain had as complete a naval presence. France was unique among the Europeans in its intelligence and reconnaissance contribution: the Helios observation satellite, Mirage aircraft, heliborne ["Horizon"] radar, drones, and electronic intercept assets.[60]

Although French contributions in the intelligence and reconnaissance areas were modest compared to those of the Americans, they were arguably out in front of the other Europeans:

In the area of intelligence, the permanent nature and the complementarity of American capabilities were such that our own national means were quite relative. However, France was able to put together a panoply that no other European country possesses: its satellite means (piloted and nonpiloted) or its heliborne observation capability furnished quality results in spite of the limitations due to unfavorable climatic conditions. Beyond this, in the area of strategic intelligence, the Mirage IV P, by its flexibility of use and other aerial vectors, permitted the gathering of precious information. In terms of intercept and observation, the technical means served to verify information furnished by other sources.[61]

Still, the report acknowledged that France was far from achieving autonomy of action in the intelligence area: "A permanent, all-weather capability, together with an ensemble of varied, complementary and even redundant means, as well as assets for rapid dissemination, appear as the conditions necessary for national autonomy in terms of an appreciation of the situation."[62]

In terms of engagement on the ground, parallel difficulties were noted in the Defense Ministry's report on Kosovo: "Our insufficiency in terms of real-time capabilities at times limited our ability to react.... A capability for real-time linkage, and in particular the transmission of optical or radar imagery should be studied for all weapons systems. Already, there was progress accomplished in the utilization of Helios [satellite] images by the units."[63]

Overall, the French contribution could have been more important, the report stated, "if we had been present in the areas where the American technological superiority was notable: long-distance and all-weather weapons (cruise missiles, [smart] bombs using the Global Positioning System (GPS), [high] performance radar), exploitation of information and imagery in real time, offensive jamming, all-weather observation capability, and medium altitude drones."[64]

Noting that efforts were underway to close this technological gap, the report acknowledged that there were certain technologies that the Americans possessed (for example, stealth technology), which the French had not mastered. Furthermore, the satellite global navigation system (GPS) was controlled by the United States.[65]

In addition to the Defense Ministry's appreciation of the gaps in French military capabilities, "The Lessons of Kosovo" was tart in its criticism of the way NATO functions and in the way the campaign was conducted. At the level of command and control, certain deficiencies in the NATO system were emphasized: "in spite of the imperative of unity of command, which is recognized by all, we are forced to conclude that part of the military operations were conducted by the United States outside the strict framework of NATO and its procedures. The commander in chief of the operation—the SACEUR—is responsible not only before the Atlantic Council but also before his [own] national hierarchy at the highest level."[66] The criticism referred to the fact that the United States used its national means (B-1 bombers, ship-launched cruise missiles, etc.) autonomously, without consultations within NATO.[67]

The Kosovo report, without being specific, called for improvement in NATO's "silence procedure," a method whereby if a member country does not object to a proposal, it is considered agreed to by that country after a certain length of time has passed. This helps to streamline NATO decision-making. However, the French report called for an amelioration in the system in such a way that the hierarchy of the system, on the one hand, and the demand for a quick response, on the other, could be better reconciled.[68]

On the higher political level, the Defense Ministry's report asserted that the Kosovo air campaign had shown that, "The evolution of the Atlantic Alliance has not been completed. On this issue, the lessons of the conflict should be drawn. The adaptation of the Alliance should continue and should result in an organization and a redistribution of responsibilities such as to maintain the transatlantic contact while at the same time taking into account the rise in power of the European actor."[69]

For the French Defense Ministry, the way ahead was clear. Europe must achieve a certain military autonomy:

the crisis in Kosovo reinforces our determination to give to the European Union the capability for deciding, conceiving and conducting a major military operation in the framework of the missions included in the Amsterdam Treaty. . . . Europe must provide itself progressively with autonomous strategic capabilities, particularly in the field of intelligence, [air] transport and command [systems]. . . . The transformation of the Euro-Corps into a projectable rapid reaction force will allow, if need be, for its headquarters to command a multinational force of the KFOR type.[70]

But in addition to the perception of European military weakness, there was a political dimension to the turn toward autonomy: in the tergiversations of American policy and in the fractionated system of decision-making in the United States. As André Dumoulin put it, "In any case, Europe cannot identify with American world interests which are engaged on a case-by-case basis, in a reactive and unpredictable manner, and according to the fluctuations of the Congress and the voters of the Middle West. Were not the interventions in Bosnia and Kosovo [approved] by a very small majority? Is not Europe at the mercy of internal American divergences?"[71]

There was also another factor in this "turn toward autonomy": the problems that NATO enlargement had caused in the West's relations with Russia, compounded by the new tensions that arose in NATO-Russian relations as a result of the Kosovo war, conducted without a clear UN Security Council mandate. There arose a new impulse among European thinkers to end the divisions in Europe and, in particular, to look anew toward EU enlargement as a more benign way of uniting Western and Eastern Europe, and as an insurance policy against further unrest developing in the Eastern European region.[72]

THE NATO SUMMIT IN WASHINGTON, APRIL 1999

The NATO Summit in Washington in April 1999 was to have been a grand celebration of NATO's fifty years years of existence and the occasion for welcoming the three new members of the Alliance. Instead, it came at an embarrassing moment. NATO's air campaign, a month old, showed no signs of forcing Slobodan Milosevic to give in. There were no indications of preparations for a ground offensive, President Clinton having ruled out that option as far as the United States was concerned from the opening of the air campaign on March 24.

The Washington Summit communiqué and a new Strategic Concept, both issued on April 24, 1999, straddled the issue of where a European defense would be situated. On the one hand, the communiqué stated, "We acknowledge the resolve of the European Union to have the capacity for autonomous action so that it can take decisions and approve military action where the Alliance as a whole is not engaged."[73]

On the other hand, the new Strategic Concept affirmed that, "On the basis of decisions taken by the Alliance in Berlin in 1996 and subsequently, the European Security and Defense Identity will continue to be developed within NATO."[74] But the Washington Summit, "building on the Berlin decisions," offered new arrangements to facilitate European Union access to NATO military assets for operations in which the Alliance as a whole was not engaged. These became known as the "Berlin plus" provisions and were described as follows in the summit communiqué:

- Assured EU access to NATO planning capabilities able to contribute to military planning for EU-led operations;

- The presumption of availability to the EU of preidentified NATO capabilities and common assets for use in EU-led operations;
- Identification of a range of European command options for EU-led operations, further developing the role of DSACEUR [Deputy SACEUR] in order for him to assume fully and effectively his European responsibilities;
- The further adaptation of NATO's defense planning system to incorporate more comprehensively the availability of forces for EU-led operations.[75]

Despite these apparent concessions on the part of NATO, the EU went forward with its drive towards autonomy. It began referring to ESDI as ESDP—the "P" standing for policy. According to one NATO official, this is essentially a French invention, to give a sense of autonomy (since ESDI has always been referred to as "within the Alliance") and also to make the term more congruent with the Common Foreign and Security Policy (CFSP) of the EU.[76]

In three other major respects, the Washington NATO Summit took decisions that had significant implications for the future. Most importantly, it pledged to accept new members, thereby laying its credibility on the line: "We pledge that NATO will continue to welcome new members in a position to further the principles of the Treaty.... The ongoing enlargement process strengthens the Alliance and enhances the security of the Euro-Atlantic region. The three new members will not be the last."[77]

The summit communiqué mentioned in particular the progress made by the two disappointed candidate countries who were not admitted into the first group at the previous Madrid Summit: Romania, sponsored by France, and Slovenia, sponsored by Italy. But the communiqué also implied that the following countries might one day be able to join: the three Baltic countries, Bulgaria, Slovakia, Macedonia, and Albania.

The Washington NATO Summit also gave a legal covering for NATO to enter the crisis management area and, thus, go beyond its traditional role of collective defense: "To stand ready, case-by-case and by consensus, in conformity with Article 7 of the Washington Treaty, to contribute to effective conflict prevention and to engage actively in crisis management, including crisis response operations."[78]

However, Article 7 of the Washington Treaty contains only a vague reference to "the maintenance of international peace and security": "This treaty does not affect, and shall not be interpreted as affecting, in any way the rights and obligations under the Charter of the parties which are members of the United Nations, or the primary responsibility of the Security Council for the maintenance of international peace and security."[79]

Finally, the Washington Summit launched a Defense Capabilities Initiative, aimed at ensuring the effectiveness of operations across the full range of Alliance missions, with special attention toward improving interoperability among Alliance forces and, where applicable, between Alliance and Partner forces.[80]

THE SUMMIT OF ALL THE DANGERS: COLOGNE (JUNE 1999)

The next step toward autonomy in European defense took place at the EU Summit in Cologne in early June 1999, just as the Kosovo campaign was coming to an end, and Slobodan Milosevic finally was giving in to Western and Russian pressure. The winding down of the war did nothing to lessen the EU's impulsion toward autonomy. The nearly unsuccessful air campaign and the continuing European perception of American reluctance to take casualties caused a further alienation of Europe from its American partner, compounded by the pervasive sense of European military inferiority that the air war had engendered. The air war, while wreaking widespread damage, had made hardly a dent on the Serbian military in Kosovo, which had basically survived intact.[81] According to an article in *Newsweek*, published in May 2000, NATO reportedly destroyed fourteen Serbian tanks during the campaign and not 120, as earlier claimed.[82]

In its communiqué issued at Cologne on June 4, the EU stated that

> The European Council should be in a position to take decisions dealing with the range of activities aimed at conflict prevention and missions of crisis management, defined in the European Union Treaty as "Petersberg missions." To this end, the Union must have a capacity for autonomous action supported by credible military forces, have the means for deciding to have recourse to them and be ready to do so in order to react to international crises, without prejudice to actions taken by NATO.[83]

The communiqué also called for a structure and a capability to give body to the concept of an autonomous European defense. In what was particularly disturbing to some American officials, it seemed to contradict the decisions of the recently concluded Washington NATO Summit in April, which, as noted previously,[84] had found a justification in the Washington Treaty for NATO to become involved in crisis management. To some in Washington, Cologne appeared to represent an attempt to "fence in" NATO as an "Article 5" organization, leaving crisis management as the purview of the EU.[85] Indeed, there is no specific mention of NATO as carrying out "Petersberg tasks," which, as the report of the German presidency to the Cologne Summit notes, were incorporated into the mission of the EU by the Amsterdam Treaty, which had gone into effect on May 1, 1999. There is only mention of the EU either using NATO assets to carry out Petersberg tasks, or else carrying them out on its own, using "national" or "multinational" assets of the EU countries themselves.[86] There is no mention in the German presidency report to the Cologne Summit or in the summit declaration itself of a "Petersberg-type" mission being carried out under the aegis of NATO.

Although the declaration, on the one hand, stated that the foundation of "the [Atlantic] Alliance remains the collective defense of its members," collective defense is not crisis management, which the EU took upon itself to do "without prejudice to actions taken by NATO." This left the impression that the EU was intent on creating a separate and independent defense organization. Furthermore, the Cologne Summit implicated the EU as a whole; the St. Malo declaration was only an Anglo-French position. Thus the Cologne Summit was considerably more of an unwelcome surprise in Washington than was St. Malo. The fact that the Cologne documentation was put together by the German rotating presidency on behalf of the EU was a fresh indication that the new "Berlin Republic" was staking out a position that was less linked to Washington than was the previous Christian Democratic Government of Helmut Kohl.

NOTES

1. ⟨http://www.nato.int/docu/pr/1997/p97–081e.htm⟩, p. 3.
2. James M. Goldgeier, *Not Whether But When: The U.S. Decision to Enlarge NATO* (Washington, D.C.: Brookings Institution, 1999), p. 106.
3. See p. 90.
4. Jolyon Howorth, "Britain, France and the European Defence Initiative," *Survival*, vol. 42, no. 2 (summer 2000): 33–34.
5. George Robertson, "OTAN: les leçons du Kosovo," interview with Brigitte Adès, *Politique Internationale* (summer 2000): 212.
6. Peter Rodman, *Drifting Apart? Trends in U.S.–European Relations* (Washington, D.C.: Nixon Center, June 1999), p. 19.
7. ⟨http://britain-info.org/bistext/fordom/defence/4dc98–2.stm⟩, p. 1.
8. Ibid.
9. United Nations Treaty Series, vol. 211, 1955, p. 346. See also p. 9.
10. Pascal Boniface, ed., *L'Année stratégique 2001* (Paris: Éditions Michalon, 2000), p. 54.
11. ⟨http://britain-info.org/bistext/fordom/defence/4dc98–2.stm⟩, p. 1.
12. See p. 98.
13. President Chirac's speech to the Institute of Higher Studies of National Defense (IHEDN), June 8, 1996, p. 9. N.D.L.R. The different projects referred to include the Euro-Corps, the air operations cooperation between France and Great Britain, and the maritime operations cooperation among France, Italy, and Spain.
14. *Le Monde*, December 9, 1998 (cited in *L'Année Stratégique 2001*, p. 26).
15. "NATO in the New Millennium," *NATO Review*, no. 4, (1999): 6.
16. Thierry de Montbrial and Pierre Jacquet, eds., *Ramses 2001* (Paris: Dunod for the Institut Français des Relations Internationales, 2000), p. 168.
17. Ibid.
18. ⟨http://www.state.gov/www/regions/eur/ksvo_rambouillet_text.html⟩. (Cited in Barry R. Posen, "The War for Kosovo: Serbia's Political-Military Strategy," *International Security*, vol. 24, no. 4 [spring 2000]: 44.)
19. Posen, "The War for Kosovo," p. 44.
20. Interview with a French diplomatic official.
21. *L'Année Stratégique 2001*, p. 23.
22. ⟨http://www.defense.gouv.fr/actualites/dossier/d36/information2.htm.⟩
23. *Ramses 2001*, p. 168.

24. *L'Année Stratégique 2001*, p. 24.

25. André Dumoulin, "Les ambitions de l'Europe: de l'après-Kosovo aux indicateurs de cohérence," *Politique Étrangère*, vol. 2 (summer 2000): 489–90. N.B. Although the individual in question was not cited, the reference is to Air Force General Michael C. Short, NATO's Joint Air Force Component Commander, who testified before the U.S. Congress in the aftermath of the war. The unnamed country was France.

26. As of January 2001, KFOR consisted of 38,000 troops, of whom only 5,200 were Americans. (*New York Times*, January 25, 2001, p. A6.)

27. Robertson, "OTAN: les leçons du Kosovo," p. 217.

28. Posen, "The War for Kosovo," p. 67.

29. Ibid., p. 210.

30. The German reaction to the Kosovo campaign is reflected in two reports, one by the blue-ribbon Weizsacker Commission and the other by Defense Minister Rudolph Scharping, issued respectively in May and June 2000. Though differing in some respects, notably the size of the Bundeswehr, the proportion of draftees, and the size of budget reductions, both agreed that the Bundeswehr was out of step with national interests and should convert itself to more of a crisis management than a territorial defense force. (Remarks of Professor Helga Haftendorn, a member of the Weizsacker Commission, to a Harvard University conference at Talloires, France, June 17, 2000.) As for Italy, which participated in most UN interventions in the 1990s, and whose contribution was vital in the Kosovo campaign through the use of its airbase facilities, the coordination with the Italian military was excellent. The problem with Italy during this period was the nervousness of the Italian public due to the protracted air campaign so close to its shores.

31. Howorth, "Britain, France and the European Defence Initiative," pp. 38–39.

32. T. D. Kilvert-Jones, "One Year Later: The U.K. Strategic Defense Review," ⟨http://www.navyleague.org/seapower/one_year_later.htm⟩, p. 3.

33. On January 17, 2001, British Defense Minister Geoff Hoon announced that a Memorandum of Understanding had been signed in Washington for the next stage of the development of the JSF in a co-production arrangement. The STOVL variant of the JSF is to replace the British Harrier aircraft of the Royal Navy. The regular JSF will replace the Tornado of the Royal Air Force.

34. Kilvert-Jones, "One Year Later," p. 3.

35. Ibid.

36. Ibid.

37. "Kosovo—Lessons from the Crisis," June 6, 2000, ⟨http://www.mod.uk/news/kosovo/lessons/chapter6.htm⟩, p. 4.

38. Ibid.

39. ⟨http://www.kosovo.mod.uk/lessons/chapter5.htm⟩, p. 3.

40. Ibid., pp. 3–4.

41. Ibid., p. 4.

42. ⟨http://www.mod.uk/news/kosovo/lessons/chapter6.htm⟩, p. 10.

43. See above this page.

44. ⟨http://www.kosovo.mod.uk/lessons/chapter5.htm⟩, p. 2.

45. ⟨http://www.mod.uk/news/kosovo/lessons/chapter1.htm⟩, p. 1.

46. Ibid.

47. ⟨http://www.kosovo.mod.uk/lessons/chapter5.htm⟩, p. 1.

48. ⟨http://www.kosovo.mod.uk/lessons/chapter1.htm⟩, p. 2.

49. See p. 104.

50. R. E. Utley, *The French Defence Debate: Consensus and Continuity in the Mitterrand Era* (London: Macmillan, 2000), p. 208.
51. Ibid., pp. 157–58.
52. Ibid., p. 207.
53. Ibid., p. 156.
54. ⟨http://www.defense.gouv.fr/actualites/dossier/d36/intro.htm⟩, p. 2.
55. *Le Monde*, November 23, 2000, p. 7.
56. *Le Monde*, December 23, 2000, p. 8.
57. See p. 104.
58. ⟨http://www.defense.gouv.fr/actualites/dossier/d36/intro.htm⟩, p. 3.
59. ⟨http://www.defense.gouv.fr/actualites/dossier/d36/avantpropos.htm⟩, p. 1.
60. ⟨http://www.defense.gouv.fr/actualites/dossier/d36/intro.htm⟩, p. 2.
61. ⟨http://www.defense.gouv.fr/actualites/dossier/d36/capacites2.htm⟩, p. 2.
62. Ibid.
63. ⟨http://www.defense.gouv.fr/actualites/dossier/d36/capacites6.htm⟩, p. 1.
64. ⟨http://www.defense.gouv.fr/actualites/dossier/d36/technologie1.htm⟩, p. 2.
65. Ibid.
66. ⟨http://www.defense.gouv.fr/actualites/dossier/d36/intro.htm⟩, p. 3.
67. *L'Année Stratégique*, p. 120.
68. ⟨http://www.defense.gouv.fr/actualites/dossier/d36/juridique2.htm⟩, p. 1.
69. ⟨http://www.defense.gouv.fr/actualites/dossier/d36/intro.htm⟩, p. 3.
70. Ibid., p. 4.
71. Dumoulin, "Les ambitions de l'Europe: de l'après-Kosovo aux indicateurs de cohérence," p. 488.
72. See p. 10 for a declaration to this effect by a group of European intellectuals in August 1999.
73. ⟨http://www.nato.int/docu/pr/1999/p99-064e.htm⟩, p. 6.
74. ⟨http://www.fas.org/man/nato/natodocs/99042411.htm⟩, p. 7.
75. ⟨http://www.nato.int/docu/pr/1999/p99-064e.htm⟩, p. 7.
76. Interview with a NATO headquarters official.
77. ⟨http://www.nato.int/docu/pr/1999/p99-064e.htm⟩, p. 4.
78. Ibid., p. 3.
79. Henry W. Degenhardt, ed., *Treaties and Alliances of the World, 9, North Atlantic Treaty Organization (NATO)* (Detroit: Gale Research, 1986), p. 204.
80. ⟨http://www.nato.int/docu/pr/1999/p99-064e.htm⟩, p. 7.
81. Talk by Professor Barry Posen at Harvard University, March 6, 2000.
82. Referred to in *L'Année stratégique*, p. 28.
83. *Bulletin d'Etudes de la Marine*, no. 16, November 1999, p. 3.
84. See p. 111.
85. Interview with a State Department official.
86. *Bulletin d'Etudes de la Marine*, no. 16, p. 5.

CHAPTER 6

The European Union Becomes a Defense Organization (July 1999– December 2000)

THE RECTIFICATION AT HELSINKI (DECEMBER 1999)

American policymakers were concerned that a clear conflict might emerge as a result of the Cologne EU Summit in June 1999, but the subsequent Helsinki EU Summit at the end of the year seemed, in one State Department official's words, to "bring the process back together."[1] There had been considerable disquiet in the period between the two summits (of June and December 1999). After Helsinki, a high-ranking official of the Defense Department observed to a European visitor, "We were concerned. We beat up on you. You shifted your ground."

The "beating up on you" refers in part to two resolutions passed by the House of Representatives and the Senate in November 1999 expressing concern that the Europeans were going off on their own in matters of defense, as evidenced particularly by the Cologne Summit. As for the "shifting of the ground," this was evident from the results of the Helsinki Summit:

- First, the centrality of NATO was recognized;
- Second, crisis response was not excluded from the NATO purview ("NATO remains the foundation of the collective defense of its members and will continue to play an important role in crisis management"[2]); and
- Third, the EU's action role was limited to those situations in which NATO would not be involved ("The European Council emphasizes its determination to develop an autonomous capability to decide, in cases where NATO is not involved per se, and then launch and conduct military operations under the direction of the EU in response to international crises"[3]).

The key phrase in question was "where NATO is not engaged," and this was more or less in conformity with the New Strategic Concept language enunciated at the Washington NATO Summit of April 1999 ("in which the Alliance is not engaged militarily"[4]), in contrast to the EU's Cologne Summit language ("the Union must have a capacity for autonomous action supported by credible military forces, have the means for deciding to have recourse to them and be ready to do it so in order to react to international crises, without prejudice to actions taken by NATO"[5]). The Cologne language had seemed to indicate that NATO and the EU would act independently of each other.

Significantly, the State Department official referred to above noted that, at the diplomatic level, the British negotiators were not of much help in arriving at this compromise language, in contrast to those of the host country, Finland, and to a lesser extent those of the Netherlands. According to another American official knowledgeable of the negotiations,[6] it took a U.S. intervention at the highest level, to Tony Blair, to persuade Jacques Chirac, at the Anglo-French summit that preceded the Helsinki meeting, to accept the compromise language. A key element here is that, as Jolyon Howorth has pointed out, Tony Blair supported the idea of deferring first to NATO. Blair's position was given emphasis by the new British minister of defense, Geoffrey Hoon, in a statement on December 20, 1999, in the aftermath of the Helsinki summit:

> I have to say I have sometimes been disappointed at the rather curious misrepresentation of what we are trying to do. . . . The whole process which the Prime Minister set in hand last year . . . will strengthen both Europe and NATO. . . . NATO is and will remain the cornerstone of our security. We will always look to NATO for our territorial defence and in most circumstances the Alliance will be our choice for most other crisis management operations. But equally, Europe must make a stronger and more coherent contribution to NATO and must be able to act effectively where the Alliance as a whole is not engaged. Our work in the Balkans has shown how important this is. This does not mean creating a European Army. Helsinki is explicit on this point.[7]

While the phrase, "where the Alliance as a whole is not engaged," does not explicitly give NATO a "right of first refusal," it comes close to suggesting it, and this is something that the French keenly wanted to avoid. They preferred that the choice of whether an operation is conducted with NATO or autonomously be made independently.[8] For the French, giving NATO a "right of first refusal" was tantamount to putting the EU in a subordinate position.[9] What is clear is that, behind these nuances of language, as between the British and the French, is not a matter merely of emphasis but of real strategic substance, as Howorth also has pointed out.[10]

THE "HEADLINE GOAL" AND THE INTERIM COMMITTEES

The Helsinki EU Summit provided for a number of concrete measures as a follow-up to the principle of an autonomous European defense decreed at the previous summit at Cologne in June 1999. First, the EU would create by 2003 a multinational mobilizable force of the equivalent of an Army corps (fifteen brigades) totaling 50,000–60,000 troops. This so-called "Headline Goal" would constitute a "capability" or a mobilizable structure rather than a permanent formation. It would be, in effect, a rapid reaction force capability with an air and naval component, capable of being deployed within the space of two months and self-sufficient to the extent that it could remain deployed for one year.[11] Subsequent projections indicate that the force would be based on a reservoir of more than 100,000 personnel and that the air and naval component would consist of approximately 400 planes and 100 ships.[12]

In addition, the Helsinki Summit decided that, as part of the Common Foreign and Security Policy (CFSP), three committees would be set up to direct the gamut of crisis management or "Petersberg missions." For the time being these would be designated as interim bodies (these bodies had been prefigured in the report of the German presidency to the previous EU Summit at Cologne):

- An Interim Political and Security Committee (IPSC, or COPSi in French) that would be based in Brussels at the ambassadorial level and would provide the political and strategic direction that would lead to effective and rapid EU decisions.
- An Interim Military Committee composed of the Chiefs of Defense Staffs of the member countries or their designees. This committee would provide recommendations to the IPSC.
- A military staff to provide military expertise to support the Common Foreign and Security Policy, including in the conduct of EU-led military operations.[13]

THE "THIRD OPTION"

In operational terms, the "turn toward autonomy," which began formally at St. Malo, came to encompass, at least in the French view, three options for action instead of two. The original idea in the Alliance was that either NATO would act or the Europeans would act where NATO declined to become involved. In the latter case, NATO assets would be loaned out for use under the direction of the WEU/EU (but, it was understood in Washington, subject to monitoring and recall if a higher priority arose in NATO). The officer in charge of this action would be Deputy SACEUR, who is a European (but, it was understood in Washington, the deputy would retain his responsibilities to the SACEUR).[14] This was essentially the U.S. view of the meaning of a European Security and Defense Identity within the Alliance.

Now there is a third option, as viewed and promulgated principally by Paris: a purely European action, using European assets only, and with a separate and completely European chain of command. The three options were spelled out by French Defense Minister Alain Richard in a speech at Georgetown University on February 23, 2000:

The first option is that the 19 members of the Alliance conduct a military operation and launch it using the full potential of the NATO machinery and of its members.

In the second option, the EU would take overall responsibility for a crisis management operation.... It would make use ... of the chain of command under [the] Deputy SACEUR for the command of the operation, and of the operational headquarters and troops earmarked [by] NATO for its implementation.

The third option [would] rely on strictly European capabilities to run an operation [should the NATO Allies decide not to commit themselves]. In the short term this option will ... be available only for more limited military operations. We believe this is a workable option [and] an indispensable one if we want all our nations to have a real choice when they decide in the future.[15]

The so-called third option, though largely theoretical, was an important point of principle to the French. (However, the British and the Germans did not buy explicitly this French proposal.) Foreign Minister Hubert Védrine made clear the French view in a press conference in Paris on November 16, 1999: "When France speaks, we think of a European pillar within the Alliance or autonomous."[16] As noted previously, the British position, while subscribing to the principle of autonomy from St. Malo onward, emphasized NATO's primacy,[17] which had the effect of rendering the so-called third option an even more remote possibility. Peter Rodman viewed this third option of an all-EU chain of command in the starkest of terms: "This all-EU scenario is relevant to one particular contingency that is hardly ever discussed, namely the (hypothetical) case of a European military enterprise that the United States actively opposes and would therefore block the use of NATO assets for. This is the contingency that dare not speak its name. But it should be faced."[18]

A less mordant perspective would tend to regard this third option as a gauge of Europe taking responsibility for its own defense. This is a view that has been pressed, as we have seen, by French officials such as Foreign Minister Védrine and Defense Minister Richard, and it is one that seems destined to gain increasing adherents over time, though perhaps not in a linear progression. It cannot be expected that a Europe taking on responsibility for defense will be satisfied with a "European Security and Defense Identity within the Alliance," a mantra that continues to be repeated in NATO communiqués. On December 15, 1999, four days after the conclusion of the Helsinki EU Summit, NATO Foreign Ministers meeting in Brussels issued a reminder of this principle, noting that, "We have set in train work on the development of the European Security and Defense Identity within the Alliance as set out in the Washington Summit Communiqué and the Strategic Concept."[19]

This same NATO Ministerial of December 1999 did recognize, however, the changing circumstances brought about by the chain of meetings from St. Malo through the EU summits in Cologne and Helsinki. In language virtually identical to that of Helsinki (and to that of the Washington NATO Summit of April 1999), the Brussels communiqué stated, "We acknowledge the resolve of the European

Union to have the capacity for autonomous action so that it can take decisions and approve military action where the Alliance as a whole is not engaged. We note this process will avoid unnecessary duplication and does not imply the creation of a European army."[20]

Clearly some distance remained between the two formulas of an "ESDI within the Alliance" and the EU's "capacity for autonomous action." But for the French, and to some other Europeans, a truly autonomous European defense capability, whether or not it is ever put to practice, is an important theoretical point. As the late Colonel Nelson Drew observed, "While as a practical matter the NATO chain of command has already been adopted . . . [in] the former Yugoslavia, resolution of the theoretical debate [concerning NATO command arrangements] is crucial if the Alliance is to move beyond crisis response to developing standard doctrine and long range planning for peace support operations."[21]

INSTITUTIONALIZING THE EU-NATO RELATIONSHIP

What was evident post-Helsinki, and as reflected in the Brussels Ministerial communiqué of December 15, 1999, was that NATO clearly recognized that its interlocutor for European defense matters was henceforth the EU—an organization that, though existing in the same city (Brussels), had had very little interface with NATO. Starting in 1999, Lord Robertson, the new secretary-general of NATO, and his predecessor, Javier Solana, who became both the secretary-general of the European Council and the high representative for the EU's Common Foreign and Security Policy (CFSP), began to meet on a nearly weekly basis.[22]

But meetings at the top were a far cry from institutionalizing the relationship between the two institutions, and NATO (again read the United States) wanted to accomplish this without delay. In its December 15, 1999, Brussels communiqué, NATO sought to clarify the relationship between itself and the EU, "ensur[ing] the development of effective mutual consultation, cooperation and transparency, [and] building on the mechanisms existing between NATO and the WEU."[23] The "Europeanists," or "autonomists," within the EU were in no hurry for such a clarification. The French position was that the interim committees created to manage the autonomous EU defense force needed to be set up first, before the EU got into a fixed relationship with NATO. In part this anticipated the next EU presidency—that of France (July–December 2000)— and in part it reflected the French desire that the EU organs remain intergovernmental and not be drawn into the NATO integrated command orbit.[24]

Before long, the principle of transparency between the two institutions appeared to gain the ascendancy. At the following semiannual meeting of the European Council at Maria da Feira, Portugal, on June 19 and 20, 2000, the Portuguese presidency proposed that a "Security Task Force" be created to set up liaison mechanisms between the EU and NATO, envisaging in general a close tie-in between the two organizations. This included attendance of the Deputy SACEUR at meetings of the EU Military Committee, in the case of an EU operation conducted with NATO military assets.[25]

In the wake of the Feira Summit, there began an institutionalization of the relationship between NATO and the EU, despite some French hesitations. The first-ever meeting of the ambassadors representing the countries of the EU and NATO was held on September 19, 2000, in the form of the new supreme body for European defense, the Interim Political and Security Committee (IPSC or COPSi in the French version), and the North Atlantic Council (NAC). In July 2000, four joint committees began work on the following subjects: military capabilities of the Europeans; questions of security, principally in the exchange of documents; utilization by the Europeans of the military assets of NATO; and permanent ties between NATO and the EU.

In November 2000, a Capabilities Pledging Conference was held in which the various EU members' contributions to the Headline Goal were established. Whether NATO was to be allowed to assess the results of this conference on a continuing basis was not fully established, as the French, in particular, did not want NATO to help in the planning of the Headline Goal, out of concern that the United States would come to dominate it.[26] NATO's position was that it must be involved, under the rationale of the need to avoid duplication, as NATO had become involved in a similar exercise following the Washington NATO Summit of April 1999. This was the so-called "Defense Capabilities Initiative"[27] and was NATO's effort at assessing its own military requirements and the contributions expected from the NATO member states.

In the preparations for the Capabilities Pledging Conference, EU officials identified some 500 line items that would be required for the Headline Goal force.[28] As far as Washington was concerned, the key question was whether the Europeans would sustain the effort to fulfill these targets once they had set them.

According to *Le Monde*, the "Declaration of Commitment of Capabilities," issued on November 20, 2000, at Brussels by the Foreign Ministers of the EU, who were joined by the Defense Ministers, included the following list of country-by-country contributions to the Headline Goal:

Austria: 2,000 troops.

Belgium: 1,000 fully trained troops, plus another 3,000 for a maximum of six months; 25 aircraft; 9 ships.

Denmark: no contribution because of its allowed derogation on defense in the Amsterdam Treaty.

Finland: 2,000 troops.

France: 12,000 troops, 75 combat aircraft; 15 ships; and the Helios spy satellites.

Germany: 13,500 troops; 93 aircraft; 20 ships.

Great Britain: 12,500 troops; 72 aircraft; 18 ships.

Greece: 3,000 troops.

Ireland: 1,000 troops.
Italy: 6,000 troops.
Luxembourg: 100 troops.
Netherlands: 5,000 troops.
Portugal: 1,000 troops.
Spain: 6,000 troops; 40 aircraft; and an air-maritime group to be attached to an aircraft carries.
Sweden: 1,500 troops.[29]

COOPERATIVE ARRANGEMENTS IN THE BALKANS

In the meantime, on the ground in the Balkans, compromises that would have seemed improbable a few years earlier generally were worked out, reflecting, perhaps, an awareness between Europeans and Americans of their dependence upon each other, the latter in terms of their overwhelming superiority in sophisticated weaponry, and the former in terms of preponderance of troops on the ground.

As of April 18, 2000, the headquarters organization of the Allied force in Kosovo (KFOR) was placed in the hands of the Euro-Corps headquarters, under the command of Spanish General Juan Ortuno.[30] KFOR remained in a chain of command under the SACEUR, who in turn is responsible to the North Atlantic Council (NAC). The next rotational cadre for KFOR headquarters, beginning on October 16, 2000, came out of a regional NATO headquarters based at Naples and was headed by Italian General Carlo Cabigiosu.[31]

In the meantime, six years after the enunciation of the CJTF concept at the Brussels Summit of January 1994, its implementation had not been not completed. Two exercises were held, both in 1998, aimed at testing command and control capabilities under the CJTF concept for maritime operations, for land operations, and for the transition from the former to the latter. As of 2000, the nuclei of three CJTFs had been set up: one in NATO's Regional Command South, one in Regional Command North, and one in the Commander-in-Chief Atlantic (CINCLANT) fleet at Norfolk. Positions within these NATO commands were designated as double-hatted positions whose occupants could be deployed externally as a CJTF to undertake a specific non–Article 5 operation.[32] Also as of 2000, a number of French officers had been designated for assignment to these CJTFs, should the French decide to participate.[33] In fact, there were some French officers already present in the headquarters nuclei (the Joint Operations Command) at NATO's Regional Command South at Naples, but they were analogous to "liaison officers," since France was not part of the NATO integrated command.

As of fall 2000, however, the CJTFs were being pushed into the background in favor of a new concept called Rapidly Mobile Commands. This change meant, in effect, following the Kosovo example rather than the Bosnia example. In

Bosnia an ad hoc command arrangement was put together à la a CJTF. In Kosovo, already constituted headquarters elements were used.[34]

HELSINKI AND EU EXPANSION

At the Helsinki Summit, and in part in response to European public opinion, the EU decided somewhat precipitously to put six postulant countries into the same basket with the six already accepted candidate countries and not to exclude a thirteenth—Turkey—from eventually being considered for membership: "The European Council confirms the importance of the enlargement process started at Luxembourg in December 1997 . . . [and] reaffirms the inclusive character of the adhesion process, which now groups together 13 candidate countries into a single category. The candidate countries participate in this process on an equal footing."[35] (According to the Luxembourg EU Summit of December 1997, the principle of EU enlargement was agreed to, and subsequent to the conference, in March 1998, six countries—Estonia, Poland, the Czech Republic, Hungary, Slovenia, and Cyprus—started negotiating with the EU on an individual basis).[36]

No firm timetable was set at Helsinki for any new admissions, only the forecast that "the [EU] should be in a position to welcome new state members starting at the end of 2002."[37] Nevertheless, expectations were raised, and this came at a time when the EU was only beginning to address anew the unwieldiness of its institutions, stemming from the fact that its structures were designed for its original six members, let alone the present fifteen or the future twenty-seven or more. This was supposed to be done by a new Intergovernmental Conference, which was to complete its work by December 2000.

Partly because of this unwieldiness and partly because the Euro did not become the strong currency that was expected, the European project as a whole came in for increasing questioning. German Foreign Minister Joshka Fischer, in a bold initiative favoring a federation of the states of Europe enunciated in Berlin on May 12, 2000, declared that the method of Jean Monnet has run its course: the communitarian method of putting together Europe from the bottom up, without a political authority at the top to realize the unity of Europe, was proving more and more difficult as the Union expanded from six to fifteen members. As it goes beyond this number, as the Union has now pledged to do, the lack of unity, as well as the lack of a purpose ("la finalité de l'Europe"), will be even more evident. Both Fischer and Jacques Delors, the former head of the European Commission in an earlier initiative, tried to square the idea of a community of nations with that of a federal government that could speak for all of them. Fischer even suggested that there could be a president of such a federal government elected by universal suffrage.[38]

THE EU SUMMIT AT NICE

At the Nice Summit in December 2000, following the end of the Intergovernmental Conference (IGC) on the reform of EU institutions, voting weights for qualified majority voting in the European Council were decided upon, as regards both the present members and the candidate members. The fact that the prospective members were counted in as part of the new voting mechanism, gave a further fillip of ineluctability to EU enlargement, and this was the chief accomplishment of Nice. Even so, there was still no firm timetable for accession of any of the prospective new members. In a press conference at the end of the meeting, the president of the summit, Jacques Chirac, made the following statement: "At Helsinki . . . the European Union made a commitment, namely to open its doors on January 1, 2003, to those who fulfill the conditions, of course, for crossing the threshhold. [The Union] will keep its word. There is no doubt of that."[39]

The voting weights in the European Council ranged from twenty-nine for the largest countries (Germany, France, Great Britain, and Italy) down to two for the smallest (Luxembourg, Cyprus, and Malta). The new apportionment gave greater weight to the larger countries, but still the smaller countries had relatively more votes than their mere population would suggest. (Luxembourg, with 400,000 people, still gets two votes, while Germany, with 82 million people, gets twenty-nine.)

In the new system decided upon at Nice, 73.4 percent of the votes will be required to form a qualified majority. But the new system will also require that the decision of the Council be supported by countries representing 62 percent of the total population of the enlarged EU.[40] This provision represents a compensation to Germany, which had acceded to France's insistence that Germany not have more votes in the Council than France (even though France's population is 59 million compared to Germany's 82 million).[41] However, although Germany, France, Great Britain, and Italy all have twenty-nine votes in the Council, another compensation given to Germany was that it did not have to reduce the number of its deputies in the new European Parliament comprising the candidate countries as well. The other large countries—Britain, France, and Italy—had to reduce the number of theirs.

In the matter of qualified majority voting, not much progress was made at Nice in extending this procedure and, thereby, streamlining decision-making in the Council as it eventually expands from fifteen to twenty-seven members. As *The Economist* noted, "Before the Nice summit, some 70 treaty articles—representing about 20 percent of EU decisions—were still subject to national vetoes. Twenty-nine of these articles will now be subject to majority voting, but the most far-reaching were kept off the table."[42]

According to *The Economist*, the most notable advance in the matter of qualified majority voting was in the area of "trade negotiations in services [that] will now be decided by majority vote, although France has preserved its veto on issues related to culture and education. Some immigration and asylum issues are [also] no longer subject to national vetoes. And the head of the European Commission will also be appointed by majority vote."[43]

Also at Nice, it was decided that any group of eight or more countries could engage in so-called "enhanced cooperation," that is, they could pursue greater integration in certain areas. According to *The Economist*, it was at British insistence that defense was excluded from those areas in which "enhanced cooperation" could be applied.[44] The Treaty of Nice states that "Enhanced cooperation . . . cannot concern questions having military implications or [those] in the defense area."[45]

At Nice, the defense bodies of the European Union that were created on a temporary basis at Helsinki were made permanent: the Political and Security Committee (PSC), the Military Committee, and the Military Staff. The role of the PSC was incorporated into the European Union Treaty (Article 25): "a political and security committee follows the international situation in the areas related to the Common Foreign and Security Policy and contributes to the definition of policies in giving its opinions to the [European] Council, at the request of the latter or on its own initiative. In the framework of the present title, the Committee exercises, under the responsibility of the Council, political supervision and strategic control of crisis management operations."[46]

At the Nice Summit, the report of the French presidency on European security and defense, developed in the course of the Intergovernmental Conference, was approved in its entirety. Furthermore, it was decided that the defense provisions would not have to await the ratification of the Treaty of Nice before being implemented:

In conformity with the texts approved by the European Council of Nice concerning the European Security and Defense Policy (report of the Presidency and its annexes), the objective of the European Union is to be rapidly operational. A decision to this effect will be taken by the European Council as soon as possible in the course of the year 2001, and at the latest by the European Council of Laeken/Brussels, on the basis of the existing clauses in the treaty. As a consequence, the ratification of the treaty does not constitute a precondition [for proceeding].[47]

The French presidency's "Report on the European Security and Defense Policy"[48] restated the principles of the December 1999 Helsinki Summit, emphasizing "its determination to develop an autonomous capacity to take decisions [in the security and defense field] and, where NATO as a whole is not engaged, to launch and conduct EU-led military operations in response to international crises. For that purpose, Member States have decided to develop more effective military capabilities. This process, without unnecessary duplication, does not involve the establishment of a European Army."[49] In annexes to the French presidency's report are spelled out arrangements of the EU concerning non-EU European NATO members and other countries who are candidates for accession to the EU (Annex VI) and arrangements for consultation and cooperation between the EU and NATO (Annex VII).[50] In both cases, these are guiding principles more than fully worked out rules of procedure.

There is nothing in the French presidency report to suggest any backtracking from the EU's aim of an "autonomous capacity for military action." Furthermore, there is implicit in the report the retention of the French "Third Option"—that is, an action distinct from operations conducted by NATO and from operations conducted by the EU with NATO assets: "In the event of a European Union operation conducted without NATO assets: throughout the period in which the European Union conducts an operation without NATO assets, or if NATO conducts a crisis management operation, each organization will keep the other informed of the general progress of the operation."[51] The "Third Option"—of European operations without NATO assets—however improbable it seemed in the face of NATO's overwhelming military capability, continued to be an important point of principle for the French.

However, although the Nice Summit approved the provisions of the French presidency report, its contents were not reflected in the public statement at the end of the summit. Though the French wanted the points reaffirmed in the public declaration, the British toned the declaration down, limiting the defense references to two sentences[52]—suggesting, perhaps, that the British might have considered they had gone too far in accommodating the French viewpoint. Also, there may have been a certain British backpedaling in view of the fact that the Blair government had to face the electorate in 2001 and, therefore, sought to appear acceptable to as wide a swath of voters as possible. An additional reason for British caution was that the Blair government wanted to wait and see how the new Bush administration would act in general foreign and security policy terms and inside NATO before deciding how much further European defense will go.[53]

On December 7, 2000, at the start of the Nice Summit, Jacques Chirac declared to the press, "European defense would naturally be coordinated with the [Atlantic] Alliance, but as regards its preparation and execution, it must be independent with respect to the NATO command." Immediately thereafter, Tony Blair stated to the BBC, "If someone claims that we have a capability independent of NATO, that would be absolutely false. For Great Britain, there is neither a proposal, a desire or a decision to have a separate military capability."[54] The British prime minister was more explicit in his statement to the House of Commons on December 11, 2000, immediately after the summit: "Any significant operation will require NATO assets and any such operation will be planned at NATO by the planning staff at SHAPE. This underlines the EU's aim to develop a strategic partnership with NATO."[55]

The verdict of *The Economist* following the Nice Summit was that "the terms of a deal between NATO and the Union seem clear in outline, with NATO doing the planning and lending its European friends military equipment that is not needed elsewhere. But many details still need to be worked out."[56] Indeed, the debate on this issue continued with a meeting of NATO foreign ministers at Brussels on December 14–15, 2000, which ended inconclusively. While hailing the fact that "significant progress [had been made], notably with an agreement on NATO's approach to permanent arrangements between the Alliance and the EU," the ministers noted that "work remains to be done in the area of modalities for EU access to NATO assets and planning," and they concluded that "nothing will be agreed till everything is agreed."[57] (NATO planning issues will be discussed in detail below.)

The Brussels NATO meeting also was marked by divergences on the more fundamental issue of how distinct the EU's defense effort was to be from NATO. Jacques Chirac even had used the word "independence" in relation to European defense.[58] In the margins of the Brussels meeting, the Quai d'Orsay issued a statement emphasizing that "European defense should naturally be coordinated with the Alliance, but as regards its conception and application, it should be independent of SHAPE: coordinated but independent." Hubert Védrine, the French foreign minister, was more specific in remarking on December 15, 2000, at the NATO Brussels meeting that when the Europeans made use of NATO assets, they would go through SHAPE planning procedures; on the other hand, when they did not use NATO assets, this planning would be assured by "the headquarters of European countries." Lord Robertson, the secretary-general of NATO, observed in response that this was a question of "very small-scale operations," which could be managed by French and British planning staffs and which would not involve creating a "new SHAPE."[59]

The debate at Brussels drew a sharp reaction in Washington, where John Bolton, an adviser on security matters to incoming President George W. Bush, warned that French proposals for the European defense force are "a dagger pointed at NATO's heart." He added that unless NATO and the EU force worked together, the United States would have to deny intelligence to the British. Said Bolton, "We would have to pose the stark question [to Britain]: are you with us or with them?" Bolton's remarks, reported in the *London Sunday Times*, "followed America's failure at a meeting of Alliance Foreign Ministers on [December 15] to lock the Euro[pean] army into NATO's structures." Jon Kyl, a Republican senator from Arizona and a close friend of George W. Bush, was reported as stating flatly that "This [European] force cannot exist outside NATO." The newspaper quoted the SACEUR, General Joseph Ralston, as favoring "a system of integration in which Alliance staff would help the EU plan military action."[60]

THE DILEMMA OVER PLANNING

Planning became a simmering issue between NATO and the EU once the idea of an autonomous defense for Europe surfaced. In January 2000, right after the Helsinki EU Summit, U.S. ambassador to NATO Alexander Vershbow expressed publicly his concern at having separate, duplicative systems for the EU and NATO.[61] By the end of 2000, planning had become the core problem in the NATO-EU defense relationship, in essence because it relates to the question of who is in charge in Europe.

The issue was not on the level of *strategic* planning but, rather, on the level of *operational* planning. NATO conceded an independent role for the EU in strategic planning. In the words of Secretary of Defense William Cohen, "we have no intention somehow to diminish the EU's capability for independent decision and direction, which understandably would include planning at a strategic level."[62]

Operational planning involves most pertinently the question of how actual operations are going to be carried out by the Europeans with the use of NATO assets. At his final NATO Defense Ministers meeting at Brussels on December 5, 2000, Secretary Cohen evoked "the need to support the creation of this EU rapid reaction capability—provided that it was not seen as being in competition with NATO itself, [and provided] that we should not have dual [operational] planning institutions."[63]

At the same time, Secretary Cohen emphasized "the need to assure the EU access to NATO operational planning machinery." Added Cohen: "Assured access to NATO's operational planning has other advantages: it would provide a forum to work out the arrangements for the EU to use NATO assets in EU-led operations, and it would provide a flexible and generous approach to participation by non-EU allies."[64]

In sum, NATO considered it should do the operational planning for both NATO and the EU. In return, it offered *assured* access to NATO planning machinery and *presumed* access to NATO operational assets–*presumed* meaning that access would be accorded to a preidentified "catalogue" of NATO assets. This formula harked back to the "Berlin-plus" principles developed at the Washington NATO Summit of April 1999.[65] These ideas stemmed from proposals originally put forward at the NATO Berlin Ministerial Meeting in 1996 and adapted and strengthened at the Washington Summit of 1999—hence the rubric of "Berlin-plus."[66]

A complicating factor in the "Berlin-plus" principles is that only certain assets are, properly speaking, NATO assets–in essence the physical plant, headquarters capabilities, communications systems, and the Airborne Warning and Control System (AWACS) planes. These would be put into the category of the "catalogue" of preidentified NATO assets to which the EU would have presumed access. The rest are national assets, mostly American, and the United States is not about to give automatic access to these without first examining the situation on a case-by-case basis. A complicating factor here is that the Turks contended that the availability of *all* NATO assets should be decided on a case-by-case basis and that there should not be a category of "presumed."

What is more, in December 2000 the Turks, while agreeing to an accord on "permanent arrangements" between the EU and NATO, refused to give their assent on a text dealing with "assured access" to NATO planning. The Turks' sticking point was that they wanted to have a seat at the EU table not just when NATO assets were to be used but also when any military action in the region was contemplated. This would replicate the arrangement they had with the WEU.[67]

In sum, as of the end of the year 2000, the procedures had yet to be worked out for how these national assets–mostly American–are going to be loaned out for European-only operations. Another aspect of planning that had yet to be established between NATO and the EU was that of *force planning*—that is to say, the reconciliation of the EU's Headline Goal requirements and those of NATO's Defense Capabilities Initiative.[68]

The overall planning issue also is related to the role of the deputy European commander—the deputy SACEUR—who is a European and who would direct a European-only operation using NATO assets. Again, this relates to the "Berlin-plus" principles—"developing the role of DSACEUR" and "incorporat[ing] more comprehensively the availability of forces for EU-led operations."[69] Here the problem is twofold: first, how can the Deputy SACEUR's terms of reference be adapted so that he becomes an arbiter, or an accountant, so to speak, regarding management of a common pool of forces and its employment in support of both NATO and European-only operations; and second, how can NATO planning be improved so that these NATO assets can be made more readily available to the Europeans.

From the NATO point of view, making available NATO assets involves two conditions: first, that NATO have the right to monitor the use of these assets and, if necessary, call them back into NATO for use in higher priority NATO contingencies; second, that the Deputy SACEUR would retain at all times his responsibilities toward his military chief, the SACEUR. Though the emergence of a European Deputy SACEUR to run European-only operations using NATO assets represents, to some degree, a Europeanization of the Alliance, the insistence that he maintain his "responsibilities" (in other words, his command subordination) to the SACEUR, constitutes another "red line" for the United States.

The position outlined above, which can be termed the U.S. interpretation of "Berlin-plus," represented a pragmatically based effort at making NATO assets (mostly American) available to the Europeans without letting the process get out of hand (and however skeptical the Americans remain about any operation of magnitude run by Europeans alone). But in this attempt at "making the thing work," the Atlanticists within NATO vitiated the Europeanists' cherished principle of an autonomous European defense. This impasse of views relates back to the problem of the American-led integrated command of NATO—its military strength but its present political liability—which will be among the subjects discussed in the next, summary chapter.

NOTES

1. Interview with a State Department official.
2. ⟨http://www.diplomatie.fr/actual/evenements/helsinki/c.l.html⟩. ("Conclusions of the Presidency," Annex IV, p. 22.)
3. Ibid., Section II, paragraph 27.
4. ⟨http://www.fas.org/man/nato/natodocs/99042411.htm⟩, p. 7.

5. *Bulletin d'Etudes de la Marine*, no. 16 (November 1999): 3.
6. Interview with a Washington expert on NATO.
7. ⟨http://www.mod.uk/index.php3?page=119⟩, p. 2.
8. Jolyon Howorth, "Britain, France and the European Defence Initiative," *Survival*, vol. 42, no. 2 (summer 2000): 47.
9. Interview with a French diplomatic official.
10. Howorth, "Britain, France, and the European Defence Initiative," p. 39.
11. *Le Monde*, December 12–13, 1999, p. 3. (Also, interview with U.S. defense official.)
12. Balance-sheet of the French Presidency of the European Union, January 3, 2001 ⟨http://www.diplomatic.govr.fr/europe/presidence/pfuebilan1.htm l⟩, p. 3.
13. Interview with a U.S. defense official. N.B. The Military Committee is largely double-hatted with its NATO counterpart, and the Military Staff will probably turn out to be largely transferred from the WEU. (Source: a State Department official.) It also should be noted that one reason these bodies were designated as "interim" was that a determination was to be made as to whether their creation would require an amendment to the European Treaty language. This turned out not to be the case, and the bodies became permament with the EU's Nice Summit in December 2000.
14. Interview with a U.S. defense official.
15. Speech to Edmund Walsh School of Foreign Service (text of French Embassy, Washington). Note: this was not the first articulation of the "third option" concept, which had been presented before by other French officials.
16. ⟨http://www.ambafrance.org.uk⟩. (British Press and Information Service text, p. 18.)
17. Howorth, "Britain, France and the European Defence Initiative," p. 47. Also see p. 118.
18. Peter Rodman, *Drifting Apart? Trends in U.S.–European Relations* (Washington, D.C.: Nixon Center, June 1999), p. 21.
19. ⟨http://www.nato.int/docu/pr/1999/p99-166e.htm⟩, p. 8. N.B. The Washington NATO Summit of April 1999 enunciated a new Strategic Concept for the Alliance.
20. Ibid., p. 9.
21. S. Nelson Drew, *NATO from Berlin to Bosnia* (Washington, D.C.: Institute for National Strategic Studies, National Defense University, McNair Paper 35, January 1995), p. 18.
22. *Le Monde*, February 29, 2000, p. 4. There is also a proposal that, in addition, Solana preside over the EU's new IPSC organ, rather than this being done by EU Defense Ministers on a rotating basis. (Ibid.)
23. ⟨http://www.nato.int/docu/pr/1999/p99-166e.htm⟩, p. 8.
24. Interview with a U.S. defense official.
25. *Le Monde*, February 29, 2000, p. 4.
26. Interview with a U.S. defense official.
27. See p. 111.
28. Interview with an official of a Washington think tank.
29. *Le Monde*, November 22, 2000, p. 3.
30. For the first period of its existence, the KFOR headquarters consisted of elements of the Allied Rapid Reaction Corps (ARRC) from Germany, under the command of a British General, Sir Michael Jackson. For the next period, elements from NATO's Allied

Command Europe Mobile Force Land (AMF[L]) in Germany formed the KFOR headquarters complement, under the command of a German general, Klaus Reinhardt.

31. *Le Monde*, October 15–16, 2000, p. 7.
32. Interview with a U.S. defense official (who also noted that Article 5 operations are not ruled out for CJTFs).
33. Interview with a U.S. defense official; interview with a British defense academic.
34. Interview with a State Department official.
35. ⟨http://www.diplomatie.fr/actual/evenements/helsinki/cl.html⟩, p. 1
36. Pascal Boniface, ed., *L'Année Stratégique 2001* (Paris: Éditions Michalon, 2000), p. 40.
37. ⟨http://www.diplomatie.fr/actual/evenements/helsinki/cl.html⟩, p. 1.
38. *Le Monde*, May 14–15, 2000, p. 15.
39. ⟨http://www . . . page-dossier6htm?dossier=01853&nav=6&lang=6&page=1&rubrique=0173⟩, p. 5.
40. *The Economist*, December 16–22, 2000, p. 25.
41. Ibid., p. 27.
42. Ibid.
43. Ibid.
44. Ibid.
45. ⟨http://www.presidence-europe.fr/pfue/dossiers/01862-fr.pdf⟩ (Treaty of Nice, SN 533/1/00 REV 1), p. 16.
46. Ibid., p. 7.
47. Ibid. N.B. The Laeken/Brussels European Council was scheduled to be held in December 2001.
48. ⟨http://www.ue.eu.int/en/summ.htm⟩.
49. Ibid., p. 9.
50. Ibid., pp. 32–40.
51. ⟨http://www.ue.eu.int/en/summ.htm⟩, p. 38.
52. Interview with a State Department official.
53. Interview with a British defense academic in touch with policymakers.
54. *Le Monde*, December 9, 2000, p. 3.
55. ⟨http://www.fco.gov.uk/news/newstext.asp?4489⟩, p. 2.
56. *The Economist*, December 16–22, 2000, p. 28.
57. ⟨http://www.nato.int/docu/update/2000/1213/e.htm⟩, p. 1.
58. See p. 127.
59. *Le Monde*, December 17–18, 2000, p. 3.
60. ⟨http://www.sunday-times.co.uk/news/pages/sti/2000/12/17/stifgnusa01010.html⟩.
61. Wilton Park speech, January 20, 2000. Cited in André Dumoulin, "Les ambitions de l'Europe: de l' après-Kosovo aux indicateurs de cohérence," *Politique Étrangère*, vol. 2 (summer 2000), p. 493.
62. ⟨http://www.defenselink.mil/speeches/2000/s20001010-secdef.html⟩, p. 5. (Speech at Informal NATO Defense Ministerial Meeting at Birmingham, U.K., October 10, 2000.)
63. ⟨http://www.defenselink.mil/news/Dec2000/tl2062000_t205nato.html⟩, p. 2.
64. Ibid., pp. 1–2.
65. See pp. 110–11.
66. Interview with a Defense Department official.
67. Interview with a State Department official.
68. Interview with a State Department official.
69. See p. 111.

CHAPTER 7
Epilogue

ABSORPTION VS. AUTONOMY: THE EURO-AMERICAN SECURITY DILEMMA

The continued existence of NATO, its expansion into Eastern Europe, and its embodiment institutionally as the expression of U.S. engagement (some would say hegemony), has not been without its contradictions. There *has* been a manifestation of centrifugal tendencies within the Atlantic Alliance since the end of the Cold War, and, looking back, it would have been astonishing indeed if there had not been. As Frédéric Bozo has observed, "the political-military risks outside the European area . . . multiform and unpredictable, certainly cannot take the place of a Soviet threat which was massive and directed, as a political cement for NATO."[1]

The 1990s represented the decade in which the military limitations of Europe's three major powers, Britain, France, and Germany, were put most graphically on view, as the end of the Cold War brought in its wake a series of regional conflicts—from the American-dominated military triumph in the Gulf War, to the European politico-military failure in the former Yugoslavia in the first half of the decade, followed by the successful American-led intervention in Bosnia in 1995, and then to the costly but finally triumphant air war over Kosovo and Serbia in 1999. The contrast was striking with the situation prevailing at the beginning of the twentieth century, when the major powers of the Old Continent, with their enormous war machines, were preparing for what seemed to be a probable conflict, while the isolationist United States remained aloof from this looming struggle.

Perhaps the most signal reflection of the centrifugal tendencies that set in with the perceived failure of NATO reform to go further in europeanization was the Anglo-French declaration at St. Malo in December 1998, which set Europe squarely on the road toward autonomy in matters of defense. That this only could have been accomplished with the willing consent of America's closest ally, Tony Blair, is an indication of the depth of these centrifugal tendencies and of the yearning in Europe's political class for military self-sufficiency—a yearning long suppressed during the Cold War, but which reached traumatic levels with the demonstration of European military inferiority in the air campaign over Kosovo and Serbia in the spring of 1999. As the Kosovo campaign receded into the background, the atmosphere began to change somewhat, in that the peak of the Europeans' frustration at their inferiority in military technology and at the presumptive way they perceived they had been treated during the air war subsided.

Still, as the twenty-first century begins, one is drawn to the conclusion that Europe cannot and will not remain indefinitely an area of relative military impotence or, as Zbigniew Brzezinski has put it, with his characteristic acerbity, "a *de facto* military protectorate of the United States."[2] Pascal Boniface has seen in the rise of European defense the maturation of the European project as a whole: "It became less and less logical for a power [that was] economic, commercial, cultural, technological, etc. to remain a minor power on the strategic plane. It amounted to an historical incongruity."[3]

The trend in Europe toward autonomy in defense, therefore, seems ineluctable. Whether this trend will reduce NATO to a "relic of the past," an apprehension voiced by Secretary of Defense William Cohen in December 2000,[4] remains an open question, as does the larger issue of whether Western Europe and the United States can maintain a harmonious strategic relationship over the long term. As the authors of "NATO's Triple Challenge" have argued, NATO, despite having survived a number of crises in the 1990s, is inherently in a fragile condition: "The key characteristic of NATO as a political organization continues to seem to be, not robustness, but on the contrary, political fragility."[5] They point to the following: "Relations with Moscow have at best been strained; questions arise over the military implications of the Alliance's restructuring; and 'ten years after the Berlin Wall came down, the spectre of decoupling is once again haunting trans-Atlantic relations.' "[6] In short, NATO is fragile because the transatlantic link itself is fragile in the absence of the massive threat, first German and then Russian, that existed throughout much of the twentieth century.

What has been going on in the transatlantic relationship since the end of the Cold War could be characterized in the formula of *absorption* versus *autonomy*, representing the two extremes of, on the one hand, a United States that is powerful but geographically removed, desirous of retaining its status as the sole superpower, and wanting to remain in Europe and, therefore, in control in Europe; and, on the other hand, a congeries of European nations led by France, increasingly jealous of American power and increasingly disabused at the way the United States exercises this power. Thus, in addition to the previous affirmation that, in Pascal Boniface's words, Europe cannot "remain a minor power on the strategic plane," one is drawn to a second conclusion: that the tie between

Europe and the United States will inevitably weaken as the Alliance discipline imposed by the rigors of the Cold War continues to fade away. A decade after the fall of the Berlin Wall, the now "sole superpower" has less capacity to impose its will on its Allies than it was able to during most of the Cold War.

Underlying it all is the American concern about being shut out of Europe. The Americans want to consider themselves, and to be considered, as a European power. Some Europeans would contest this, including the very articulate Foreign Minister Hubert Védrine. Said Védrine, "The concept of the 'euro-atlantic world,' which NATO is so keen on, has no reality in the public mind here."[7]

NATO AND THE EU: THE CONTEST FOR ENLARGEMENT

With the EU hanging back from its own enlargement during most of the decade of the 1990s, a combination of forces began to look toward NATO enlargement, in particular the Eastern European leaders themselves and certain activists in the Clinton administration. At first glance, it seemed justified that the three prospective new adherents, especially Poland and the Czech Republic, deserved to be safeguarded from attack, considering how the Western European allies had not tried to help them when they were invaded in 1939—Poland not just from Germany but from Russia as well. Guaranteeing their security was a way of wiping away the sins of the past. Hungary, though an ally of Nazi Germany in World War II, had been attacked by the Soviet Union in 1956 and therefore qualified, though to a lesser degree, for Western protection. Furthermore, all three countries belong to the culture of Western Christendom, in the framework of Samuel P. Huntington's controversial theme in "The Clash of Civilizations." This consideration was probably not absent at least from the subconscious of American planners, nor from, more palpably, the minds of the large numbers of persons of Polish and, to some extent, Czech and Hungarian descent living in the United States.

But among those who did not favor NATO enlargement, some posed the question of whether these three countries were seriously threatened by Russia, other than existentially. As one French official put it, the problem with this first round of NATO enlargement was that it protected those who were secure and left unprotected those who were insecure—that is, the Baltic states. The authors of "NATO's Triple Challenge" argue, however, that a sort of security assurance already exists for the Baltic states through Article 8 of the Framework Document of the Partnership for Peace (PfP), which provides for consultation with partner countries facing direct external threats. Furthermore, the authors cite the security reinforcement represented by the development of interoperability and other forms of military cooperation with these states as members of the PfP.[8]

But more crucially, taking the step of enlarging NATO meant that sooner or later the question of what to do about the Baltic countries would have to be addressed. Not to have expanded NATO would not have opened this question at all. But NATO did expand, and this has left in suspense the question of the next moves. Admitting the Baltic countries to NATO would constitute a clear affront to Russia and could produce an unacceptable level of stress in the East-West relationship. Yet doing nothing would only increase the sense of hollowness and ambiguity that has begun to envelop the NATO enlargement exercise. "It is no surprise," note the authors of "NATO's Triple Challenge," "that enthusiasm for further enlargement has waned significantly within NATO."[9]

In the view of a senior U.S. official familiar with NATO affairs, at least one additional country will have to be admitted when the next round of consideration of new members, which is scheduled to take place in 2002, gets underway. This is a necessity in order for NATO to remain credible, and the likely country would be Slovenia, according to this official.[10] According to a decision of the Washington NATO Summit in April 1999, a Membership Action Plan was established that was designed to place the nine aspirant countries in a better position to achieve membership. The nine aspirants are the three Baltic states, Slovenia, Slovakia, Bulgaria, Romania, Albania, and Macedonia.

In Washington, there arose in the course of 2000 the idea of a "Big Bang." Though this was by no means a majority view, the proposal being advanced was that NATO, at its next summit in 2002, should invite all the nine aspirant countries to join the Alliance. The nine are nearly, but not quite, the same as the twelve countries currently in negotiations to join the EU. Some of the more energetic of the NATO enlargement proponents in Washington saw a scenario of more "Little Americas" at the table in NATO deliberations—in other words, more weight in favor of American positions—a trend that already has been underway since NATO has moved out to the East. While not specifying which countries should be considered for inclusion in NATO, Zbigniew Brzezinski has recommended that "the 1999 NATO decision to return to the issue of enlargement no earlier than 2002 should be revised and that a serious effort to decide on new members should be made in 2001."[11]

A more modest solution was proposed by the authors of "NATO's Triple Challenge." In their view, the next NATO enlargement, which could take place some time after 2002, could include Romania, Bulgaria, Slovenia, and Slovakia, plus any of the European neutrals who might choose to join. This limited, or "consolidationist," enlargement "would allow NATO to save face in the light of its public commitments, would provide a reward to Sofia and Bucharest for their practical support of Operation Allied Force [in Kosovo], and would avoid (unlike the entry of the Baltic states) an irreparable break in relations with Moscow."[12]

As noted earlier,[13] the problems that NATO enlargement caused in the West's relations with Russia and the new tensions that arose in NATO-Russian relations as a result of the Kosovo war gave rise at the end of the 1990s to a renewed impulsion in favor of EU enlargement. At the end of 1999, the Helsinki EU Summit, while still not setting a firm timetable, put EU enlargement anew on the agenda. It scheduled for 2000 an Intergovernmental Conference (IGC) for the reform of EU institutions, to be followed by the admission of new members, in principle starting by January 1, 2003, for those countries qualifying for admission. The IGC, particularly in setting voting weights in the European Council both for present and prospective members, and as modified and incorporated by the Nice Summit of December 2000, paved the way for the EU's enlargement. The Nice agreement, announced Tony Blair, "removes all the remaining obstacles to enlargement."[14] At Nice, Jacques Chirac, exercising the EU rotating presidency, reaffirmed that the EU would keep its word and open its doors by the beginning of 2003 to those that qualify for membership.[15]

THE FINALITY OF RUSSIA

At the turn of the century, a new concern arose about a resurgent and more unreliable Russia. This coincided with the transition from the chaos of the Yeltsin period to the strong-man rule of Vladimir Putin that took place in 1999. By January 2000, Russia had come up with a new "National Security Concept" in reaction to NATO's New Strategic Concept of April 1999 and, most particularly, to the NATO enlargement announced at that time at NATO's Washington Summit.

Moscow's new "Concept," announced on January 14, 2000, stated that "The Russian Federation envisages the possibility of utilizing all the forces and all the means at its disposition, including nuclear weapons, in a case in which all the other means for settling a crisis situation are exhausted or are insufficient." This marked a clear difference from the same passage in the previous "Concept," formulated at the end of 1997 under the Yeltsin regime, which took a more restricted view of the use of nuclear weapons: these would be employed only if Moscow were faced with "an armed aggression that appeared to be a threat to the existence of the Russian Federation."[16]

There were other straws in the wind, including the announcement of a new strategic partnership between Russia and India at the end of April 2000, and, one might also say, in the adoption, by the Russian Duma, of the former Soviet national anthem (albeit with changed words) in December 2000. In January 2001, it was announced that Russia and China were considering a bilateral strategic relationship. If one were to put a word on it, this new phase might be termed "cool war." Alexander Dougin, an ultranationalist thinker close to the Kremlin, called in January 2001 for the revival of Russia as an empire: "The new Eurasian empire will be built on the fundamental principle of the rejection of the common enemy—the atlantist doctrine [and] the strategic control of the United States; and [on] the refusal to allow ourselves to be dominated by liberal values."[17]

A study in the spring of 2000 by a Russian think tank under the Ministry of Foreign Affairs and the Kremlin, while clearly reflecting disillusion with the Russian-American relationship, advocated a policy of prudence. The Council on Foreign Relations and Defense cautioned that Russia should not allow itself to be "dragged into an international confrontation," while at the same time recommending that a pragmatic policy vis-à-vis the United States, one concentrated on Russia's own "vital interests," would serve to limit the damage. At the same time the Russian experts warned that Russian-American relations were in a state of "larval crisis" that could "dangerously intensify." In any event, concluded the Russian experts, "Constructing a partnership with the United States on a model of parity is doomed to failure."[18]

A long-term solution to the Russian problem was hinted at by President Clinton in a speech at Aachen, Germany, on June 2, 2000; that is, to finesse the question of boundaries altogether by including Russia as part of the West. Said Clinton: "Russia should be an integral part of Europe, which means that no door should be closed to her, neither that of the European Union nor NATO."[19] That Russia might also join the EU was mentioned, thus, for the first time by a U.S. president.

However, the vision of the outgoing president was hardly that of NATO. While anxious not to close any doors, the secretary-general of NATO, Lord Robertson, made clear his preferences in an interview published in the summer of 2000:

The entry of Russia into NATO would imply very profound changes both in Russia and in the [NATO] Organization. One cannot therefore envisage it except in a long term perspective.... The [need for a] deepening of economic reforms, [and] the consolidation of democratic institutions [indicates that] the road is still a long one before Russia can knock at the door of NATO. In this respect, the "Partnership for Peace" presents a framework perfectly adapted to a step-by-step strategy.[20]

In the unlikely event that Russia were to join both the EU and NATO, this would transform both institutions into much more diffuse groupings than either has constituted to date. In effect, NATO would become a low-intensity alliance. Inclusion of Russia would transform out of recognition what was NATO's cachet of success during the Cold War: the integrated military command. It is doubtful whether the American (or the European) leadership would accept reverting to what would be an OSCE-type organization as a means of bringing Russia "into the reservation."[21]

THE EURO-ATLANTIC RELATIONSHIP

The 1990s—the first decade of the post–Cold War era—has seen the former bipolar system of confrontation between two superpowers evolve into a new system that has yet to define itself. Though many have attempted to describe what has happened, as in Thomas Friedman's "globalization" and as in Allen Hammond's "Market World," it is clear that we are in a transitional phase that will eventually lead to a constellation of regional powers. In this evolution, the relationship between Europe and the United States will be a critical determinant of the stability of this new system. As former National Security Adviser Zbigniew Brzezinski put it, "The transatlantic alliance is America's most important global relationship. It is the springboard for U.S. global involvement, enabling America to play the role of arbiter in Eurasia—the world's central arena of power—and it creates a coalition that is globally dominant in all the key dimensions of power and influence.... How the U.S.–European relationship is managed, therefore, must be Washington's highest priority."[22]

AMERICAN ATTITUDES TOWARD EUROPEAN DEFENSE

On the American side, in reaction to the drive toward European defense, there emerged post-Kosovo a new willingness to let the Europeans do more of the heavy-duty activities. These are the so-called "high end" Petersberg tasks—forcible interventions in regional crises, including the separation of contending parties. In this context, one began to hear the phrase in Washington, "We want the Europeans to do the next Kosovo." Yet at the same time, many in Washington doubted that the major European powers had the will to commit the resources necessary to accomplish an *aggiornamento* in defense. In this respect, the American concern was that the new European defense organization would complicate NATO's life and weaken it while, at the same time, not producing the kind of capability for conducting the "high-end" Petersberg operations. As one Washington official stated in the fall of 2000, the new European force is likely to be only a constabulary force, not a warfighting force.[23]

There is a certain disillusion within the political class in the United States, especially on the Right, concerning a perceived ungrateful attitude on the part of Europe toward the United States on the issue of European defense. This sentiment is rather widespread in the U.S. Congress, where, for example, there have been one or two notoriously heated exchanges between staffers on Capitol Hill and French official visitors. There is a strong isolationist current in an important faction of the Republican Party, which expressed itself notably in an article by Senator Kay Bailey Hutchinson in the *Washington Post*. Hutchinson stated in substance that if the Europeans wanted to create their own defense capability, this was well and good: it would make it all the more easy for the United States to withdraw its troops from Europe.[24]

Congressional freedom of expression is, of course, much greater than in the administration itself, where one is supposed to put a good face on things and, as much as possible, maintain good relations externally, especially with America's principal allies in Western Europe. In private, within the U.S. administration, it is another thing. Following the Cologne EU Summit of June 1999, one heard in the corridors of the Department of State the following observation, uttered with a mix of exasperation and grudging admiration: "The thing is, the French now think they're winning."

There is a sort of ambiguous mix in the attitude of U.S. senior officials toward France, especially in function of the wars in ex-Yugoslavia and the involvement of French forces in the NATO dispositions there. On the one hand, it is recognized, especially in the Pentagon, that France and Great Britain are the two major European countries with both a significant capability and a will to intervene outside the traditional defensive zone of the member countries of NATO. In this sense, France is considered "a willing ally." On the other hand, there exists a sort of exasperation at never being able to satisfy the demands of the French. One often hears the following formula: each time a concession is offered to the French, they simply pocket it and go on with the negotiating, offering nothing in return.

But, as is often the case in French-American relations, although the two countries seem to approach an abyss from time to time, they always walk back from it. There is never a rupture (except, perhaps, that of de Gaulle in 1966, but this was not a real rupture, far from it). When all is said and done, these two countries are the world's oldest allies (a formula, however, which often seems denied by the reality). As of December 2000, the principal unknown was the attitude of the incoming Bush administration, which was generally expected to be less permissive on the subject of European defense than the preceding Clinton administration had been. On the right wing of the Republican foreign policy community there was evidence of a sharply critical attitude toward France, as indicated by the following statement by Richard Perle, former Pentagon official, in an interview with *Le Monde*:

France has always been the most difficult ally and she is all the more so today. Your leaders have a tendency to define themselves in opposition to the United States. You don't like the idea of a dominating power like [the United States], and you want to cut its wings. France is not alone but it is she who gives us the most worry, and [she] is today playing the role of agent provocateur. Under her lead, Europe wants to invest in defense systems identical to ours, like spy satellites.... I hope that things are not going to deteriorate, but I note some disquieting signs.[25]

Generally in the American policy community, critics of the European Common Security and Defense Policy (ECSDP) have displayed two attitudes. First, there is a sort of relaxed skepticism, bordering on deprecation, that the Europeans would be willing to commit the resources to match the rhetoric of the so-called "Headline Goal," as called for in the Helsinki EU Summit.[26] Second, there is a more concerned view that the rhetoric surrounding ESDI could increase the level of American annoyance, resulting in a weakening of the transatlantic link without the emergence of a European alternative that is real.[27]

A parallel concern voiced in Washington is that European energies will be channeled into the new autonomous defense force to the detriment of NATO. And, by bringing defense issues into the EU, the usual transatlantic quarrels over bananas and beef and American films and the like will enter the defense area, as already began to take place with the sharp debates over national missile defense and the American use of depleted uranium munitions in the Gulf War and in the Balkans. There is clearly less of a need for a show of transatlantic unity over defense—a constraint that was in effect to a large extent during the Cold War.

The European-American relationship in the next several decades will evolve in many forms and along many fronts, from monetary policy to trade to culture, and the defense and security component will be a key element in this evolution. The absence of the former threat from the Soviet Union will inevitably produce an impulsion toward greater European independence in all of these areas. In the realm of defense, as far as Europe is concerned, France will play a preponderant part, along with Great Britain, until such time as Germany recovers its strategic legs, both operationally and psychologically.

In the Euro-Atlantic orbit, the position toward the United States of the three leading countries of Europe—Great Britain, France, and Germany—will be of crucial importance, as will the relationship among these three powers. Here, as will be discussed below, the chief variables are the French-German relationship and the Anglo-French one. An Anglo-German close relationship failed to materialize at any point during the Cold War. Britain never has given up fully its century-old policy of "balancing" against Germany as the strongest power on the Continent. And in Britain, memories of World War II run deep. Its death struggle with Germany, honorably waged, left Britain greatly diminished and brought about the end of its term as a great power.

THE FRENCH-GERMAN IMBALANCE AND ITS ADJUSTMENT

A great security anomaly in Europe, left over from the Cold War and, one might also say, World War II, is the relative strategic weakness of Germany. Over the long run it will be difficult for Germany to accept the strategic imbalance between itself and France (or, for that matter, between itself and Britain), especially with the institution of the European Common Security and Defense Policy (ECSDP). The closer integration of European militaries, especially those of France, Germany, and Britain, as implied in the creation of the autonomous defense force, will stand in stark contrast to France's "sanctuary" policy in the nuclear domain. Put another way, it would seem in the order of things that, if France aspires to the military co-leadership of Europe with Britain and Germany, it should logically accept cooperation and greater integration in all areas of military activity, including the nuclear one. The same holds true for Britain.

It remains to be seen whether and how a nuclear compromise in Europe can be worked out. It cannot be expected, at least in the short term, that France will share its nuclear weapons technology with other European powers. The focus instead could be on a central control, by the EU, of the stocks of nuclear weapons held by France and Britain. There is a precedent for this (although it did not include Britain) in the accords that created the WEU in 1954, but it remained a dead letter. According to the final act of the London Conference (September 28–October 3, 1954), which incorporated the Paris Accords of October 23, 1954,

"As regards the weapons [atomic, chemical, and bacteriological] specified in paragraph 2A above, when the [continental European member] countries which have not renounced the right to manufacture them have gone beyond the experimental stage and have begun effective production of these weapons, the level of stocks that they will be authorized to retain on the continent will be established by the Council of the Brussels Pact on the basis of a majority vote."[28]

As the unity of Europe proceeds, it seems inevitable that, on the nuclear and political planes (the latter symbolized by the seats of France and Great Britain on the UN Security Council), the privileged position of these two countries will be more and more contested, especially by Germany. Once Germany thoroughly exorcises its inhibitions against the use of military force, and once the German military becomes completely independent of American presence and command, it is hardly likely that Germany will accept a military role inferior to that of France (or Britain).

Throughout the Cold War, or more properly since 1963, it was the French-German alliance that was the constant of the European political scene. It was as though that three-generation period when Germans hated Frenchmen and Frenchmen hated Germans was a thing of the past, and reconciliation had become a permanent necessity. The many links built up since the Élysée Treaty of 1963, especially in the military area with the Euro-Corps, are vibrant testimonials to this new fact of life in Europe.

Of course it is possible, although hard to visualize, that the coalition of France and Germany will fall apart. Whatever happens in the coming years, there will be no European unity, let alone coherence, without this coalition. As Victor Hugo wrote in the nineteenth century, "[Europe] is composed essentially of France and Germany. The alliance of France and Germany is the constitution of Europe.... Civilization is essentially Germany and France.... It is necessary, for the universe to be in equilibrium, that there be in Europe, as the double keystone arch of the continent, two great states of the Rhine."[29]

The world has changed, and the French-German "couple" has changed since the end of the Cold War, and this requires adjustments. As Arnaud Leparmentier observed,

A problem in the French-German relationship is that for a long time it was dominated by France. Today, a reunified Germany is asking for a re-equilibrium—reform of the Common Agricultural Policy, lowering of its contribution to the [EU] budget at Brussels, taking into account its demographic weight in qualified majority voting in European Council, and the use of the German language [in the EU]—[all of] which are not illegitimate, but they call into question French pre-eminence.[30]

The fall of the Berlin Wall presaged German reunification and, therefore, the end of French ascendancy in Europe. As France's foreign minister, Hubert Védrine, reflected, Europe was a multiplier of influence for France, until the 1990s.[31] A German diplomat put it in a more disabused way in December 2000 on the occasion of the European Union Summit at Nice: "Europe is the continuation of France by other means."

Notwithstanding the German diplomat's acid comment, it was the Nice Summit which rang down the curtain on France's ascendancy in the EU. As Daniel Vernet put it,

> Europe will no longer be a "jardin à la française," as defined by a former adviser to Chancellor Helmut Kohl, [by way of] emphasizing that the Common Market and then the European Community had been conceived in Paris and constructed according to the principles of the French administration.... The European Council of Nice in many respects marked a point of rupture.... The intellectual hegemony that France exercised over European integration, from Jean Monnet to Jacques Delors, belongs definitely to the past.[32]

Though France, during the Nice Summit, successfully prevented Germany from getting more votes than itself in the European Council's qualified majority voting (QMV), a supplemental arrangement included in the treaty required that 62 percent of the EU's population must also approve a measure in the QMV mode. Thus Germany's greater population weight was recognized, after all, by this "double majority" provision and also by its significantly larger number of seats in the future European Parliament.[33]

Voting weights in the European Council also were set at Nice for the candidate members from the East, opening the way for these applicants to come in, though a definite timetable for their entry still was not established. *The Economist* noted the significance of the fact that "after the EU's expansion, the Germans will be at the geographical hub of the Union, rather than at its eastern edge."[34] What seems to be in prospect post-Nice, therefore, is both the end of French ascendancy in the EU and a readjustment in the power balance between France and Germany, perhaps even leading to a reversal of the situation that developed throughout the Cold War. Whether Germany has the ambition to play a leading role in Europe, in the way that France has repeatedly demonstrated its vocation in this regard, is open to question, at least in the short run. There is still a disposition in Germany to recognize France's preeminent role in the construction of Europe, as acknowledged by German Foreign Minister Joshka Fischer: "the idea that Germany wants to play a directing role [in the EU] is stupid. The question doesn't arise. France, a permanent member of the [UN] Security Council and a nuclear power, is politically stronger than Germany for historical reasons. And she will remain so. It is a reality that one cannot change."[35]

French "hegemony," based on its nuclear deterrent and what was the deterrent's deepest aim, an ascendancy over Germany, disappeared with the sudden end of the Cold War, the reunification of Germany, and the collapse of the Soviet Union. But for some, the reflexes live on: in the preparations for the Nice EU Summit, French diplomats, arguing for parity with Germany in voting weights in the European Council, made the point that, although it has 20 million fewer people than Germany, it has nuclear weapons! Such assertions, commented *Le Monde*, feed the traditional criticism, notably in Germany, concerning the arrogance of "la grande nation."[36]

Another French reason advanced for maintaining parity with Germany, rooted in history but equally out of touch with the times, was that there was a compact at the outset of the European Coal and Steel Community, proposed by Jean Monnet and agreed to by Konrad Adenauer: namely, that Germany and France would remain in a state of perpetual equality. Monnet recounted in his memoirs that "When he [the chancellor] received me in Bonn on April 4, [1951], I told him in beginning our talk, 'I am authorized to propose to you that the relationship between Germany and France in the Community be governed by the principle of equality in the Council and in the Assembly, and in all the European institutions now or in the future ... regardless of whether Germany [comprises] West Germany or is reunified.' "[37]

Paradoxically, at the end of the decade of the 1990s, it was the Germans who were pushing for the further integration of Europe, whereas at the beginning, the French were in the lead in this regard, seeking to anchor Germany firmly to the West through the means of the Euro.

At the Nice EU Summit in December 2000, it was the Germans who gained approval, despite some French reticence, for the holding of a new Intergovernmental Conference (IGC) in 2004 to set clearer demarcations of functions among the three institutions of the EU: the Commision, the European Council, and the European Parliament. The new IGC also could take up the issue of the framing of a constitution for the EU.

In the German view, the construction of Europe should proceed in the direction of more integration and less intergovernmentalism, part of which means strengthening the role of the Commission. This would involve further transfers of sovereignty, which are easier for the Germans than for the French. For the latter, especially in an enlarged EU, French influence is preserved more easily through the European Council. The German view, as expressed by a German diplomat, is that "Areas like defense, where soldiers are sent to risk their lives, will remain for a long time in the intergovernmental domain. [But] if we want Europe to become more and more a global actor, foreign policy should go beyond [the realm of] the intergovernmental."[38]

THE ENTENTE CORDIALE: HAS IT REALLY BECOME CORDIAL?

Our greatest hereditary enemy was not Germany, it was England. From the Hundred Years War to Fashoda, she has scarcely ceased struggling against us. And since then, she has had difficulty in not opposing our interests.... She continually forms a bloc with America.... She wants to prevent us from making the Common Market a success. It is true that she was our ally during the two wars, but she is not naturally inclined to wish us well.

With Germany, on the other hand, it is clear that our interests meet, and that they meet more and more. She needs us as much as we need her.

Much has passed since Charles de Gaulle uttered these words to Alain Peyrefitte in 1962.[39] With the turning point of St. Malo, in December 1998, and more generally, there is the feeling that Anglo-French differences are a thing of the past. According to Hubert Védrine: "They are out of date. Besides, what would they be based on? Neither in the Near East nor in Africa are there rivalries or contradictions, simply occasional memories and different tropisms, but which are fading away."[40]

But at the time de Gaulle made his private remarks to Peyrefitte, his information minister then, there was much dissatisfaction—and it was mutual—between France and Great Britain. Earlier, the weak France of the postwar period had turned in the first instance toward an alliance with its prewar ally, Britain. The hopes of yet another revival of the Entente Cordiale, emerging in early 1948, quickly evaporated. The new partnership of Britain and France rapidly turned into a duel, as Maurice Vaïsse has put it.[41]

Throughout the entire postwar period, France was never able to fix its position vis-à-vis Great Britain satisfactorily. She was never able to draw even with Great Britain in the eyes of the United States. There was a sort of implicit complicity between the British and the Americans aimed at maintaining France at a level below that of Britain. The European Defense Community—if it had come to pass—would have obliged the French, but not the British, to meld themselves into a European defense ensemble and, thereby, surrender some elements of their national sovereignty.

Thus, when the occasion arose in the 1960s, during which General de Gaulle twice vetoed the entry of Great Britain into the Common Market, it was not so much a sign of ingratitude toward his ally of World War II as it was a way of demonstrating to the world the end of this ephemeral disequilibrium that existed between Great Britain and France between 1940 and the 1960s. And it was also to mark France's desire for hegemony over the continent of Western Europe. As the American ambassador to Paris, Charles Bohlen, was later to observe:

It would appear to me that the real French objection [to the Multilateral Force] is the recognition that any form of NATO (or outside NATO) nuclear force in which some continental Europeans would participate would inevitably do away with the French monopoly of European nuclear weapons. . . . The French undoubtedly feel that [they] could easily retain in the future under any circumstances the advance [they] have over Germany in this field. . . . This central aim of French policy has rarely been enunciated and does not figure among the public chief objections to the MLF.[42]

THE FATE OF THE INTEGRATED COMMAND

Eleven years after the fall of the Berlin Wall, NATO's integrated command persists, and both the United States and Europe are still coming to grips with the underlying fact that a hegemonic power for Europe is no longer needed. Some European observers, like Paul-Marie de la Gorce, even affirm that hegemony has expressly been the hallmark of American policy throughout the 1990s: "More than ever, the Atlantic Alliance, which survived its first mission—to face up to the Soviet Union—remains the instrument of American hegemony in Europe.... The common will of American leaders since the end of the Cold War ... has been to assure that the United States maintain its rank of sole superpower, and to prevent the resurgence of a rival power analogous to what the Soviet Union was after World War II."[43]

By the end of the decade of the 1990s, with the EU summits of Cologne, Helsinki, Feira, and Nice, the way appeared to have been cleared for Europe, over time, to cut off its moorings to America in matters of defense. Whether, or when, this will become a reality is not certain. The Europeans are faced with the problem of forging an effective military machine for a continent that is still far from political union and in which the mechanism of a defensive alliance represented by NATO has already been in place for many years. As Catherine Guicherd put it in 1991, in an observation that is still valid, "The challenge is to combine the effectiveness of military arrangements in the Atlantic Alliance with the development of the European defense identity carried out by the European Union project."[44]

Most important, the "European defense identity," to be credible and politically viable, theoretically should have a large measure of autonomy vis-à-vis NATO so that the commitment of resources and the transfers of sovereignty implied in its creation will appear to have been worthwhile. As the *Financial Times* put it, "The banner of European integration provides the political impetus for governments that would not otherwise put higher defence spending on the top of the list of priorities."[45]

And yet, as the authors of "NATO's Triple Challenge" argue, attaining such autonomy is unlikely: "EU member states in the short term are unlikely to be able individually or cooperatively to rationalize and increase their defense expenditures to the degree necessary to build up missing military capabilities far enough so that they would not have to request help from NATO or the United States. Hence, until the EU member states are able to provide the requisite military capabilities in and of themselves, the EU will be dependent on NATO."[46]

Paradoxically, and in political terms, it is the EU that, having finally taken on a defense role for itself, now has a larger potential vocation in this area than does NATO. As a "European" entity, the EU can expand into Eastern Europe and help assure stability in the region more legitimately than can the "North Atlantic" alliance. Some Europeans see the European Union as having a larger vocation in the security realm than NATO itself. In an interview in *Le Monde*, General Jean-Pierre Kelche, the chief of staff of the French Armed Forces, stated: "In the future, we would like it that, when a crisis develops, Europe would be able to analyze the elements and seek solutions in all possible areas of action, including military, and then engage the means. The solutions will not necessarily be only military ones. *The field of responsibility of the European Union is more vast than that of NATO.*" (Italics added.)[47] But in military terms, a European force is not, and may never be, the equivalent of an American-led force in terms of power and unity.

What changed the whole transatlantic negotiating equation was the British agreement at St. Malo, after nearly fifty years of opposition,[48] to let defense be part of the European Union. The British turnabout paved the way for the eventual disappearance of the Western European Union, which had always been, by treaty, in a position of subordination to NATO in matters of defense. This change put the Europeans, now represented by the EU, in a position of equilibrium vis-à-vis the United States, as the dominant member of NATO. There is little doubt that the St. Malo declaration of December 1998 constituted the pivotal event of the decade in the development of a European defense capability.

Protecting American security and the American presence in the European area while ceasing to exercise its right of *primus inter pares* is at the heart of the United States' post–Cold War transition problem. Protecting European security while moving toward greater union is the parallel problem of the EU. Creation of a truly autonomous European defense force necessarily would bring about a weakening of Europe's military posture in terms of command arrangements and losses of sovereignty, at least for a transition period, which might, however, last for years. The power and the facility of command implied in the existence of Europe's individual national armies would inevitably undergo modification (and dilution) if and as these military entities became a coordinated instrument of European political union and will.

The American troop drawdown in Europe to 100,000—which is slightly less than a third of what it was during the Cold War—is leading, whether explicitly or not, to a redefinition of the relationship on both sides of the Atlantic. This redefinition cannot be expected to take the form of a deeper, more "integrated" defense commitment: the ties between the United States and Europe have continued and inexorably will continue to loosen, given the disappearance of the Soviet threat.

In sum, the continued viability of NATO would seem to require that, at some point, perhaps later rather than sooner, the United States will have to relinquish, to some degree, the power involved in its sole exercise of the NATO integrated command. An American military commander for Europe was a logical arrangement when the West was faced with an overarching nuclear and conventional threat from the Soviets. In historical terms, the end of the Cold War, the reunification of Germany, and the collapse of the Soviet Empire, in effect, have bypassed NATO's strategic deterrent.

At the same time, it is difficult to visualize a non-American commander of NATO as long as there is a major American military presence in Europe. This has never been in the American tradition. Even in World War I, as François de Rose has noted,[49] General John J. Pershing, the commander of the American

Expeditionary Force, would go only so far as to accept "advice" from Marshal Ferdinand Foch, the overall Allied troop commander. American forces were not "integrated" within the French command.

However, the day is likely to come when the United States will no longer be the vital element in coping with threats to the European region. In terms of sheer numbers, the United States cannot expect to maintain the leading role in the defense of Europe if, and as, its troop commitment continues to decline. Already the number of American troops in Europe—100,000—is considerably less than the number of European troops committed to NATO: 300,000. Given these numbers, it would seem logical that a rotation in the NATO command could become the pattern in time, although this would introduce in turn a new element of competition and dissension among the principal European countries that would be contenders for the position. To date, a "European SACEUR" has been a consistent "red line" for the United States, including since the end of the Cold War: Washington has been able to kill this idea each time it has come up.

If, indeed, the integrated command of NATO were modified into some form of rotating SACEUR, it should make, theoretically at least, for easier relations between the United States and France—relations that were disturbed almost continuously in the 1950s and 1960s over U.S. attempts to impose multilateral instruments on France while retaining for itself the benefits of the integrated command structure—through such devices as the European Defense Community (notwithstanding that the EDC was originally a French idea) and the Multilateral Force (MLF). Yet another attempt at preserving such benefits in the 1990s, this time based on weaker grounds, given the end of the Cold War, resulted in the turn toward autonomy in European defense. This turn took place following the Madrid NATO Summit of July 1997, as described in chapter 5.

Another difficulty between NATO and the EU, and not a minor one, is the so-called participants issue, involving the six European countries that are NATO members but not EU members. Here the problem has been with Turkey, which has been perceived by some in the EU as trying to get into the EU via the back door. The preferred U.S. position was to leave it to the EU to come up with proposals that were satisfactory enough so that the United States then could sell to the Turks. However, convincing the Turks may prove to be a problem that keeps recurring, particularly if Turkey continues to be prevented from actually entering into negotiations for joining the EU. As we have seen in the previous chapter,[50] in December 2000 the Turks refused to give their agreement to an "assured access" text making NATO planning facilities available to the EU. They had insisted, unsuccessfully, that they be brought in from the beginning on any discussions concerning possible military actions in the European region.

In the wake of the European Council meeting at Feira in June 2000, it was agreed that there will be twice-yearly meetings between the fifteen EU members and the six so-called participants: Turkey, Poland, Norway, Hungary, the Czech Republic, and Iceland. This was confirmed and extended at the Nice Summit, with the frequency of meetings changed to three times a year.

NATO AND THE EU: THE FUTURE

There is a general view in Washington that the EU and NATO are compatible and complementary and that they should enlarge at their own pace with the expectation that their memberships will eventually converge. One can pose the question of whether, to use the phrase of Talleyrand, "Il est urgent d'attendre" ("It is urgent to wait"). In other words, for the next round, might it not be wiser to wait for the EU to go first? To be sure, it may turn out to be a long time to wait before the EU moves eastward, perhaps much longer than the EU's theoretical starting point of the beginning of 2003. If the EU does expand eastward, a subsequent corresponding move by NATO would seem at that point to be less objectionable to the Russians.

In the fall of 2000, NATO expert Lawrence S. Kaplan echoed the growing doubts that have arisen about proceeding with NATO enlargement in the near run: "NATO enlargement must be counted as a major achievement of the Clinton Administration's foreign policy. But its success was in the short run. Further expansion of the Alliance in light of the potential consequences would not be in the interest of the next President.... The relative silence on the subject as the Presidential election approaches suggests appropriate bipartisan doubts about further enlargement in the immediate future."[51]

The above having been said, the Russians would not regard an EU enlargement with complete equanimity, especially now that the EU is taking on a defense role for itself. In a document conveyed to the EU Summit in Helsinki in December 1999, Russia, for the first time, registered its concern at EU enlargement. The document noted that the adhesion of the Eastern European countries to the Single European Market could hurt Russia's own commercial interests; it stated that the EU should not establish privileged relations with the former states of the Soviet Union if these would be detrimental to Soviet interests in these areas; and it claimed it should have a say in whether the Baltic states join the EU because of the Russian minorities living there. The latter was, by way of protesting the Helsinki Summit's decision, to open membership negotiations with Latvia.[52]

But such reserves, expressed regarding the EU, pale beside the resistance that can be expected if and when NATO expands into the Baltic states. Moreover, Russia's attempts at rapprochement with Europe, under Vladimir Putin's policy of restoring the strength of the Russian state and placing Russia in opposition to American aims, would seem to indicate eventual Russian acquiesence in an EU expansion to the East. This was evident in the joint communiqué issued in Paris on October 30, 2000, on the occasion of the sixth summit held since the signing of the EU-Russian Partnership and Cooperation Accord: "The EU has informed Russia of the process of enlargement which, since the European Council of Helsinki [in December 1999] has gone into high speed. Our common objective is to take advantage of the potential that enlargement of the EU will have for increasing the exchanges between an enlarged EU and Russia, and between the latter and the candidate countries."[53]

The same joint communiqué acknowledged the validity of the EU's new defense initiatives: "We are pleased with the progress accomplished in the Common European Security and Defense Policy, whose objective is to contribute effectively, and in conformity with the principles of the United Nations, to crisis management."[54]

Russia's policy of rapprochement with Europe earned it the restoration of its voting power in the Council of Europe, which had been withdrawn because of the Russian repression in Chechnya. Although widely criticized, this action was voted on by the Parliamentary Assembly of the Council, 88 to 20, with 11 abstentions, on January 25, 2001. On the same date, Azerbaijan and Armenia were admitted to the Council, reviving, it is perhaps not too much to say, the ancient Gaullist vision of a Europe "from the Atlantic to the Urals."

There is now, as has not existed heretofore, an ambiguity and a contradiction in having two defense organizations—NATO and the EU—trooping around in Europe. This may become more acute in time, as, for the moment, the European autonomous defense force represents only a call-up capability. Or, to put it in another way, as one Washington official observed, "people are not afraid of the Europeans." Nevertheless, the existence of two defense organizations on the European continent will pose a contradiction over the long term. It is a contradiction that will have to be faced somehow, but the resolution of it has been made more difficult by the events of the 1990s. For just as there is no turning back the clock on NATO enlargement, there is no turning back the clock on European defense.

NOTES

1. Frédéric Bozo, *La France et l'OTAN: de la guerre froide au nouvel ordre européen*, (Paris: Masson, 1991), p. 166.
2. Zgibniew Brzezinski, "Living With a New Europe," *The National Interest* (summer 2000): 17.
3. Pascal Boniface, ed., *L'Année Stratégique 2001* (Paris: Éditions Michalon, 2000), p. 22.
4. *Le Monde*, December 17–18, 2000, p. 3.
5. Stuart Croft, Jolyon Howorth, Terry Terriff, and Mark Webber, "NATO's Triple Challenge," *International Affairs*, vol. 76, no. 3 (2000), p. 496.
6. Ibid., p. 495. The quotation is from Ivo H. Daalder, "Europe and America Aren't Divorcing," *Wall Street Journal*, December 10, 1999.
7. Hubert Védrine, dialogue avec Dominique Moïsi, *Les cartes de la France à l'heure de la mondialisation* (Paris: Fayard, 2000), p. 74.
8. Croft et al., "NATO's Triple Challenge," p. 503.
9. Ibid., p. 501.
10. Interview with a former senior U.S. diplomatic official.
11. Brzezinski, "Living With a New Europe," p. 27.

12. Croft et al., "NATO's Triple Challenge," p. 502.
13. See p. 110.
14. ⟨http://www.fco.gov.uk/news/newstext.asp?4489⟩, p. 1. (Statement to the House of Commons, December 11, 2000.)
15. ⟨http://www . . . /page-dossier6.htm?dossier=01853&nav=6&lang=6&page=1&rubrique=0173⟩, p. 5. (Final press conference of the presidency, December 11, 2000.)
16. *Le Monde*, January 16–17, 2000, p. 4.
17. *Le Monde*, January 18, 2001, p. 16.
18. *Le Monde*, June 4–5, 2000, p. 2.
19. Ibid.
20. George Robertson, "OTAN: les leçons du Kosovo," interview with Brigitte Adès, *Politique Internationale* (summer 2000): 219.
21. Organization for Security and Cooperation in Europe (OSCE) includes all the European countries plus Canada and the United States and makes its decisions by unanimity.
22. Brzezinski, "Living With a New Europe," p. 17.
23. Interview with a congressional staffer dealing in foreign affairs.
24. Kay Bailey Hutchinson, "A New Division of Labor for a New World Order," *Washington Post*, January 3, 1999, p. C7.
25. *Le Monde*, January 21–22, 2001, p. 3.
26. Interview with a prominent U.S. defense Academic.
27. Interview with a State Department official.
28. Paragraph 3 of Title II of the Final Act, *Le Monde*, October 5, 1954. N.B. The U.K., which is not on the continent of Europe, was outside the zone of WEU arms control though a member of the WEU.
29. Claude Julien, "L'outil et le projet," *Le Monde Diplomatique*, April 1996, p. 16.
30. Arnaud Leparmentier, "Les relations entre la France et l'Allemagne connaissent de nouvelles tensions," *Le Monde*, November 29, 2000, p. 2.
31. Védrine, *Les cartes de la France*, p. 102.
32. *Le Monde*, December 15, 2000, pp. 1, 19.
33. See p. 125.
34. *The Economist*, December 16–22, 2000, p. 26.
35. *Le Monde*, January 13, 2001, p. 1.
36. *Le Monde*, December 7, 2000, p. 3.
37. *Le Monde*, December 2, 2000, p. 5.
38. *Le Monde*, February 1, 2001, p. 2.
39. Alain Peyrefitte, *C'était de Gaulle*, vol. 1 (Paris: Fayard, 1994), p. 153.
40. Védrine, *Les cartes de la France*, p. 131.
41. Maurice Vaïsse, "L'Échec d'une Europe franco-britannique ou comment le pacte de Bruxelles fut créé et délaissé," in *Les Débuts de la construction européenne* (Brussels: Bruylant, 1986), p. 369.
42. Lyndon Baines Johnson Library, National Security Files, Europe and USSR, Box 170, France: vol. 5, 12/64–2/65, Paris telegram 3978, January 5, 1965, section 2, pp. 1–2.
43. Paul-Marie de la Gorce, "L'Alliance atlantique, cadre de l'hégémonie américaine," *Le Monde Diplomatique*, April 1999, p. 4.
44. Catherine Guicherd, *A European Defense Identity: Challenge and Opportunity for NATO* (Congressional Research Service Report for Congress, June 12, 1991), p. 62.

45. *Financial Times*, February 6, 2001, p. 14.
46. Croft et al., "NATO's Triple Challenge," p. 514.
47. *Le Monde*, December 9, 2000, p. 3.
48. The Western European defensive alliance, known as the Brussels Pact, was signed on March 17, 1948. The European Coal and Steel Community, forerunner of the European Union, went into effect on July 25, 1952.
49. Interview with François de Rose, June 18, 1992.
50. See p. 129.
51. Lawrence S. Kaplan, "The Enlargement of NATO, 1994–1999," *Report to the President-Elect 2000. Triumphs and Tragedies of the Modern Presidency: Seventy-Six Case Studies in Presidential Leadership* (Washington, D.C.: Center for the Study of the Presidency, 2000), pp. 170–74.
52. *Le Monde*, January 16–17, 2000, p. 4.
53. Text of French embassy, Washington, D.C.
54. Ibid.

Appendix

The immensely complicated interaction between these two regional organizations—NATO and the EU—which for decades existed resolutely apart, needs to be more closely examined in order to assist in an understanding of the unforeseen events of the last decade—the first decade of the post–Cold War era. As an aid to this examination, we have included the following schematic, which is a time line consisting mainly of decisions taken at the semiannual European Council and NATO Council meetings. Principal external events also are keyed in along this time line.

EU	NATO	External
1989		
Strasbourg European Council. November 1989. EMU engaged.		Fall of Berlin Wall. November 1989.
Mitterrand calls for European Confederation. December 1989.		
1990		
	London Summit. June 1990. New Strategic Concept mooted.	
		Saddam invades Kuwait. August 1990.

EU	NATO	External
1991		
		End of Gulf War. February 1991.
Mitterrand & Kohl Propose monetary & political conferences by end of the year. April 1991.		
	Copenhagen North Atlantic Council. June 1991.	
Mitterrand proposal at Prague for European Confederation. June 1991.		
		Serb attacks in Slovenia/Croatia. June–July 1991.
	Rome Summit. New Strategic Concept approved. November 1991.	
Maastricht Summit. Common Foreign & Security Policy (CFSP). December 1991.	North Atlantic Cooperation Council. December 1991.	Collapse of Soviet Union. December 1991.
		German recognition of Slovenia & Croatia. December 1991.
1992		
		EC member states follow suit. January 1992.
Maastricht Treaty signed. February 1992.		
		Euro-Corps established. May 1992.
Western European Union (WEU) assigns itself "Petersberg" Tasks. June 1992.		
Single European Market: end of 1992.		

Appendix

EU	NATO	External
1993		
		Clinton assumes presidency. January 1993.
	Euro-Corps under NATO in a crisis. January 1993.	
		Operation Deny flight. April 1993.
		Christopher failed "Lift And Strike Demarche. May 1993.
Copenhagen EU Council. Admission of Eastern Europeans "in principle." June 1993.		
	Travemünde DefMins Meeting. October 1993. Partnership for Peace mentioned.	
1994		
	Brussels Summit. PfP and Combined Joint Task Forces Announced. Principle of enlargement enunciated. January 1994.	
		Markale market explosion. February 1994.
		Sarajevo ultimatum to Bosnian Serbs. February 1994.
		Contact group for ex-Yugoslavia. April 1994.

EU	NATO	External
Essen Summit. Eastern Europeans as observers. December 1994.		
1995 Turkey into Customs Union. Cyprus into 1st tier of applicants. Spring 1995.		
		Rapid Reaction Force in Bosnia. June 1995.
		Srebrenica Massacre. July 1995.
		London Conference ends dual key. July 1995.
		Croatian attack in Krajina. August 1995.
	Williamsburg DefMins IFOR agreed. October 1995.	
		Dayton Agreement on Bosnia signed. November 1995.
	France returns to NATO Military Committee. December 1995.	
		IFOR deployed to Bosnia. December 1995.
1996	Berlin Ministerial WEU to use NATO "separable but not separate" assets. CJTFs and NATO	

EU	NATO	External
	reform to be implemented. June 1996.	
	French-U.S. dispute over Southern Command at Naples. Fall 1996.	
1997	NATO-Russia Founding Act. May 1997.	
		Arrival of "New Labor" government in Britain under Tony Blair. May 1997.
		Socialist-led government in France after snap election. May 1997.
Amsterdam Treaty goes into effect. Post of High Representative of CFSP created. "Petersberg" tasks incorporated into EU. June 1997.		
	Madrid Summit invitations issued to Poland, Czech Republic, and Hungary. French return to NATO halted. July 1997.	
1998		Holbrooke-Milosevic Accord on Kosovo. October 1998.
		Anglo-French Declaration at St. Malo on

EU	NATO	External
		European defense. December 1998.
1999		
		Rambouillet Conference on Kosovo. February 1999.
		Bombing campaign over Kosovo and Serbia starts. March 1999.
	Washington NATO Summit. Poland, Czech Republic, Hungary admitted. New Strategic Concept. April 1999.	
Cologne EU Summit. Autonomous European defense. June 1999.		
		End of Kosovo War. June 1999.
Helsinki EU Summit. Use of EU only where NATO not involved. "Headline Goal" announced. December 1999.		
2000 European Council Feira. Working groups for NATO-EU relations. June 2000.		
Strategic Partnership Declaration between EU and Russia. Paris, October 2000.		
Capabilities Pledging		

EU	NATO	External
Conference for Headline Force Goals. November 2000.		
Nice EU Summit Entry of new members programmed, but without timetable. CFSP excluded from enhanced cooperation. December 2000.		
	NATO Ministerial at Brussels unable to finalize EU-NATO Agreement. December 2000.	
		New Bush administration prepares to take over in United States. December 2000.

Selected Bibliography

BOOKS

L'Année Stratégique 2001. Edited by Pascal Boniface. Paris: Éditions Michalon, 2000.
D'Armaillé, Bernardette. *L'Architenture européenne de sécurité*. Paris: CREST, 1991.
Attali, Jacques. *Verbatim III, 1988–1991*. Paris: Fayard, 1995.
Auriol, Vincent. *Mon septennat 1947–1954*. Paris: Gallimard, 1970.
Aybet, Gülnur. *A European Security Architecture after the Cold War: Questions of Legitimacy*. London: Macmillan, 2000.
Baker, James A., III, with Thomas M. DeFrank. *The Politics of Diplomacy: Revolution, War and Peace, 1989–1992*. New York: G. P. Putnam's Sons, 1995.
Bertram, Christoph. *Europe in the Balance: Securing the Peace Won in the Cold War*. Washington, D.C.: Carnegie Endowment, 1995.
Bozo, Frédéric. *La France et l'OTAN: de la guerre froide au nouvel ordre européen*. Paris: Masson, 1991.
Bozo, Frédéric, Pierre Mélandri, and Maurice Vaïsse, eds. *La France et l'OTAN, 1949–1996*, Brussels: Editions Complexe, 1996.
Chevènement, Jean-Pierre. *Une certaine idée de la République m'amène à. . . .* Paris: Albin Michel, 1992.
Cogan, Charles G. *Oldest Allies, Guarded Friends: The United States and France since 1940*. Westport, Conn. Praeger, 1994.
———. *Forced to Choose: France, the Atlantic Alliance, and NATO—Then and Now*. Westport, Conn.: Praeger, 1997.
Cohen, Samy, ed. *Mitterrand et la sortie de la guerre froide*. Paris: Presses Universitaires de France, 1998.
David, Dominique, ed. *La Politique de Défense de la France: textes et documents*. Paris: Fondation pour les études de Défense Nationale, 1989.
Doise, Jean, and Maurice Vaïsse. *Diplomatie et outil militaire 1871–1991*. Paris: Seuil, 1992.

Drew, S. Nelson. *NATO from Berlin to Bosnia*. Washington, D.C.: Institute for National Strategic Studies, National Defense University, McNair Paper 35, January 1995.

Les enseignements du Kosovo. Paris: Ministry of Defense, 2000. ⟨http://www.defense.gouv.fr/actualites/dossier/rubriques0.htm⟩.

Favier, Pierre, and Michel Martin-Roland. *La Décennie Mitterrand, Vol. 3, Les défis (1988–1991)*. Paris: Seuil, 1996.

———. *La Décennie Mitterrand, Vol. 4, Les déchirements (1991–1995)*. Paris: Seuil, 1999.

Gautier, Louis. *Mitterrand et son armée 1990–1995*. Paris: Grasset, 1999.

Gnesotto, Nicole. *La Puissance et l'Europe*. Paris: Presses de Sciences Po, 1998.

Goldgeier, James M. *Not Whether But When: The U.S. Decision to Enlarge NATO*. Washington, D.C.: Brookings Institution, 1999.

Gordon, Michael R., and General Bernard E. Trainor. *The Generals' War: the Inside Story of the Conflict in the Gulf*. Boston: Little Brown and Company, 1995.

Gordon, Philip H. *A Certain Idea of France: French Security Policy and the Gaullist Legacy*. Princeton: Princeton University Press, 1995.

Grosser, Alfred. *Affaires extérieures: la politique de la France 1944–1989*. Paris: Flammarion, 1989.

Guelton, Frédéric. *La guerre américaine du Golfe*. Lyon: Presses Universitaires de Lyon, 1996.

Guicherd, Catherine. *A European Defense Identity: Challenge and Opportunity for NATO*. Congressional Research Service Report for Congress, June 12, 1991.

Holbrooke, Richard. *To End a War*. New York: Random House, 1998.

Huntington, Samuel P. *The Clash of Civilizations and the Remaking of World Order*. New York: Simon and Schuster, 1996.

Jacquet, Pierre and Thierry de Montbrial, eds. *Ramses 2001*. Paris: Dunod for the Institut Français des Relations Internationales, 2000.

Kaplan, Lawrence S. *NATO and the United States: the Eduring Alliance*. Boston: Twayne, 1988.

———. *The Long Entanglement: NATO's First Fifty Years*. Westport, Conn.: Praeger, 1999.

Keohane, Robert O., Joseph S. Nye, and Stanley Hoffmann, eds. *After the Cold War: International Institutions and State Strategies in Europe, 1989–1991*. Cambridge: Harvard University Press, 1993.

Kissinger, Henry A. *Diplomacy*. New York: Simon and Schuster, 1994.

Kosovo-Lessons from the Crisis. London: Ministry of Defense, June 6, 2000. ⟨http://www.mod.uk/news/kosovo/lessons/htm⟩.

Mitterrand, François. *De l'Allemagne, de la France*. Paris: Odile Jacob, 1996.

Rodman, Peter. *Drifting Apart? Trends in U.S.–European Relations*. Washington, D.C.: Nixon Center, June 1999.

Schmitt, Général Maurice. *De Diên Biên Phu à Koweït City*. Paris: Grasset, 1992.

Stern, Brigitte, ed. *Guerre du Golfe: le dossier d'une crise internationale*. Documents assembled by Habib Gherari and Olivier Delorme. Paris: La Documentation Française, 1993.

Treaties and Alliances of the World, 9, North Atlantic Treaty Organization (NATO). Edited by Henry W. Degenhardt. Detroit: Gale Research, 1986.

Utley, R. E. *The French Defence Debate: Consensus and Continuity in the Mitterrand Era*. London: Macmillan, 2000.

Védrine, Hubert. *Les mondes de François Mitterrand. À l'Élysée 1981–1995*. Paris: Fayard, 1996.
———. Dialogue avec Dominique Moïsi. *Les cartes de la France à l'heure de la mondialisation*. Paris: Fayard, 2000.

ARTICLES

Andréani, Gilles. "La France et l'OTAN après la guerre froide." *Politique Étrangère*, no. 1 (1998): 77–92.
———. "In Defence of Europe." *Survival*, vol. 40, no. 1 (spring 1998): 152–57.
———. "Le rebond européen." *Politique Étrangère*, no. 1 (1999): 35–44.
———. "Why Institutions Matter." *Survival*, vol. 42, no. 2 (summer 2000): 81–95.
Asmus, Ronald D. "L'Amérique, l'Allemagne et la nouvelle logique de réforme de L'Alliance." *Politique Étrangère*, no. 3 (1997): 247–59.
Asmus, Ronald D., Richard L. Kugler, and F. Stephen Larrabee. "Building a New NATO." *Foreign Affairs*, vol. 2, no. 4 (September/October 1993): 28–40.
Bensahel, Nora. "Separable But Not Separate Forces: NATO's Development of the Combined Joint Task Force." *European Security*, vol. 8, no. 2 (summer 1999): 52–72.
Biden, Joseph R., Jr. "Unholy Symbiosis: Isolationism and Anti-Americanism." *The Washington Quarterly*, vol. 23, no. 4 (2000): 7–14.
Bildt, Carl. "Force and Diplomacy." *Survival*, vol. 42, no. 1 (spring 2000): 141–48.
Boniface, Pascal. "Révolution stratégique mondiale, continuité et inflexions de la politique française de sécurité." In *Mitterrand et la sortie de la guerre froide*, edited by Samy Cohen, 157–85. Paris: Presses Universitaires de France, 1998.
Bozo, Frédéric. "De la 'bataille' des euromissiles à la 'guerre' du Kosovo: l'Alliance atlantique face à ses défis (1979–1999)." *Politique Étrangère*, vol. 3 (1999): 587–600.
———. "France." In *NATO and Collective Security*, edited by Michael Brenner, 39–80. London: Macmillan, 1999.
Bruckner, Pascal. "L'Amérique diabolisée." Interview with Brigitte Adès. *Politique Internationale*, no. 84 (summer 1999): 99–114.
Brzezinski, Zgibniew. "Living With a New Europe." *The National Interest* (summer 2000): 17–32.
———. "Living with Russia." *The National Interest* (fall 2000): 5–16.
Calleo, David P. "The Strategic Implications of the Euro." *Survival*, vol. 41, no. 1 (spring 1999): 5–19.
Croft, Stuart, Jolyon Howorth, Terry Terriff, and Mark Webber, "NATO's Triple Challenge." *International Affairs*, vol. 76, no. 3 (2000): 495–518.
Deloche-Gaudez, Florence. "La France et l'élargissement de l'Union européenne." *Les études du CERI*, no. 46 (October 1998): 2–39.
Dumoulin, André. "Les ambitions de l'Europe: de l'après-Kosovo aux indicateurs de cohérence," *Politique Étrangère*, vol. 2 (summer 2000): 485–98.
Gaddis, John Lewis. "History, Grand Strategy and NATO Enlargement." *Survival*, vol. 40, no. 1 (spring 1998): 145–51.
Gautier, Louis. "L'Europe de la défense au portant." *Politique Étrangère*, vol. 2 (summer 1999): 233–43.

Gnesotto, Nicole. "Introduction: L'OTAN et l'Europe à la lumière du Kosovo." *Politique Étrangère*, vol. 2 (summer 1999): 9–17.

Gorand, François. "La défense européenne après Helsinki." *Commentaire*, vol. 23, no. 89 (spring 2000): 5–13.

Gorce, Paul-Marie de la. "L'Alliance atlantique, cadre de l'hégémonie américaine." *Le Monde Diplomatique* (April 1999): 4–5.

Gordon, Philip H. "Their Own Army? Making European Defense Work." *Foreign Affairs* (July/August 2000): 12–17.

———. "The French Position." *The National Interest* (fall 2000): 57–65.

Grant, Charles. "Intelligence Test." *Prospect* (June 2000): 21–25.

Guéhenno, Jean-Marie. "The Impact of Globalisation on Strategy." *Survival*, vol. 40, no. 4 (winter 1998–99), 5–19.

———. "Américanisation du monde ou mondialisation de l'Amérique." *Politique Étrangère*, vol. 1 (spring 1999): 7–20.

Haski, Pierre. "Mitterrand et la réunification de l'Allemagne." In *Mitterrand et la sortie de la guerre froide*, edited by Samy Cohen, 9–22. Paris: Presses Universitaires de France, 1998.

———. "Le Barbare et le Bourgeois." Interview with Thomas Hofnung and Jean-Christophe Thiabaud. *Politique Internationale* (summer 1999): 81–98.

Hassner, Pierre. "L'Amérique et le monde. Théorie et pratique." *Études* (October 1998): 293–303.

Heisbourg, François. "Alliance atlantique: la crise de la cinquantaine." Interview with Thomas Hofnung. *Politique Internationale*, no. 83 (spring 1999): 67–80.

———. "L'Europe de la défense dans l'Alliance atlantique." *Politique Étrangère*, vol. 2 (summer 1999): 219–32.

———. "États-Unis 1979–1999: portée et limites de la puissance." *Politique Étrangère*, vol. 3 (fall 1999): 505–18.

———. "American Hegemony? Perceptions of the US Abroad." *Survival*, vol. 41, no. 2 (winter 1999–2000): 5–19.

———. "Europe's Strategic Ambitions: The Limits of Ambiguity." *Survival*, vol. 42, no. 2 (summer 2000): 5–15.

Hoffmann, Stanley. "French Dilemmas and Strategies in the New Europe." In *After the Cold War: International Institutions and State Strategies in Europe, 1989–1991*, edited by Stanley Hoffmann, Robert O. Keohane, and Joseph S. Nye, 127–47. Cambridge: Harvard University Press, 1993.

———. "La France dans le Monde, 1979–2000." *Politique Étrangère*, no. 2 (2000): 307–17.

Howorth, Jolyon. "Renegotiating the Marriage Contract: Franco-American Relations since 1981." Paper delivered to the Conference on US-European Interactions, University of Washington, April 16–18, 1999, 18 pp. In *U.S.–European Interactions Since the End of the Cold War*, edited by Christine Ingebritsen and Sabrina Ramet. Boulder: Rowman and Littlefield, 2000.

———. "Britain, France and the European Defence Initiative." *Survival*, vol. 42, no. 2 (summer 2000): 33–55.

Hunter, Robert E. "Solving Russia: Final Piece in NATO's Puzzle." *The Washington Quarterly*, vol. 23, no. 1 (2000): 115–34.

Julien, Claude. "L'outil et le projet." *Le Monde Diplomatique* (April 1996): 16.

Kamp, Karl-Heinz. "NATO Entrapped: Debating the Next Enlargement Round." *Survival*, vol. 40, no. 3 (autumn 1998): 170–86.

———. "L'OTAN après le Kosovo: ange de paix ou gendarme du monde?" *Politique Étrangère*, vol. 2 (summer 1999): 245–56.

Kilvert-Jones, T. D. "One Year Later: The U.K. Strategic Defense Review." ⟨http://www.navyleague.org/seapower/one_year_later.htm⟩, 1–7.

Kramer, Steven Philip. "Les relations franco-américaines à l'épreuve de la crise du Kosovo." *Politique Étrangère*, vol. 2 (summer 2000): 359–74.

Kupchan, Charles A. "In Defence of European Defence: An American Perspective." *Survival*, vol. 42, no. 2 (summer 2000): 16–32.

Lequesne, Christian, "Une lecture décisionnelle de la politique européenne de François Mitterrand." In *Mitterrand et la sortie de la guerre froide*, edited by Samy Cohen, 127–48. Paris: Presses Universitaires de France, 1998.

Naumann, General Klaus (Ret.). "Implementing the European Security and Defense Policy: A Practical Vision for Europe." *The Atlantic Council of the United States; Institute for National Strategic Studies, National Defense University* (2000).

"Nomion." "François Mitterrand et le système militaire français," In *Mitterrand et la sortie de la guerre froide*, edited by Samy Cohen, 441–52. Paris: Presses Universitaires de France, 1998.

Parmentier, Guillaume. "Après le Kosovo: pour un nouveau contrat transatlantique." Draft paper (May 5, 2000): 26 pp.

———. "Redressing NATO's Imbalances." *Survival*, vol. 42, no. 2 (summer 2000): 96–112.

Posen, Barry R. "The War for Kosovo: Serbia's Political-Military Strategy." *International Security*, vol. 24, no. 4 (spring 2000): 39–84.

Richard, Alain. "Défense européenne: l'ardente obligation." Interview. *Politique Internationale*, no. 85 (fall 1999): 151–60.

Robertson, George. "OTAN: les leçons du Kosovo." Interview with Brigitte Adès. *Politique Internationale* (summer 2000): 209–24.

Rollat, Alain. "Jeu de patience à l'Elysee." *Le Monde*, October 19, 1991, 9.

Ruiz-Palmer, Diego A. "La coopération militaire entre la France et ses alliés, 1966–1991: entre le poids de l'héritage et les défis de l'après-guerre froide." In *La France et l'OTAN, 1949–1996*, edited by Frédéric Bozo, Pierre Mélandri, and Maurice Vaïsse, 567–618. Brussels: Editions Complexe, 1996.

Sa'adah, Anne. "Franco-German Relations in the Mitterrand Years." Draft paper for presentation at "France in Europe—Europe in France," Harvard University, (December 3–5, 1999): 1–34.

Sanguinetti, Antoine. "French military equipment, too expensive and outmoded." *Le Monde diplomatique* (July 1992): 10.

Schake, Kori, Amaya Bloch-Lainé, and Charles Grant. "Building a European Defense Capability." *Survival*, vol. 41, no. 1 (spring 1999): 20–40.

Schoutheete, Philippe de. "L'avenir de l'Union européenne." *Politique Étrangère*, vol. 3 (1997): 263–77.

Serre, François de la. "La politique européenne de François Mitterrand." In *Mitterrand et la sortie de la guerre froide*, edited by Samy Cohen, 109–25. Paris: Presses Universitaires de France, 1998.

Sloan, Stanley R. "Les États-Unis et la défense européenne." *Institut d'Études de Sécurité, Union de l'Europe occidentale* (April 2000): 1–57.

Subtil, Marie-Pierre. "L'échec du projet de défense européenne," *Le Monde*, August 20–21, 1989, 2.
Tatu, Michel. "Kosovo: une chance pour l'Europe." *Politique Internationale*, no. 85 (autumn 1999): 195–208.
Tertrais, Bruno. "Faut-il croire à la 'révolution dans les affaires militaires?" *Politique Étrangère*, no. 3 (1998): 611–29.
Vernet, Daniel. "La révolution stratégique chiraquienne." *Le Monde*, June 8, 1996, 12.
———. "Mitterrand, l'URSS et la Russie." In *Mitterrand et la sortie de la guerre froide*, edited by Samy Cohen, 23–46. Paris: Presses Universitaires de France, 1998.
Winnerstig, Mike. "Rethinking Alliance Dynamics." Draft paper for presentation at the annual convention of the *International Studies Association*, Toronto. March 18–22, 1997, 1–45.
Yost, David S. "The New NATO and Collective Security." *Survival*, vol. 40. no. 2 (summer 1998): 135–60.

Index

Absorption *vs.* autonomy, 133–35
Acquis communautaires, 78
Adenauer, Konrad, 19, 144
Africa, 17
AFSOUTH. *See* Southern Command (AFSOUTH) dispute
Aggiornamento, 61, 139
Ailleret-Lemnitzer accord, 5, 13
Airborne Warning and Control System (AWACS) planes, 129
Aircraft, 48, 104–5, 108, 114n.33
Aircraft carriers, 104–5, 107
Air operations: cooperation between France and Great Britain, 113n.13; Kosovo campaign, 112, 158; strikes against Bosnian Serbs, 71; strikes against Iraq, 101
Albania, 101, 103, 136
Albright, Madeleine, 100
"All-azimuth" strategy, 29, 30, 31
Allied Command Europe (ACE) Mobile Force, 59n.72
Allied Command Europe Mobile Force Land (AMF[L]), 132n.30
Allied Rapid Reaction Corps (ARRC), 53, 54, 131n.30
Al-Sabah, Shayk Jabar, 45

Amsterdam NATO Summit (May 1997), 98
Amsterdam Treaty, 93, 98, 157
Andréani, Jacques, 34
Anglo-Italian proposal, 54–55
Arab-Israeli problem, 46
Arafat, Yasir, 43
Armaments Group, 99
Armenia, 150
Arms control, 151n.28
Arms embargo: against Iraq, 41; against Serbia and KLA, 101
Aron, Raymond, 29
ARRC. *See* Allied Rapid Reaction Corps
Asmus, Ronald D., 77–78
Aspin, Les, 65
Assets: availability of, 110, 129, 130; NATO, xii, 104, 110, 129, 130, 156; "separable but not separate," xii, 85, 110, 156; strategic, 104
Atlanticists, 26, 97, 130
Atlantism, 22
Austria, 93, 122
Autonomists, 92, 121
Autonomy: absorption versus, 133–35; discourse of, 72; EU capacity for autonomous action, 120, 121; of forces

versus of decision, 43; French quest for, 104; turn toward, 97–115
AWACS planes. *See* Airborne Warning and Control System (AWACS) planes
Azerbaijan, 150
Aziz, Tariq, 46

Baker, James, 18, 22–23, 27, 68; and Gulf War, 40, 46
Balkans, 123–24
Balkan wars, 17, 63, 67–72
Baltic states, 135, 136, 149
Bartholomew, Reginald, 49
Belgium, 4, 122
Berlin dispute (1958–1961), 42
Berlin Ministerial Meeting (June 1996), 83–84, 89, 156
Berlin-plus principles, 110–11, 129, 130
Berlin Republic, 113
Berlin Wall, fall of, 17–38
"Big Bang," 136
Blair, Tony, 94, 100, 101, 118, 134, 137, 157; Kosovo campaign, 98–99, 102; Nice EU Summit (December 2000), 127; St. Malo Declaration, 11
Bohlen, Charles, 145
Bolton, John, 128
Bosnia, 5, 8, 12, 61–83; American-led intervention in, 133; Contact Group for, 69, 72; Dayton Agreement, 71, 72, 156; humanitarian intervention in, 68; Implementation Force (IFOR) deployment to, 71, 76, 156; as independent state, 68; "lift and strike" proposal for, 68, 155; Muslim-Croat federation in, 69; Operation Deny Flight, 72, 155; Operation Joint Endeavor, 71; Rapid Reaction Force in, 71, 156
Bosnia-Herzegovina, 76
Bozo, Frédéric, 1, 49
Britain. *See* Great Britain
Brussels Ministerial Meeting (December 1999), 128, 129, 159
Brussels NATO Summit (January 1994), 64, 65, 67, 79, 155
Brussels Pact, 2, 3, 152n.48
Brussels Treaty, 3, 99
Brzezinski, Zbigniew, 134, 136, 138–39

"Building a New NATO" (Asmus, Kugler, and Larrabee), 77–78
Bulgaria, 136
Bundeswehr, 114n.30
Bundy, McGeorge, 30
Burden sharing, 50
Bush, George H.W., 18, 21–22, 28, 46, 49
Bush, George W., 128
Bush administration (1988–1992), 46, 68
Bush administration (2000–2004), 140, 159

Canada, 151n.21
CAP. *See* Common Agricultural Policy
Capabilities Pledging Conference (EU), 122, 158–59
Carbigiosu, Carlo, 123
CFSP. *See* Common Foreign and Security Policy
CJTFs. *See* Combined Joint Task Forces
Channel Command, 88
Charles-de-Gaulle (aircraft carrier), 107
Chechnya, 150
Cheney, Dick, 18, 53
Chevènement, Jean-Pierre, 42, 47
China, 17, 137
Chirac, Jacques, 13, 26, 63, 71, 89, 118; AFSOUTH dispute, 87; Gaullist consensus, 83; Kosovo campaign, 102; Nice EU Summit (December 2000), 127; nuclear deterrence, 74, 75; rapprochement with NATO, 72–73, 77, 89, 90; support for EU expansion, 125, 137
Christopher, Warren, 91, 92; "lift and strike" proposal, 68, 155
Clemenceau (aircraft carrier), 43, 107
Clinton administration, 5, 6, 68, 91, 139, 155; AFSOUTH dispute, 87; and Bosnia, 68, 69, 70; Kosovo campaign, 101, 103, 106; "lift and strike" proposal, 68, 155; Russian problem, 138; support for NATO enlargement, 91–92, 97
Cohabitation, 81n.73
Cohen, William, 87, 129, 134
Cold War, 5, 21; post–Cold War expecta-

tions, 17–18; post–Cold War world order, 23
Cologne EU Summit (June 1999), 112–13, 139, 158
Combined Joint Task Forces (CJTFs), 65–67, 86, 156; announcement of, 155; implementation of, 123; key role of, 84
Commisariat for Atomic Energy (CEA), 30–31
Common Agricultural Policy (CAP), 7
Common European Security and Defense Policy (CESDP), 150
Common Foreign and Security Policy (CFSP), 8, 64, 154, 159; British policy toward, 99; constructive abstention in, 95n.57; High Representative to, 93, 98, 157; interim committees, 118–19; military staff support to, 119; operationalization of, 66; progressive definition of, 93
Common Market, 145
Communism, 17
Communist Bloc, 21
Communitarianism, 1, 2, 7, 124
Conference on Security and Cooperation in Europe (CSCE), 23. *See also* Organization for Security and Cooperation (OSCE)
Contact Group for Bosnia, 69, 72
Contact Group for former Yugoslavia, 72, 155
"Contract with America" (Republican Party), 91
"Cool war," 137
Cooperation, enhanced, 93, 126
Copenhagen EU Council (June 1993), 155
Copenhagen North Atlantic Council, 154
COPSi. *See* Interim Political and Security Committee
Council of the Brussels Pact, 3
Crisis management, 5, 39, 64; arcs of crisis, 77–78; CJTF operations, 86; endorsement of, 98; NATO options, xii, 39, 111; objective for, 84; Third Option, xii, 119–21, 127, 131n.15. *See also* Petersberg tasks or missions
Critical theory, viii

Croatia, 63, 67–68, 69, 71, 154, 156
CSCE. *See* Conference on Security and Cooperation in Europe
Cultural values, 17
Currency, single, 6, 8, 20
Customs Union, 156
Cyprus, 124, 125, 156
Czech Republic, 5, 6, 135; admission to EU, 124, 157, 158; admission to NATO, 6, 77, 79, 91, 92, 97; meetings with EU, 148

Daguet Division, 44
Dayton Agreement, 71, 72, 156
Declaration of Commitment of Capabilities (EU), 122
Declinists, 17
Defense Capabilities Initiative, 111, 122
Defense Ministers, 90
Defense Planning Committee (DPC), 53, 54
De Gaulle, Charles, 12, 19, 145; "all-azimuth" strategy, 29, 30, 31
De la Gorce, Paul-Marie, 146
Delors, Jacques, 8, 75, 124
Delors Report, 8, 20
Democracy, 5
Denmark, 122
Deputy SACEUR, 111, 119, 130
Dougin, Alexander, 137
DPC. *See* Defense Planning Committee
Dragoons, 43
Drew, S. Nelson, 67
DSACEUR. *See* Deputy SACEUR
Dumas, Roland, 28, 53
Dutch forces, 71

Eastern Europe, 5–6, 10, 156. *See also specific states*
East Germany, 21, 22
Economic and Monetary Union (EMU), 5, 9, 20–23, 61; creation of, 8, 25; engagement of, 153
Economic sanctions, 101
ECSC. *See* European Coal and Steel Community
ECSDP. *See* European Common Security and Defense Policy

EDC. *See* European Defense Community
Eden, Anthony, 2
EEC. *See* European Economic Community
Eisenhower, Dwight D., 11, 15n.36, 88
Eisenhower administration, 31
Élysée Treaty. *See* Franco-German Treaty of Friendship and Cooperation
Embargo: against former Yugoslavia, 3; against Iraq, 41; against Serbia and KLA, 101; against Serbia-Montenegro, 4
EMU. *See* Economic and Monetary Union
English Channel, 88
Enhanced cooperation, 93, 126
Entente cordiale, 144–145
ESDI. *See* European Security and Defense Identity
ESDP. *See* European Security and Defense Policy
Essen EU Summit (December 1994), 156
Essentialism, 17
Estonia, 124
EU. *See* European Union
Euro, 6, 8, 9, 20
Euro-Atlantic relationship, 138–39
Euro-Atlantic world concept, 135
Euro-Corps, 4, 54, 64, 113n.13, 155; establishment of, 154; Lanxade-Naumann-Shalikashvili agreement, 13
Europe: areas of deficiency, 105; as continuation of France, 143; integration of, 144, 146; military inadequacy of, 104; relationship with U.S., 134–35, 138–39, 141; Russian rapprochement with, 150; Strategic Concept, 110; strategic identity, 1, 13, 27; transformation of, 23–25, 40; U.S. troops in, 76, 147, 148
European Central Bank, 8
European Coal and Steel Community (ECSC), 7, 19, 144, 152n.48
European Common Security and Defense Policy (ECSDP), 1–2, 14, 140, 141
European Community. *See* European Union (EU)
European Confederation proposal, 7, 24, 153, 154

European Corps. *See* Euro-Corps
European Council, 10, 93; enlargement of, 150; qualified majority voting, 125; Security Task Force, 121–22; voting weights, 124–25, 143–44, 150
European Council Feira, 121–22, 158
European defense, 134, 146; Americans and, 133–35, 139–41; bicephalic role for, 99–100; concept of, 8; creation of, 55–57, 89; dream of, 11; French attempts to establish, 3; lack of military self-sufficiency, 98; progressive definition of, 93; vocation of, 61
European Defense Community (EDC), 1–2, 145, 148
European Economic Community (EEC), 19, 78
Europeanists, 26, 34, 51, 52, 56, 97, 121
European Market, 154
European Monetary System, 8
European Monetary Union, 98
European Political Community plan, 7, 8, 25
European Political Cooperation, 8, 25
European SACEUR, 52
European Security and Defense Identity (ESDI), 3, 13, 14, 66, 100; within Alliance, 119, 120, 121; development of, 50, 97, 120; emergence of, 64, 66; objective for, 84; reaffirmation of, 84, 85; Strategic Concept, 110; tactical instrumentalization of, 66. *See also* European Security and Defense Policy (ESDP)
European Security and Defense Policy (ESDP), 3, 111, 126; "Report on the European Security and Defense Policy" (French presidency), 126
European Union (EU), 15n.17, 35n.14, 56; access to NATO military assets, 110; *acquis communautaires,* 6; autonomy of, 97–115, 120–21; British policy toward, 98–99; Capabilities Pledging Conference, 122, 158–59; capability, 119, 120, 121; Cologne Summit (June 1999), 112–13, 158; Common Foreign and Security Policy (CFSP) (Pillar Two), 2, 8, 93; Community matters

(Pillar One), 1, 93; Copenhagen Council (June 1993), 155; Declaration of Commitment of Capabilities, 122; deepening of, 5–6, 20, 61–62, 78; as defense organization, 7–10, 14, 93–94, 117–32; Essen Summit (December 1994), 156; expansion of, 6, 9–10, 78, 91, 93, 99, 124, 135–37, 146; expression of, 24–25; field of responsibility of, 147; foreign policy, 62; future directions, 149–50; Headline Force Goals, 159; Headline Goal, 118–19, 122–23, 140, 158; Helsinki Summit (December 1999), 117, 118–19, 124, 136, 158; Intergovernmental Conference (IGC) (March 1996-May 1997), 93; Intergovernmental Conference (IGC) (2000), 136; Interim Military Committee, 119; Interim Political and Security Committee (IPSC or COPSi), 119, 131n.22; Kosovo campaign, 101; Luxembourg Summit (December 1997), 124; meetings, 148; membership, 93; Military Committee, 126; Military Staff, 126; new defense initiatives, 150; Nice Summit (December 2000), 124–28, 137, 144, 159; operations conducted without NATO assets, 127; outreach to Eastern Europe, 5–6; Petersberg tasks, 157; planning dilemma, 128–30; Police and Judicial Cooperation in Criminal Matters (Pillar Three), 93; Political and Security Committee (PSC), 126; political-military role, 93; Pörtschach Summit (October 1998), 98; post-Cold War, 78; recognition of Bosnia, 68; recognition of Croatia, 68, 154; recognition of Slovenia, 68, 154; relationship with NATO, 14, 63–64, 110, 121–23, 127–28, 128–30, 149–50, 159; relationship with WEU, 93–94; "Report on the European Security and Defense Policy" Annexes (French presidency), 126; restructuring, 10; and St. Malo declaration, 101; strategic partnership with Russia, 158; working group for NATO relations, 158

European Union Treaty, 126
EU–Russian Partnership and Cooperation Accord, 149
Expeditionary warfare, 104

FAR. *See* French Rapid Action Force
Federal institutions, 1
Federal Republic of Yugoslavia. *See* Yugoslavia
Feira European Council Summit (June 2000), 121–22, 158
Finland, 93, 122
Fischer, Joshka, 124, 143
Flexible response doctrine, 37n.79
Foch (aircraft carrier), 107, 108
Foch, Ferdinand, 148
Force projection, 48
Fortuna, viii
Fouchet Plan, 25
France: agreements with NATO, 13, 30; ambition of, 1, 63–64; as autonomist, 92, 104; and Bosnia, 70; and CJTFs, 67; cohabitation governments, 13, 90, 106, 157; Contact Group for Bosnia, 69; contributions to Headline Goal, 122; cooperation with Germany, 54, 142; cooperation with Great Britain, 11, 113n.13; cooperation with Italy and Spain, 113n.13; defense policy, 8–9, 26–27, 28, 33, 72; defense strategy, 9, 29, 30, 31, 34; entente cordiale, 144–45; and EU-NATO relationship, 121; and European transformation, 24–25; Europe as continuation of, 143; Gaullist consensus, 83; and German reunification, 18–20; and Gulf War, 41, 42, 43–45, 45–46, 47–49; independence of, 10–11, 30–31, 33; as keeper of the temple, 61; Kosovo campaign, 101, 102–3, 107–8; "The Lessons of Kosovo" ("Les enseignements du Kosovo"), 104–10; mediation efforts during Gulf War, 45–46; military capability, 75–76, 107, 133; military deployment in Saudi Arabia, 43–45, 58n.50; nuclear deterrent, 28–32, 40, 74, 75, 143–44; as outsider, 12–13, 77; pro-Arab policy, 41; rapprochement with NATO, 13, 61–

83, 84, 89, 90, 97–98, 156, 157; relationship with Britain, 141, 145; relationship with Germany, 141–44; relationship with NATO, 10–14, 73–74, 76, 83; relationship with United States, 28, 32, 44, 139–40; "Report on the European Security and Defense Policy," 126; security of, 34; self-overestimation of, 22; Southern Command (AFSOUTH) dispute, 87–90, 157; *la spécificité française,* 47–49; sponsorship of Romania, 95n.53; St. Malo declaration, 157; strategic doctrine of deterrence, 40; strategy of action, 76; Third Option, xii, 119–21, 127, 131n.15; U.S. policy, 141; voting weight in European Council, 125, 143–44; "White Paper" ("Livre Blanc") (1994), 106, 107
Franco-German Brigade, 54–55
Franco-German Defense Council, 54
Franco-German Treaty of Friendship and Cooperation (Élysée Treaty), 4, 19
French Army, 43, 48
French-German Corps, 4. *See also* Euro-Corps
French-German Defense and Security Council, 4
French hegemony, 143
French hostages, 43, 71
French Mediterranean Fleet, 12
French National Assembly, 1, 2
French Rapid Action Force (FAR), 43
Fundamentalism, Islamic, 42

Galvin, John, 44, 91
Gaullism, 11, 83
GDP. *See* Gross Domestic Product
Genscher, Hans-Dietrich, 20
Germany, 2, 3, 21, 22; admission to NATO, 99; admission to WEU, 99; Allied Command Europe Mobile Force Land (AMF[L]), 132n.30; Allied Rapid Reaction Corps (ARRC), 131n.30; anchoring to West, 20–23, 61; Berlin Republic, 113; Contact Group for Bosnia, 69; contributions to Headline Goal, 122; Franco-German Treaty of Friendship and Cooperation (Élysée Treaty), 4, 19; French alliance, 54, 141–44, 142, 143; French-German Brigade, 4, 54–55; French-German Defense and Security Council, 4; military limitations of, 133; Nice EU Summit (December 2000), 144; reaction to Kosovo campaign, 103, 104, 114n.30; recognition of Croatia, 154; recognition of Slovenia, 154; reunification of, 18–20, 21, 22, 40; St. Malo declaration, 101; U.S. position, 141; voting weight in European Council, 125, 143–144
Globalization, 138–39
Global Positioning System (GPS), 108, 109
Gorbachev, Mikhail, 5, 21; European Confederation proposal, 24; and European transformation, 23, 24, 40; and Gulf War, 40–41, 57n.5; mediation efforts during Gulf War, 45–46
GPS. *See* Global Positioning System
Great Britain: Anglo-Italian proposal, 54–55; Contact Group for Bosnia, 69; contributions to Headline Goal, 122; cooperation with France, 113n.13; entente cordiale, 144–45; EU policy, 98–99; and European transformation, 24–25; expeditionary capability, 104–5; and France, 11; German reunification and, 18–20; Gulf War, 47–48; Joint Rapid Reaction Forces (JRRF), 105; Kosovo campaign, 98, 101, 102, 103; "Kosovo—Lessons from the Crisis," 104–10; Memorandum of Understanding with United States, 114n.33; military limitations of, 133; NATO policy, 98; New Labor government, 157; nuclear deterrrence, 74; relationship with France, 141, 145; relationship with U.S., 11, 31, 141; reliance on NATO strategic assets, 104; St. Malo declaration, 147, 157; Strategic Defense Review (SDR), 104–5; voting weight in European Council, 125; WEU membership, 151n.28
Greece, 7, 122
Gross Domestic Product (GDP), 17

Gulf War, 3, 23, 59n.72, 101, 133, 154; Arab solution to, 45–46; balance sheet of, 47–49; French efforts in, 43–45, 45–46, 48; Operation Desert Storm, 58n.50; outbreak of, 40–43

Hadès missiles, 74–75
Hard power, 17
Harrier aircraft, 114n.33
Headline Goal (EU), 118–119, 122, 140, 158; country-by-country contributions to, 122–23
Hegemony, 27, 143, 146
Helicopters, 43
Helios observation satellite, 108
Helsinki EU Summit (December 1999), 9, 10, 124, 136, 140, 158; Headline Goal, 118–19; interim committees, 118–19; results of, 117
Hinduism, 17
Holbrooke, Richard, 6–7, 71; Kosovo campaign, 101, 102; support for NATO enlargement, 91
Holbrooke-Milosevic Accord, 157
Hoon, Geoffrey, 114n.33, 118
Horizon radar, 108
Hostages, 43, 71
Hugo, Victor, 142
Humanitarian interventions, 5, 65, 68
Hungary, 5, 6, 135; admission to EU, 124, 157, 158; admission to NATO, 6, 77, 79, 91, 92, 97; meetings with EU, 148
Hunter, Robert, 64, 65
Hussein, Saddam, 8, 23, 40, 41, 42, 45, 101; military campaign against, 48
Hutchinson, Kay Bailey, 139
Hyperpuissance, xiii, 9

Iceland, 92, 148
IFOR. *See* Implementation Force
IGC. *See* Intergovernmental Conference
Implementation Force (IFOR), 71, 76, 156
India, 137
Institutionalization, 121–23
Integrated command, 12, 73–77, 145–48
Intelligence, French, 108

Intergovernmental Conference (IGC) (March 1996-May 1997), 8, 10, 20, 93, 126
Intergovernmental Conference (IGC) (2000), 136
Intergovernmental Conference (IGC) (2004), 144
Intergovernmental institutions, 1, 8
Interim Military Committee (EU), 119
Interim Political and Security Committee (IPSC or COPSi), 119, 122, 131n.22
IPSC. *See* Interim Political and Security Committee
Iran-Iraq war, 3, 8
Iraq: arms embargo against, 41; Gulf War, 3, 40–43, 43–49, 59n.72, 101, 133, 154; invasion of Kuwait, 23, 40, 43, 153; Iran-Iraq war, 3, 8
Ireland, 7, 123
Islam, 17
Islamic fundamentalism, 42
Isolationism, American, 18, 139
Italy, 92; admission to WEU, 2; Anglo-Italian proposal, 54–55; contributions to Headline Goal, 123; cooperation with France and Spain, 113n.13; Kosovo campaign, 103, 114n.30; voting weight in European Council, 125

Jackson, Sir Michael, 131n.30
Jaguar attack aircraft, 48
Japan, 17
Joint Rapid Reaction Forces (JRRF), 105
Joint Strike Fighter (JSF), 105, 114n.33
Jospin, Lionel, 42, 90
Joulwan, George A., 66, 70, 71
Joxe, Pierre, 47
JRRF. *See* Joint Rapid Reaction Forces
JSF. *See* Joint Strike Fighter
Juin, Alphonse, 11, 88
Juppé, Alain, 75

Kant, Immanuel, vii
Kelche, Jean-Pierre, 146–47
Kennan, George, 91
Kennedy, Paul, 17
Kennedy administration, 37n.79

KFOR. *See* Kosovo Force
Kissinger, Henry, 31
KLA. *See* Kosovo Liberation Army
Kohl, Helmut, 4, 18, 19, 25, 54–55
Kosovo, 5, 8, 10, 12, 98–99; Holbrooke-Milosevic Accord, 157; Operation Allied Force, 136; Rambouillet Conference (February 1999), 158
Kosovo campaign, 101–4, 112, 133, 158; French contribution to, 107–8; German reaction to, 103–4, 114n.30; Italian contribution to, 103, 114n.30; "Kosovo—Lessons from the Crisis" (British Ministry of Defense), 104–110; "The Lessons of Kosovo" ("Les enseignements du Kosovo") (French Ministry of Defense), 104–10; NATO role, 105–6, 109, 110, 112
Kosovo Force (KFOR), 103, 106, 108, 114n.26; headquarters organization, 123, 131n.30
Kosovo Liberation Army (KLA), 101, 102
Krajina, 156
Kugler, Richard L., 77–78
Kuwait, Iraqi invasion of, 23, 40–43, 153. *See also* Gulf War
Kyl, Jon, 128

Lake, Anthony, 91
Lanxade, Jacques, 43
Lanxade-Naumann-Shalikashvili agreement, 13
Larrabee, F. Stephen, 77–78
Latin America, 17
Latvia, 149
Leadership, American, 23
"The Lessons of Kosovo" ("Les enseignements du Kosovo") (French Ministry of Defense), 104–10
"Lift and strike" proposal, 68, 155
"Little Americas," 136
London Conference (September 28-October 3, 1954), 141–42, 156
London NATO Summit (July 1990), 40, 62, 153
Long-Term Study, 84
Luxembourg, 4–5, 123, 125

Maastricht Summit, 55–57, 93, 154
Maastricht Treaty, 8, 20, 35n.14, 55–57, 61, 154
Macedonia, 101, 108, 136
Madrid NATO Summit (July 1997), 79, 90–93, 92, 97, 157
Major, John, 46
Malta, 125
Maritime operations, 113n.13
Market World, 138–39
Mendès France, Pierre, 2, 30
Middle East Command, 88
Military assets. *See* Assets
Military Committee (EU), 90, 126, 131n.13
Military intervention, 5, 52–54; air strikes, 71, 101; American-led, 133; authority for, 3; autonomy of forces, 43; in Bosnia, 61–83, 133, 156; cooperation between France, Great Britain, and Italy, 113n.13; European-only operations, 13, 127, 130; expeditionary warfare, 104; force projection, 48; Gulf War, 40–43, 43–49, 101, 133, 154; Kosovo campaign, 101–4, 104–10, 112, 133, 158; maritime operations, 113n.13; Operation Allied Force, 136; Operation Allied Shelter, 108; operational planning, 128–30; Operation Daguet (Stag), 43; Operation Deny Flight, 72, 155; Operation Desert Fox, 101; Operation Desert Storm, 58n.50; Operation Joint Endeavor, 71; Operation Sharp Guard, 3–4; U.S. troops in Europe, 76, 147, 148
Military Staff (EU), 126, 131n.13
Millon, Charles, 87
Milosevic, Slobodan, 70, 71, 102, 103, 112; Holbrooke-Milosevic Accord, 157
Mirage aircraft, 108
Mirage IV P, 108
Missiles, 75
Mitterrand, François, 9, 13; and Bosnia, 68–69; Brussels Summit (January 1994), 67; European Confederation proposal, 7, 24, 153, 154; European Corps plans, 4; French nuclear deterrent, 30, 75; and German reunification,

18, 19, 21, 22; and Gulf War, 40–47; and Kohl, 19, 54–55; London NATO Summit (July 1990), 33–34, 40; National Meetings for Europe, 62; and NATO expansion, 62, 95n.53; and NATO reform, 27–28, 77; October suprise, 54–55; and political union for Western Europe, 25; and single currency, 20; summits with Bush, 49; view of new world order, 23

MLF. *See* Multilateral Force

Modeling of international politics, vii

Modified Brussels Treaty, 3, 99

Modrow, Hans, 18

Monnet, Jean, 7, 19, 124, 144

Mostar, 4

Moynihan, Patrick, 91

Multilateral Force (MLF), 75, 148

Muslims, 68, 69

NACC. *See* North Atlantic Cooperation Council

National Meetings for Europe, 62, 75

NATO. *See* North Atlantic Treaty Organization

NATO Enlargement Facilitation Act (U.S.), 91

NATO Expansion Act (U.S.), 91

NATO Participation Act (U.S.), 91

NATO-Russia Founding Act (U.S.), 92, 97, 157

Netherlands, 123

New Strategic Concept (NATO), 39, 49–52, 57, 62, 117–18, 153, 158; approval of, 154

Nice EU Summit (December 2000), 10, 124–28, 137, 142–43, 144, 148, 159

North Africa, 88

North Atlantic Alliance, 11

North Atlantic Cooperation Council (NACC), 64, 84, 154

North Atlantic Council, 12, 28, 50, 73, 122

North Atlantic Treaty, 91

North Atlantic Treaty Organization (NATO): Amsterdam Summit (May 1997), 98; assets, xii, 104, 110, 129, 130, 156; Berlin Ministerial Meeting (June 1996), 83–84, 89, 156; blockage in, 90–93; and Bosnia, 70, 71; Brussels Ministerial Meeting (December 1999), 128, 129, 159; Brussels Summit (January 1994), 64, 65, 67, 79, 155; "Building a New NATO" (Asmus, Kugler, and Larrabee), 77–78; Central Command, 88; Channel Command, 88; Commander-in-Chief, Atlantic (CINCLANT), 123; creation of, 11; crisis management, xii, 39, 111; Defense Capabilities Initiative, 111, 122; Defense Planning Committee (DPC), 53, 54, 84–85; disunity in, 63–64; enlargement of, 2, 3, 5–6, 27, 52, 62, 77–79, 90, 91, 92, 95n.53, 97, 99, 110, 135–37, 149, 155; ESDI within, 120, 121; and EU, 14, 63–64, 78–79, 121–23, 127–28, 128–30, 149–50, 158, 159; European-only operations, 127, 130; European troops, 148; flexible response doctrine, 37n.79; Foreign Ministers, 92, 120; foundation of, 112–13; and France, 10–14, 30, 61–83, 73–74, 76, 77, 83, 84, 97–98, 157; functions of, 51; future directions, 149–50; in Gulf War, 49; Implementation Force (IFOR) in Bosnia, 71; integrated command structure, 11–12, 13, 53, 73–77, 75, 84, 89, 123, 145–48; Kosovo campaign, 101–4, 105–6, 110, 112; London Summit (July 1990), 32–34, 40, 62, 153; Madrid Summit (July 1997), 79; maintenance of, 27; Membership Action Plan, 136; Middle East Command, 88; Military Committee, 73, 77, 84, 88, 156; Military Committee Standing Group, 88, 89; military operations, 3–4, 39; Ministers of Defense, 73; missions of, 51; nature of, 17–38; New Strategic Concept, 32–33, 39, 49–52, 57, 62, 117–18, 158; Nuclear Planning Group, 85; objectives, 79n.18, 84; participants issue, 148; Partnership for Peace (PfP) initiative, 66; perduring of, 5–7; planning dilemma, 128–30; as political organization, 134; power balance in, 92–93; Rapid Reaction Corps, 53;

reform of, 26–28, 52–54, 83, 85, 90, 133–34; Regional Command North, 123; Regional Command South, 123; "Report on the European Security and Defense Policy" Annex VII (French presidency), 126; right of first refusal, 118; roles of, 5, 39, 52, 62; Rome Summit (November 1991), 39, 50, 51, 62, 154; and Russia, 110, 136, 138; silent procedure, 109; Southern Command (AFSOUTH) dispute, 87–90, 157; Strategic Concept, 110; Strategic Defense Concept, 88; strategic deterrent of, 147; strategic objectives, 64–65; Strategy Review Group (SRG), 49, 50; 1990s summits, 39–40; three Ds of, 100; three Is of, 100; Travemünde DefMins Meeting (October 1993), 155; UK reliance on, 104; Washington Summit (April 1999), 110–11, 158; WEU relations, 3, 63–64; Williamsburg DefMins Meeting (October 1995), 156; working group for EU relations, 158
Norway, 148
Nuclear weapons: British deterrent, 74; European doctrine, 75; French deterrent, 28–32, 74, 75, 143–44; French-German imbalance, 74–75; new NATO strategy, 32–33
Nunn, Sam, 91
Nye, Joseph, 17

Operation Allied Force, 136
Operation Allied Shelter, 108
Operational planning, 128–30; cooperative, 113n.13. *See also* Military intervention
Operation Daguet (Stag), 43
Operation Deny Flight, 72, 155
Operation Desert Fox, 101
Operation Desert Storm, 58n.50
Operation Joint Endeavor, 71
Operation Sharp Guard, 3–4
Organization for Security and Cooperation in Europe (OSCE), 23, 36n.35, 101, 151n.21
Orthodox Christianity, 17

Ortuno, Juan, 123
OSCE. *See* Organization for Security and Cooperation in Europe
Owen, David, 68

Pacific Ocean, nuclear testing in, 75
Paris Accords (October 23, 1954), 141
Partnership for Peace (PfP), 135, 138, 155; creation of, 64–65; Implementation Force (IFOR) in Bosnia, 71; launching, 66; objective for, 84; U.S. support for, 91
Peacekeeping, 5, 64, 65
Perle, Richard, 140
Permanent Joint Council, 92
Perry, William, 87
Pershing, John J., 147–48
Persian Gulf War. *See* Gulf War
Petersberg tasks or missions, 65, 86, 93, 112, 118–19; assignment of, 154; endorsement of, 98; EU incorporation, 157; high-end, 139
Peyrefitte, Alain, 145
PfP. *See* Partnership for Peace
Planning, 128–30
Poland, 5, 6, 135; admission to EU, 124, 157, 158; admission to NATO, 6, 77, 79, 91, 92, 97; meetings with EU, 148
Policy Coordination Group, 89
Political and Security Committee (PSC) (EU), 126
Political Union, 26
Poos, Jàcques, 68
Pörtschach EU Summit (October 1998), 98
Portugal, 7, 123
Positivism, viii
Powell, Colin, 18
"Prestrategic" weapons, 75
Primakov, Yevgeniy, 45–46
Projectable force, strategy of action by, 76
PSC. *See* Political and Security Committee
Putin, Vladimir, 137, 149

Quesnot, Christian, 72

Ralston, Joseph, 128
Rambouillet Conference (February 1999), 102, 158
Rapidly Mobile Commands, 123–24
Rapid Reaction Force, 71, 156
Rational choice, viii
Reconnaissance, 108
Reinhardt, Klaus, 132n.30
Republican Party, 18, 139, 140; "Contract with America," 91
Richard, Alain, 2, 107, 120; three options, 119–20
Robertson, Lord George, 98, 100, 103, 104, 121, 128
Robin, Gabriel, 49–50
Romania, 92, 95n.53, 136
Rome NATO Summit (November 1991), 39, 50, 51, 62, 154
Roosevelt, Franklin, 22
Royal Air Force, 114n.33
Royal Army, 48
Royal Navy, 106, 114n.33
Rugova, Ibrahim, 102
Russia, 21, 75–76, 92, 137–38; Contact Group for Bosnia, 69; EU-Russian Partnership and Cooperation Accord, 149, 150, 158; National Security Concept, 137; NATO relations, 91, 110, 136, 149; NATO-Russia Founding Act (U.S.), 92, 97, 157; Operation Joint Endeavor, 71; partnership with India, 137; relations with United States, 137–38; strategic relationship with China, 137; voting weights in European Council, 150

SACEUR. *See* Supreme Allied Commander Europe
Saudi Arabia, 42, 43–45
Scharping, Rudolph, 114n.30
Schmitt, Maurice, 43, 44, 47
Schuman, Robert, 19
Schwarzkopf, Norman, 44
Scowcroft, Brent, 91
SDR. *See* Strategic Defense Review
Security Task Force (European Council), 121–22

"Separable but not separate" assets, xii, 85, 110, 156
Serbia, 68–71, 101, 102, 133, 154, 158
Serbia-Montenegro, 4
Shalikashvili, John, 65–66, 67, 85
SHAPE. *See* Supreme Headquarters Allied Powers Europe
Shevardnadze, Eduard, 40–41
Short, Michael C., 114n.25
Short Takeoff and Vertical Landing (STOVL) aircraft, 104–5, 114n.33
Single European Act, 7
Single European Market, 8, 149
6th Light Armored Division, 43, 44
Slovakia, 6, 91, 136
Slovenia, 63, 67–68, 154; admission to EU, 124; admission to NATO, 92, 136
Smith, Leighton, 71
Soft power, 17
Solana, Javier, 121, 131n.22
Southern Command (AFSOUTH) dispute, 87–90, 157
Sovereignty, 7
Soviet Union, 21, 154. *See also* Russia
Spain, 4, 113n.13, 123
La spécificité française, 47–49
Srebrenica Massacre, 71, 156
SRG. *See* Strategy Review Group
Standing Group, 88, 89
St. Malo declaration, 11, 97–101, 113, 133–34, 147, 157
Stoltenberg, Thorvald, 68
STOVL aircraft. *See* Short Takeoff and Vertical Landing (STOVL) aircraft
Strasbourg European Council, 153
Strategic assets. *See* Assets
Strategic Concept: "Berlin plus" provisions, 110–11; New Strategic Concept, 39, 49–52, 57, 62, 117–18, 153, 154, 158
Strategic Defense Review (SDR) (UK), 104–5
Strategy Review Group (SRG) (NATO), 49, 50
Structural Funds, 7
Suez crisis, 31
Supranational institutions, 1, 2, 7
Supreme Allied Commander Europe

(SACEUR), 3, 11, 12, 65, 89, 109; European versus American, 52, 87, 148; integrated command system, 12, 73
Supreme Headquarters Allied Powers Europe (SHAPE), 11, 15n.36, 73, 94n.19, 128
Sweden, 93, 123

Tanks, 44, 48
Thaçi, Hashim, 102
Thatcher, Margaret, 18–19, 20
Third Option, xii, 119–21, 127, 131n.15
Tornado, 114n.33
Trainor, Bernard E., 44
Travemünde DefMins Meeting (October 1993), 155
Treaty of Maastricht, 8, 20, 35n.14, 55–57, 61, 154
Treaty of Rome (1957), 78
Tridominium, 49
Triumphalism, U.S., 49
Turkey, 10, 129, 148, 156

Unipolarity, 1
United Kingdom. *See* Great Britain
United Nations: Kosovo campaign, 103, 104; Resolution 242, 46; Resolution 338, 46; Resolution 660, 41, 42; Resolution 661, 42; Resolution 670, 41; Resolution 678, 46; Resolution 681, 46; Resolution 1160, 101; Resolution 1199, 101; Resolution 1244, 103
United Nations Protection Force (UNPROFOR), 68, 69, 70, 71
United States: Brussels Summit (January 1994), 67; Bush administration (1988–1992), 46, 68; Bush administration (2000–2004), 140, 159; Clinton administration, 5, 6, 67–70, 87, 91–92, 101, 103, 106, 139, 155; Contact Group for Bosnia, 69; Eisenhower administration, 31; Euro-American security dilemma, 133–35; European defense, 139–41; flexible response strategy, 37n.79; foreign policy, 91; as global gendarme, 18; hard power of, 17; integrated command by, 12; isolationism, 18, 139; Joint Strike Fighter (JSF), 105; Kennedy administration, 37n.79; Kosovo campaign, 101, 103, 104, 106; leadership of, 22–23; "lift and strike" proposal, 68, 155; Memorandum of Understanding with UK, 114n.33; military presence in Europe, 76, 147, 148; NATO Enlargement Facilitation Act, 91; NATO Expansion Act, 91; NATO Participation Act, 91; NATO reform efforts, 85, 90; NATO-Russia Founding Act, 92, 97, 157; NATO Southern Command dispute, 87–90, 157; new NATO strategy, 32–33; OSCE membership, 151n.21; policy toward Bosnia, 71; reaction to Cologne Summit, 113; reaction to Helsinki Summit, 117–18; relationship with Britain, 11, 31; relationship with Europe, 134–35, 138–41; relationship with France, 28, 32, 139–40; relationship with Russia, 137–38; soft power of, 17; support for NATO enlargement, 97; technological superiority, 108–9; transatlantic alliance, 138–39; triumphalism, 49, 133; veto power, 26
United States Air Force, 44
United States Committee to Expand NATO, 91
United States Joint Chiefs of Staff, 89
United States Sixth Fleet, 88
UNPROFOR. *See* United Nations Protection Force

Vaïsse, Maurice, 145
Valentin-Farber agreement, 5
Vance, Cyrus, 68
Védrine, Hubert, xiii, 4, 9, 32, 34, 90, 120, 135; and Bosnia, 69; Brussels Ministerial Meeting (December 1999), 128; and European Confederation proposal, 24; and Gulf War, 40
Vershbow, Alexander, 128
Visegrad countries, 6

Warrior Armored Infantry Fighting Vehicle, 48
Washington NATO Summit (April 1999), 110–11, 158

Washington Treaty of 1949, 5, 37n.76, 51, 52, 65
Weapons of mass destruction, 75, 84. *See also* Nuclear weapons; *specific weaponry*
Weiszacker Commission, 114n.30
Western Christianity, 17, 135
Western Europe: and French nuclear deterrence, 74; military inadequacy, 104; political union for, 25–26; U.S. military presence in, 76
Western European Union (WEU), 2; affirmation of, 85; Armaments Group, 99; arms control, 151n.28; Assembly, 99; assets, 156; Council at The Hague "platform statement," 56; crisis management, 64; enlargement of, 99; EU relations, 55, 93–94, 99; failure of, 2–5; Gulf War, 49; military operations, 3–4; NATO relations, 63–64; organizational principles, 85–86; peacekeeping, 64; Petersberg tasks, 154; remnants of, 99; role of, 100
West Germany, 2, 3. *See also* Germany
WEU. *See* Western European Union
"White Paper" ("Livre Blanc") (1994), 106, 107
Williamsburg DefMins Meeting (October 1995), 156

Yugoslavia, 102, 103, 133; Contact Group for, 72, 155; embargo against, 3; hostilities, 6, 63, 67–72; Operation Deny Flight, 72, 155

About the Author

CHARLES G. COGAN is a Senior Research Associate at John F. Kennedy School of Government, Harvard University, Dr. Cogan is the author of *Forced to Choose: France, the Atlantic Alliance, and NATO—Then and Now* and *Oldest Allies, Guarded Friends: The United States and France Since 1940*, both published by Praeger.